Exploring the Life of the Soul

Exploring the Life of the Soul

Philosophical Reflections on Psychoanalysis and Self Psychology

John Hanwell Riker

LEXINGTON BOOKS
Lanham • Boulder • New York • London

Published by Lexington Books
An imprint of The Rowman & Littlefield Publishing Group, Inc.
4501 Forbes Boulevard, Suite 200, Lanham, Maryland 20706
www.rowman.com

Unit A, Whitacre Mews, 26-34 Stannary Street, London SE11 4AB

British Library Cataloguing in Publication Information Available

Library of Congress Cataloging-in-Publication Data

Library of Congress Cataloging-in-Publication Data Available

978-1-4985-4390-3 (cloth : alk. paper)
978-1-4985-4392-7 (pbk. : alk. paper)
978-1-4985-4391-0 (electronic)

∞™ The paper used in this publication meets the minimum requirements of American
National Standard for Information Sciences Permanence of Paper for Printed Library
Materials, ANSI/NISO Z39.48-1992.

Printed in the United States of America

To Marcia
Clinician, Classicist, Dancer, Pianist, Mother, Grandmother
Brimming with warmth, intelligence, and spirit
My Beloved Partner in Life

Contents

Preface

I came to psychoanalysis and self psychology through two different routes—the first being a philosophical search into questions of ethics and the second a therapeutic journey into the depths of my own soul.

As I set out on my career as a philosopher at Colorado College, I found myself intensely interested in the most fundamental of ethical questions, first asked by Socrates: how is it best to live as a human being? I did not come to this question in an abstract way, but an existential one, for like many growing up in the 1950s, I observed that although my parents and many of their friends were living the prescribed lifestyle for those in the middle and upper classes, they were not happy. Indeed, the amount of rage, alcoholism, abuse, and emptiness I experienced in my childhood let me know that modern economic culture did not have the right answer to the ethical question. I witnessed too vividly that material prosperity did not necessarily equate to a depth of human satisfaction. If it were not for a profound relation to nature (see chapter 6 for this story), I might not have survived childhood. My unhappiness went underground in later childhood and early adolescence when I surprisingly became popular at school and intensely interested in girls and sports. However, the Socratic question never left me, and when I found philosophy in college, I knew I had discovered the discipline to which I needed to devote my life. I was going to address with all the depth I could muster the ethical questions that had haunted me since childhood.

The exploration of these questions has turned out to be a lifelong adventure. However, while I was probing a promising way of dealing with the question of how to live well in terms of situating it in contemporary scientific and philosophic understandings of human nature, an event happened that changed everything in my life: I had a severe psychological breakdown. The precipitating cause was the falling apart of my first marriage and with it the mirages I had built up as to how my intelligence and ego had banished all problems and constructed a perfectly wonderful life. The unconscious erupted and the childhood trauma I had repressed came roaring back.

I began a psychoanalytic psychotherapy and within the first several hours of that therapy learned more about myself than in all the years I had spent studying philosophy. I discovered that philosophy is essential for thinking in general about what it means to be human, but that it did not have the tools to penetrate into the sufferings produced by individual traumatic life histories. I further discovered that psychoanalysis had developed brilliant theories and tools for penetrating into the unconscious that none of the other disciplines had. The question was, then, how to integrate it with the other philosophical and scientific theories I had been exploring.

My philosophical project finally resulted in *Human Excellence and an Ecological Conception of the Psyche* (1991) in which I tried to integrate the theories of human nature that I had found in the social and natural sciences with those of philosophy. I accomplished this task by collating the different basic drives/needs that these disciplines and thinkers had posited and constructing a concept of the psyche that organized basic needs and emotions ecologically rather than hierarchically, as had been advocated for most of the history of philosophy. However, I did not think into what psychic agency was to be doing the organizing. Although I knew a lot more about self psychology at this point, I was unable to distinguish the Freudian ego from the Kohutian self. Nor had I seen the tremendous implications of self psychology for ethics. However, I had found, I thought, a genuine answer to my question about how to live well: to recognize, validate, and balance all the basic needs and emotions, and integrate the unconscious mind with the conscious one. What I did not fully understand was that the key to feeling fully alive was not in attending to all the pressures in the psyche, but having a coherent, vitalized self at the core of experience. The basic needs and emotions are important, but they cannot be fully accessed or integrated without a core self.

Meanwhile, my therapy with a Freudian psychoanalyst had not proved fully effective. Although I learned a great deal about myself, I was continually re-traumatized by his unrelenting attacks on my defenses and pressure to abreact my rage. So I decided to initiate a therapy with a woman known for her effective work with women who had suffered sexual abuse. While not an official self psychologist, she had a profound sense of what it means to have a self and how to empathically go about building one. After many years of therapy with her, I finally found that I had a core at the center of my psyche rather than a dark icy pit. While this therapy was progressing, I was also progressing in my knowledge of Kohutian self psychology, a knowledge that led to a second book interconnecting ethics and psychoanalysis, *Ethics and the Discovery of the Unconscious* (1997).

On the basis of this book I was invited by Jonathan Lear to be the Kohut Professor at the University of Chicago in the fall of 2003. I was still probing the question of what kind of soul is capable of the most liveliness, especially in relation to self psychology, when I finally grasped the question that would make self psychology and psychoanalysis fully relevant to ethics: "Why is it good to be good?" That is, I discovered that the crucial problem of the modern world was not "What does it mean to be a good person," for that had been somewhat fully answered by a fusion of deontology and utilitarianism—observe the rules that we all need to follow to have livable communities and be concerned for the welfare of all, especially the underprivileged and disadvantaged. However, it became clear that in modern society many people did not feel motivated to be moral when being moral conflicted with their perceived personal gains. There seemed to be no compelling answer for secular economic people to the question of why it is good to become an ethical human being. And this is when I realized how Kohut's notion of the self involved a different notion of self-interest than that of maximizing pleasure, one which could indeed be used to show why it is not only personally good to be a good person, but why ethical life needs persons to have strong, vitalized self-affirming selves. I was now back with Aristotle in seeing how ethical life could be based on a concept of human nature and how ethics is not, as many moderns would have it, a constraint on or negation of personal interest, but its highest realization.

This book is a set of explorations of how Kohut's psychoanalytic self psychology allows us to re-conceive the notion of what it means to have or be a self, what constitutes a well-lived life, what essential practices communities need to develop in order to foster selves, why relating to difference is both so hard and necessary for human beings, and even how to go about thinking about history in new self psychological ways. That is, this book explores a new way to inhabit and think about our humanity, a new ontology.

Acknowledgments

I need to recognize a number of persons who helped bring this book into a reality. First, I am grateful to Kasey Beduhn, editor at Lexington Books, an imprint of Rowman & Littlefield, who recognized the importance of this book and who has been very helpful in improving it. The great biographer of Kohut, Charles Strozier, also made extremely important suggestions that significantly enhanced the book. I also need to acknowledge that earlier versions of chapters 9 and 10 appeared in the *International Journal of Psychoanalytic Self Psychology*. I need to thank Jonathan Lear and the Committee on Social Thought at the University of Chicago for inviting me to be the Kohut Professor during the fall of 2003. The Kohut Lecture I gave on "The Life of the Soul" is the birthplace for much of the thinking that is developed in this book. I especially need to thank the self-psychology community for being so receptive an audience for the thoughts of a non-clinician philosopher. David Terman, Arnold Goldberg, and Allen Siegel have, over the years, given me many insights into self psychology, and Donna Orange has raised stimulating questions about the relation of self psychology and ethics. And, as always, I need to acknowledge Colorado College, certainly one of the most innovative and adventurous of the liberal arts colleges, and one that has supported my strange interdisciplinary bent of scholarship for all of these years. I especially thank my colleagues Jonathan Lee and Rick Furtak for their continued interest in philosophy and psychoanalysis. What is most wondrous about Colorado College is its students, who are willing to become keenly engaged in traditional philosophical questions and keep me always thinking about them. And, finally, I need to thank Marcia, my beloved spouse, companion, and fellow traveler into the ideas and practices of psychoanalysis and self psychology. Without our daily conversations and her profoundly abiding love, I could never have authored this book.

Introduction

Psychoanalysis, Self Psychology, and the Humanistic Tradition

The aim of this book is to show how psychoanalytic self psychology can offer original and important responses to pressing philosophical and cultural questions, especially those in ethics, moral psychology, and social life. My intent is to demonstrate that psychoanalysis in general and self psychology in particular are legitimated ways of rigorously probing the human psyche, and that the theory of human nature which has evolved from them can provide novel answers to the most vexing ethical and social concerns of contemporary life. These concerns address the most fundamental of ethical questions: how ought we to live as human beings? This question might better be put: how is it best to live as human beings in a post-religious, postmodern world, a world in which we cannot posit answers by referencing God or principles of pure reason. In order to probe this question we must inquire into what human beings in fact are, and, to me, psychoanalytic self psychology offers us an extraordinarily profound and innovative conceptualization of our human nature.

I propose as an initial answer to the fundamental ethical question that the best way to live as a human being is to achieve the highest degree of liveliness in one's soul.[1] I encountered this brilliant contention in the works of Nietzsche, who exposed the traditional goal of human striving—happiness—as being a deficient final value, for it could be attained in modernity with a soporific lifestyle that had a dearth of erotic striving and creative adventure (1883). The soul, more than anything else, seeks to feel as exuberantly alive as it can, and the great philosophical/psychological inquiry that needs to be undertaken is the exploration of what kind of soul is capable of the most liveliness. This formulation of the question goes back to Plato, who discovered that there are different ways of organizing the soul and that different kinds of souls open up different forms of human life. A major thematic throughout this book is that the soul capable of the most aliveness is not Plato's rational soul, Nietzsche's unstructured free spirit, nor an economic soul seeking to maximize pleasures, but a psyche revolving around what Heinz Kohut termed "a nuclear self." Since the self is largely unconscious, it had to await the development of psychoanalysis in order to be recognized and understood. In short, Kohut's theory offers a brilliantly original answer to the question of what kind of soul is most alive—indeed, an answer so novel that I believe it constitutes an authentic new ontology, a new possibility for inhabiting our humanity.[2]

Since many of the most profound thinkers in the Western tradition, starting with Plato and progressing to Freud, Marcuse (1955), and Jean-Luc Marion (2003), have linked the liveliness of the soul with eros—erotic love, I have undertaken an exploration into the relation between the self and eros, attempting to show in a novel way why Kohut needs to include eros as the unifying force in his notion of the self. This might seem strange since Kohut attempted to disentangle self psychology from the Freudian drives, but I will show that eros, even in the late Freud, is not a drive but a very different kind of motivation from that of our usual desires. If I am right in understanding that the cohesive force within self structure is eros, then we have a way of reinterpreting the late work of Freud to see it as anticipating the need for a psychology of the self, and we will also have built a strong bridge between the wisdom of ancient philosophy, Freud, and Kohut.

A third essential question that runs through the book is "Why is it personally good to be an ethical or morally good person?" With the transformation of a Medieval religious world into a modern economic one in which agents are supposed to seek their personal best interests, the critical question arises as to why modern persons should play by the rules or be ethically concerned for others if an unethical act is perceived as producing more personal pleasure and one is likely not to be caught doing it? Why not cheat? Given the extraordinary rates of cheating in American culture from major companies cooking their books, to identity thieves, to the common person cheating a bit on their taxes or partners, it is a question that seems to have no compelling answer for modern agents (Callahan, 2004). The only adequate response to this lack of a moral basis in modernity that I have found is the radical reconceptualization of what constitutes self-interest that derives from Kohut's notion of the self. In short, I will develop the idea that the best way to achieve an erotic liveliness of soul is to have a coherent, well-developed self, and that the person most likely to develop and sustain self structure is an ethical person—a person who empathically cares for others, exhibits the moral virtues as elaborated by Aristotle, and has a prevailing sense of fairness or justice (see chapter 7 for a full elaboration of this theory).

I found I could mine further philosophical riches from self psychology in the exploration of such questions as "Why do humans have such a problem with difference—otherness—and how might it be solved?" (chapter 8) "How might we re-conceive the nature of social justice if we cease looking at humans as pleasure-seeking economic agents and begin seeing them as beings who need to develop and realize core self-values?" (chapter 9) "How might we re-conceive history from the viewpoint of narcissistic pressures rather than economic or political ones?" (chapter 10) In general what I am probing is the possibility of an ontological shift from a modern economic way of being human to one that is grounded in a psychoanalytic self-psychological understanding of what it means to be human.

I

This book is intended for three audiences: psychoanalysts or therapists who want to probe the wider social and philosophical implications of self psychology and psychoanalysis, philosophers who are concerned with questions of moral psychology and ethics, and intelligent laypersons who are dissatisfied with the values and general form of life prescribed by our contemporary economic world. Indeed, even if one is a professional philosopher or therapist, one is always, first and foremost, a human being who, if you are alive to the crucial questions of what it means to be human and how to live well, will, I hope, be intrigued by this exploration of the philosophical treasures that derive from self-psychological thought. These ideas can open up new paths to self-knowledge, new ways to think about how to live, new perspectives on our historical, cultural, and natural contexts, and new ways of optimally relating to other human beings. Because we all belong to the wider economic society that instructs us to limit our thinking to the specific areas of our expertise, allowing ourselves to think, once again, in an existential way is already to break free of an embedded social code and pursue a thought-provoking journey into new possibilities.

For those unfamiliar with self psychology, it begins with the work of Heinz Kohut, a Viennese Jew who escaped the Nazis days after receiving his MD, came to Chicago, and soon became a celebrated psychoanalyst who established himself as one of the leading Freudians in the country.[3] His break from Freudian drive theory and his development of a psychoanalytic theory of the self took place from the mid 1960s until his death in the early 1980s. In a nutshell, Kohut said that the fundamental psychological task was not the development of an ego strong enough to manage sexual and aggressive drives but the development of a core nuclear self, and he further interpreted most psychopathology as emanating from injuries to the self rather than the repression of forbidden wishes. His psychoanalytic discovery of the self and his re-thinking the nature of narcissism initially reaped scorn from most of the established psychoanalytic community but has since become the basis for an important movement within psychoanalysis that has its own yearly international conference, journal, and practitioners on all the inhabited continents. Further, Kohut's ideas on empathy, the nature of the therapeutic relation, and his theory of the self have since generated significant shifts within American psychoanalysis as a whole. Indeed, I would go so far as to say that Kohut transformed the whole field by emphasizing the centrality of empathy, the importance of the client/analyst relationship, and the care for the patient's perspective rather than a theory that is telling the analyst what must be true for everyone.

However, despite his important developments in psychoanalysis and a bit of popular fame and misunderstanding in the 1970s,[4] Kohut's thought—the most important ideas about human nature since Freud—has been almost entirely ignored by that discipline whose provenance is to be concerned about the question of what it means to be human, namely, philosophy. And so the first task of this work is to ask why, if the work of Kohut and his followers is so important, has it not gained the recognition of the philosophic world or the general public?

First, Kohut is very difficult to read. He has neither Freud's elegance nor Lacan's intriguingly evocative language and often buries his conceptual discoveries in the densest of psychoanalytic jargon. His most philosophically and socially important work, *The Restoration of the Self* (1977), starts with a question seemingly of value only to clinicians—can an analysis be complete if it only deals with compensatory structures? It is also dense, overly long, and not well organized. Unless one is convinced that there are really important insights into philosophic and humanistic questions, they will quickly put the book down. I have tried in a number of works, including this one, to elucidate Kohut's theory as clearly as I can without excessive psychoanalytic jargon or terminology.

The second explanation for why Kohut's work remains unknown outside the clinical world is that it is situated within the psychoanalytic tradition, and academia has, for the past fifty years or so, largely rejected psychoanalysis as a viable way either to understand human beings or to treat their psychological debilitations, and the general public seems to have accepted this assessment. The reasons for this shunning/discrediting are numerous and include overinflated claims by psychoanalysts in the mid-century about the efficacy of psychoanalytic treatment, as well as insurance companies not wanting to pay claims for seemingly endless analyses (Lear, 2000, ch. 2); but the core of the critiques revolve around a number of influential thinkers who proclaimed psychoanalysis to be a pseudo-science.[5] At the same time as these "exposés" of psychoanalysis as a pseudo-science were being made, psychology departments were attempting to show that psychology was a genuine science, entirely distinct from the humanistic tradition that parented it. Psychologists decided to use a scientific methodology that reduced mental phenomena to objective events in the world which are, in principle, as predictable, measurable, and understandable as the physical events studied in physics and chemistry. Rather than treating human subjectivity as an activity different from that of objects—an activity that seems to involve the ability to be free, spontaneous, and capable of agency and whose fundamental impetus is something no physical entity has, namely, the production of meanings through which we can understand ourselves and the world, academic psychologists thought it better to view the mind as simply the passive outcome of a set of empirical events—patterns of reinforcement and/or neuronal firings.[6] Mind is erased and replaced by the study of behavior and/or the brain. And, so, various forms of psychology that appear more scientific, such as behaviorism, cognitive science, and neuroscience, have taken over psychology departments, and psychoanalysis has been banished to the same realm as astrology and phrenology. Philosophy, also under the sway of the demand to be scientific, has for the most part followed suit and eschewed psychoanalysis and its strange theory of unconscious subjectivity, a theory which offends the most general value in philosophy, that of rationality.

I confront the problem of the supposed scientific inadequacy of psychoanalysis in the next chapter when I ask "Can there be a science of subjectivity?" and find that the rejection of psychoanalysis because it does not fit a standard model of scientific inquiry is unwarranted, because subjectivity is not the kind of thing that can be understood by a method designed to study objects. Many of those who reject psychoanalysis seem to think that since the scientific method has been so successful in achieving an understanding of how the world of objects works, it will, therefore, be successful in achieving knowledge for any kind of thing that exists, thereby presuming that only object-like things exist. However, without something like a subject who can do such un-object-like activities as freely examining evidence, freely coming to conclusions about the evidence, and freely generating theories to account for the evidence, there could not be science, and, hence, science cannot deny the existence of subjectivity without contradicting itself. In short, subjectivity that does not work in strict causal patterns is the precondition for the possibility of science. I will try to show that subjectivity, while not open to traditional scientific methodologies, can, in fact, be rigorously inquired into, and that psychoanalysis offers, to date, the most profound, empirically generated, complex understanding of human mentality that has ever been achieved. It is a science, if you will, but one after its own kind and one adequate to its own subject matter—subjectivity.

The problem with this solution for many is that it seems to put us back into a Cartesian dualism of two kinds of substance—mind and matter or subjects and objects—a theory which makes the intersection of the two incomprehensible. Two preliminary remarks must be made to this objection. First, if matter is posited as the only kind of thing that exists, then we need to construct a concept of matter that explains how matter can feel, think, inquire into meanings, produce scientific theories, etc., for we know these activities occur, and if we think that only matter exists, then these must be some of the capabilities of matter. That is, matter cannot simply work like an opaque object without interiority or agentive subjectivity. Second, the metaphysical presupposition that posits that everything must be either mindless matter or matter-less mind needs to be rejected. The most brilliant and largely unread metaphysician of the twentieth century, Alfred North Whitehead—also one of the most important mathematicians of all time and someone who fully grasped quantum mechanics—developed a theory in which the final realities of the world are not material things and mental things, but events, each of which has subjective and objective features.[7] For Whitehead, all subatomic particles are series of connected events and minds are too, only minds are a far more complex series of events and exhibit much more of the subjective elements of events than do electrons. The reason we can only have probabilistic knowledge of electronic activity is that even at this level there is evidence of spontaneous creativity. There is so much more at the level of mentality that predictability for individual persons can only be for very gross general patterns. I am not claiming that Whitehead has discovered the truth of ultimate reality, but am saying that he offers us a stunningly different set of concepts through which we can think of subjectivity as a reality without having to fall into an untenable dualism.

Despite the overwhelming academic prejudice against psychoanalysis, there has been a small set of thinkers (mainly in comparative literature and philosophy) who have been attracted to the psychoanalytic tradition. However, this group of thinkers stays almost religiously focused on two psychoanalytic figures—Freud and Lacan—and has almost entirely eschewed self psychology. Working with Freud is legitimate because of his importance as a historical figure. Since Freud has no theory of the self, thinkers working with his thought are not led to self psychology. Neither are the thinkers who have been drawn to Lacan, probably the largest and most important set of philosophers working with psychoanalysis. Lacan produced a concept of the unconscious as a linguistic system that fit perfectly with the linguistic turn of twentieth-century philosophy and also with the Nietzschean maxim that there is no final foundation for meaning or action. For Nietzsche, God is dead; for Lacan, the chain of signifiers lacks a final ground. Since Lacan held the notion of the self to be an illusion that severely distorted our understanding of ourselves and resulted in psychopathology, philosophers inclined toward his theory are strongly disinclined to take up Kohut's self psychology.[8]

Finally, Kohut is not known in philosophy because the great majority of American philosophers work in the analytic tradition and deal with questions of language, epistemology, metaphysics, and logic and do not, for the most part, concern themselves with the great Socratic question of what it means to be human and how to live the best of human lives. If philosophers are interested in inquiring into the nature of mind they are more attracted to cognitive science or neuroscience, as these have more current legitimacy than psychoanalysis and fit with the objectifying trend of contemporary scholarship. Since it is unconventional (even professionally dangerous) for philosophers to turn to the psychoanalytic tradition for insights into the Socratic questions about human nature and the best way to live, they simply don't.

For all the above reasons (and further ones which follow), philosophers and academic psychologists have not taken up the work of Heinz Kohut, and the general public has followed academia's lead.

While the above discussion attempts to present and respond to some of the leading objections to psychoanalysis, let me now present a brief but, hopefully, convincing set of reasons for why psychoanalysis in general and self psychology in particular are crucial not only for philosophy but for society as a whole. Psychoanalysis is a tradition exploring what it means for human mentality to involve unconscious meanings and dynamics that often profoundly influence and limit our conscious intentions and abilities to carry them out. As such it offers the most innovative and challenging understanding of what it means to have a mind since the great Greek philosophers first started to theorize about the nature of the human psyche. As in Greek philosophy, the fundamental aim of psychoanalysis is to help persons know who they are and release them from internal structures that constrict their abilities to freely choose how to live their lives. While the Greek philosophers and the philosophic tradition they spawned have found rationality to be the key to freeing the psyche from the internal tyranny of the desires, the limitations imposed by believing in overly restrictive and unjustified social concepts, and the external pressures of society to think and act in coded ways, Freud and the psychoanalytic tradition have, on the other hand, explored a realm of unconscious debilitating constrictions which are not amenable to rational transformation and, further, have exposed rationality itself as imposing irrational limitations on the nature of experience. Not only has psychoanalysis uncovered a new set of hitherto unexplored limitations on human choice, but has also been discovering in the patient/therapist interaction a novel form of human relationship that has the power to restructure the dynamics of the psyche such that it can overcome unconscious restrictions and offer persons ways of achieving psychic integration other than control by rational mandates.

What self psychology adds to the general psychoanalytic attempt to achieve freedom by lessening unconscious constrictions is the exploration of a more positive form of freedom—the freedom to discover and be oneself. This freedom to actualize oneself might seem like nothing new, as it has been an essential value in American individualism for a long time; however, "the self" that Kohut discovered is not the self championed by either modern economic society or American individualism. It is a largely unconscious psychological structure which develops out of relationships with early caregivers, is inherently susceptible to fragmentation and depletion and, hence, always in need of others. It is the repository of self-esteem, vitality, inner coherence, and meaningfulness when the developmental process goes well, but can harbor injury, trauma, rage, and an unbearable sense of emptiness when severe failures in the relational process have occurred. When the self is injured or traumatized, psychic dynamics will then involve constructing defenses so as to protect it from further injury and compensate for the lack felt within. Typical narcissistic defenses include such common contemporary phenomena as addictions to substances and activities, entitled behavior, an overblown sense of importance, over-sensitivity to criticism, and a desperate need to attain symbols of greatness. Self psychologists are exploring how empathic responsiveness and interpersonal dynamics in the consulting room have the power to heal injuries to the self and re-vitalize it.

It is self psychology's two claims that the self is the most vitalizing of psychic structures but also the most vulnerable to injury and, hence, always in need of others, that makes this theory capable of giving an answer to the question of why we should become ethical human beings. If we conceive of persons, like the economic world does, as autonomous units seeking pleasure rather than as organisms needing to create and sustain a sense of self through relationships with others, then I can find no compelling argument that can be given to individuals as to why they should restrain their pursuit of pleasure when it conflicts with the well-being of others. Without a change in how modern society conceives of the self, there are no secular reasons other than fear of censure that can be given for why anyone should adopt an ethical way of being in the world rather than a hedonistic self-serving one. It is self psychology's new way of conceiving the self and what constitutes self-interest that so attracts me and opens up a novel framework for addressing traditional ethical concerns.

There are many other important concepts about our human nature that come from self psychology and which will be elaborated in the succeeding chapters in this book. Here are some of the ideas that will be explored:

Self Psychology

- offers a new map of the human psyche in which ego functions and self functions are distinguished and this distinction will provide a new ground for understanding both personal and ethical life. The Western philosophical tradition has fully explored the rational and linguistic capacities of the ego, but has missed the most crucial of all psychological structures: the self. Plato had a sense for it when he explored *eros* in his *Symposium*, but then shifted quickly to the primacy of reason and the rational ego in his seminal work, *The Republic*. The existentialists knew that the heart of who we are is a singular, creative, erotic self, but did not have an adequate understanding of the unconscious or developmental theory to know how the self develops and what it needs to be sustained. The concept of self in distinction from the ego offers ethicists a naturalistic ground for justifying why persons should adopt a moral stance as their primary way of being in the world—indeed, I think that self psychology is the only naturalistic ground for ethics that works in a post-religious age.
- incorporates into its concept of the nuclear self Plato's insight that human life needs to revolve around ideals, Nietzsche's claim that spontaneous creativity is the essential human activity, and Hegel's notion that the soul needs always to be working out a dialectical tension between sides of itself: ideals and ambitions—universality and particularity.
- can, in contrast to existentialism, show how a person with a fully realized self need not be alienated from the wider social world.
- can offer profound reasons for why humans seek to be with those who are "same" but also why they must endure the tension of engaging otherness. It can thus offer crucial insights into the terrible social problems that plague the modern world in the fear of "the other," and the retreat to relate only to those who are the same.
- can offer those inclined towards existentialism a genuine notion of what it means to have a singular self—a notion grounded in empirical observation and the testing ground of clinical space.
- offers an alternative vision of the self from either that of the economic subject or the American rugged individual and can thereby offer a different way of thinking about self-interest than the optimizing of pleasures or the attainment of self-sufficiency.
- is discovering optimal ways for humans to relate to one another in its exploration of empathy in the therapeutic relationship.
- can offer social theorists a new concept of what humans genuinely need. It will be a variation of Hegel's theory of recognition, but offer an original account of the specific ways in which we need to be recognized in order to sustain our humanity.
- can offer philosophers of history an understanding of how narcissistic pressures influence historical eras, thereby tying together the original his-

torical theorists—Herodotus and Thucydides—with a contemporary view-point.

I believe that self psychology is needed in order for the great humanistic tradition to go forward. What I understand by the "humanistic tradition" is the ongoing historical conversation that inquires into what it means to be human and how best to live a distinctively human life. It refuses to make humanity subservient to some kind of non-human authority such as God, reduce human experience to a set of objective variables that can be empiri-cally measured, or follow Heidegger in his attempt to displace humanity from the center of concern with Being. I do not mean by the humanistic tradition the one so fiercely criticized by post-structural theory, namely, that each person has an essential, metaphysically generated self that remains identical with itself for a lifetime, for the Kohutian self is a dynamic, fragile system that is constantly evolving and constantly subject to environmental influences.[9] For me, the humanistic tradition posits that we must inquire into the question of how it is best to live by understanding what it means to be human. This tradition was initiated in the West with Socrates, Plato, and, especially Aristotle, but is a tradition which has come under severe attack from a number of sources, each quite different from the other—existential-ism, Darwinism, Foucault and social philosophy, and postmodernism.

The core of this critique is that one cannot base ethics on human nature, for there is no such thing as human nature. The biological approach would have us motivated by the same drives that motivate all mammals—sexual reproduction and survival. Existentialism—especially Sartre—would empha-size that what is crucial about human beings is their openness—that we are free to choose who we are and how to value or devalue any given part of our nature. That is, we are free to choose the ground of our choosing—nothing is a set ground for choice, certainly not a set human nature. Lacanian thought posits that there is no pre-discursive reality, no final ground for the chain of signifiers. Foucault and other post-structuralist thinkers find no essential hu-manity, for we are mere variables to be formed into particular kinds of persons by the social pressures of our regnant discursive power/knowledge systems.[10] Postmodernism would champion that there are multiple ways to be human and we should respect this diversity rather than finding an essential human nature. It is these powerful conceptual paradigms that I believe are in part responsible for the non-recognition of self psychology as a new concep-tual way to understand our humanity.

Each of the above positions contains a crucial truth that must be acknowl-edged in any new humanism—we are mammals and have a mammalian inheritance; consciousness does have an openness to possibility that is essen-tial to being human; humans are for the most part colonized by the social systems of which they are a part, and there are many different ways in which humans can occupy their humanity. Self psychology can be articulated as a position that affirms these truths about the human species, but also claims that human psychology revolves around the development of a core self, and it is this claim that provides the ground for ethical life and genuine agency, something that none of the other positions can do.

Without some notion of a substantial self that can grant meaning, resist capture by mass social pressures, and ground ethical agency, the humanistic tradition will wither and die. It is here where self psychology is most important, because it can provide a notion of the self that fits with the naturalistic cast of modern knowledge but can also be the basis for the dignity and power of the ethical subject. We will find that it acknowledges and fosters different expressions of humanity, openness of choice, and acceptance of the reality of social pressures, while being able to give a basis for choice and a ground for integrity in its concept of the self.

In sum, I hope this volume will show that the concepts of self psychology can further the great humanistic tradition that has previously helped save humans from subservience to gods and that can now rescue them from being reduced to quantifiable objects, mere pawns of socio-discursive disciplinary structures, or groundless bits of freedom with no basis for the generation of meaning. I believe that self psychology is the only empirically substantiated way to give ethical subjectivity an important ground, the only substantial ground it has had since the death of God in the nineteenth century. I suggest that self psychology offers the most compelling way to continue the Socratic and humanistic traditions of attempting to achieve freedom through attaining self-knowledge and achieving psychic integrity by developing a core self. It is not only a bastion against contemporary theoretical positions that attempt to deny the reality of self, freedom, and subjectivity, but also a position that represents a very different way of being human from the pleasure-optimizing economic subjects who roam the earth these days.

II

This book is divided into two parts. Part I first attempts to situate Kohut's concept of the self within the great philosophical tradition, extending back to Plato, that inquires into the life of the soul (ch. 2) and then offers an original metapsychology for thinking about the nature of subjectivity and the place of the self within its multiple motivational systems (ch. 3). We then plunge more deeply into crucial conceptual issues concerning the self—what is the nature of the energy that binds ideals and ambitions into a self? (ch. 4), and why should we think of the multidimensional self as singular—as a "one" rather than, as many postmodernists would have it, a "many?" (ch. 5). Finally, Kohut has no theory about the self's relation to nature, but in my own personal history, nature has been a life-saving selfobject for me. Hence, I turn to America's first great self psychologists—Emerson and Thoreau—to explore the relation of nature to the formation of the self (ch. 6).

Part II focuses primarily on the ethical, cultural, and social implications of this new concept of human nature. In particular, I will attempt to show why psychoanalytic self psychology offers our post-religious, postmodern world the only naturalistic explanation for why it is personally good to become an ethical human being (ch. 7). I will also indicate how psychoanalysis in general and self psychology in particular can offer profound understandings for why discrimination and violence against the other is such a common human phenomenon, but also why we need to relate to those who are different from us in order to grow. I further contend that self psychology's concept of empathy offers us the best understanding for what constitutes a non-objectifying relation to those who are other (ch. 8). I continue by showing how this new concept of human nature requires us to re-think what is meant by social justice, focusing not on the economic status/needs of human beings but on the needs of their selves (ch. 9). Finally, I attempt to re-think, in huge brushstrokes, the nature of modern Western history from the viewpoint of narcissistic pressures rather the vicissitudes of power or economics (ch. 10).

However, before we can dive into any of these delicious subjects, we must first confront the fact that psychoanalysis has been severely attacked and discredited as a legitimate realm of knowledge. Hence, we need first to inquire into what kind of epistemological validity psychoanalysis has, and this will constitute the subject matter of the next chapter.

NOTES

1. Like Jonathan Lear in *Open-Minded: Working Out the Logic of the Soul* (2000) and Mari Ruti in *Reinventing the Soul* (2006), I want to reclaim the word "soul" for philosophy, away from its capture by religion. "Mind" is too embedded with rationality and consciousness to be helpful in discussing a concept of human mentality that involves unconscious processes. While "psyche" is fine, it is Greek and does not have the wealth of associations that "soul" does. By "soul" I mean that subjective activity which produces meanings and through which we act. It involves all the elements of human subjectivity—thoughts, affects, meanings, and self-awareness.

2. Since Kohut wrote in the 1970s, self psychology has developed several subsidiary theories, namely, intersubjectivity and relational self psychology. I will not probe the connections and differences in these theories, as they mainly revolve around how to conceive of the analytic situation. Rather I will concentrate on the two basic features of self psychology which I think are held by all these theories: (1) that the development of a core self is the crucial psychological task, and (2) that this core self is developed from and depends upon relations with others.

3. For a full account of Kohut's life and theory, see Charles Strozier's fine biography: *Heinz Kohut: The Making of a Psychoanalyst* (2001).

4. See Elizabth Lunbeck's *The Americanization of Narcissism* (2014) for an interesting historical account of how Kohut's theory of narcissism and the self was received and misunderstood by the wider public.

5. These attacks include—most famously—those of Adolf Grünbaum (1984), Alasdair MacIntyre (1958), and Ludwig Wittgenstein (1958). Although all of these attacks have been critically taken apart, these criticisms of the attacks remain largely unknown while the original critiques are still taken as compelling. See Donald Levy's *Freud Among the Philosophers* (1996) for an excellent criticism of the critiques of psychoanalysis.

6. See Frank Summer's *The Psychoanalytic Vision* (2013) for a thorough critique of the objectifying forces at work in psychology.

7. I wrote my PhD dissertation on Whitehead in 1968 and his theory is presupposed in all of my thinking. For those who want to probe Whitehead's theory, I suggest starting with *Science and the Modern World* (1925) and then Donald Sherburne's *A Key to Whitehead's Process and Reality* (1966). Sherburne's organization of Whitehead's *magnum opus* makes its fundamental concepts far more comprehensible while keeping Whitehead's original language.

8. However, it must be noted that what Lacan and Kohut mean by the self is quite different. Kohut's self is much more fluid than the concept of self critiqued by Lacan for overly constricting psychic flow. However, it is true that Kohut's theory calls for more psychic organization than Lacan's does. For Kohut, we need self structure in order to be open to genuine adventures and alternative possibilities. Since the process of the self is never complete, it contains "lack" within it, while for Lacan, lack precedes all structure, and attempts to organize the flow of psychic processes in some sense lessens the life of the soul. For Kohut, if a person has a disorganized or absent self at the core of experience, she will be psychotic and have no world at all.

9. I need to note that although Mari Ruti's *Reinventing the Soul* (2006) is subtitled *Posthumanist Theory and Psychic Liife,* her themes of a posthumanist soul are almost the same as mine for the humanist soul. We both take the Socratic questions seriously and both think that there is a unique particularity to each person that can serve as the basis for creativity and agency.

10. See especially Foucault's *Discipline and Punish* (1975) for a powerful account of how modern disciplinary, socio-discursive power structures work to form modern subjects.

Part I

Psychoanalysis and the Nature of the Self and Soul

Chapter One

Knowledge in Psychoanalysis

Can There Be a Science of Subjectivity?

Before we can explore the concepts of self and soul in psychoanalytic self psychology, we need to confront the criticism that psychoanalysis is not a legitimate discipline because it is not a science. Psychoanalysis came into being as a discipline when Freud proclaimed that his new theory of the human psyche was a scientific discovery and that his method for curing psychological pathologies constituted a validated medical practice. These were brilliant moves on his part, given that science was the only epistemological currency worth much of anything in the first part of the twentieth century and that the methods of scientific medicine were considered the only trustworthy path to medical cure. However, psychoanalysis' claim to be a science of subjectivity has turned out to be a highly problematical contention, one that has brought devastating criticism from many quarters and turned numerous people unfairly away from its genuine worth. It has been felt that if psychoanalysis can be exposed as not being a science, then it can be dismissed as a fraud, and nothing seems to bring out more disgust and rejection than something's being shown to be a fraud.

I believe that the failure of psychoanalysis to establish its claim to be a science has been in large part responsible for its fall from preeminence in both the therapeutic and academic realms. It is not only untaught in academic psychology departments but sneered at (NYT, 11/25/07). It survives in the academy not as a science but as a theory that can be used by literature and philosophy departments to interpret literature, film, and human nature. However, nothing is quite so passé as an interpretative theory that has just been replaced by the latest theory-du-jour, and new interpretative theories seem to pop up every decade or so. In short, psychoanalysis' existence is being

3

threatened, and I think this is due in some measure to the claim it has made for its being a science of subjectivity. While I do believe that part of its work can legitimately be called "scientific," psychoanalysis is in essence not a science nor should it want or claim to be one.

If psychoanalysis is not a science, what is it? The responses to this question are usually stated in false binary oppositions: If it is not a science, then it must be an art, or a religion, or a philosophy. When certain aspects of it are emphasized to the detriment to others, psychoanalysis can appear to be a science, an art, a philosophy, high drama, and even a religion with a great founding father. It is, however, none of these but an original form of human inquiry that achieves knowledge of human subjectivity in a way different from any of the established disciplines.

What I intend to do in this chapter is to establish why psychoanalysis cannot be a traditional science by showing that there can be no such thing as a science of subjectivity. That is, it is not a fault of psychoanalysis that it is not a science but rather a necessity built into its fundamental project of knowing and transforming human subjectivity. I will then attempt to explain how knowledge operates in psychoanalysis, showing both why psychoanalysts could have thought it was a science and why its unique way of knowing and transforming subjectivity is one of the great discoveries in the history of humankind, one which constitutes a legitimate and valuable discipline that deserves a preeminent place both within the field of psychological health and the academy.

WHY PSYCHOANALYSIS CANNOT BE A SCIENCE OF SUBJECTIVITY

There have, of course, been many attempts to reveal that psychoanalysis is not a science, Adolph Grünbaum's (1984) perhaps being the most famous. These critiques generally show how psychoanalysis fails in one way or another to properly follow standard scientific protocol as outlined in standard scientific theory texts such as those of Popper (1963) and/or Hempel (1965). The problems are manifold. First, the observational data in psychoanalysis are intrinsically faulty, for minds are not directly observable through the five senses. Second, since each analysis is unique, there is no way for observers to validate its findings by replicating it. Also, psychoanalysis does not seem to follow the standard scientific method of proposing a hypothesis, designing an experiment that would validate or falsify the hypothesis, and performing the proposed experiment—an experiment that supposedly could be duplicated by anyone anywhere. Further, psychoanalysis has failed to generate any psychological laws that are so accurate and simple that they can be used to predict what any human beings would do or think when certain variables are present.

There also seems to be no standard way to calculate and measure internal psychological phenomena.

Some defenders of psychoanalysis have responded to these criticisms by saying that it is a young science that just needs a bit more time to get itself up to scientific snuff, while others have pointed to recent kinder, more inclusive concepts of science as being able to accommodate psychoanalysis. I believe such defenses to be misguided, for insofar as psychoanalysis is that discipline whose aim is to understand and transform subjective phenomena, it can never be a science. The reason why psychoanalysis cannot be a science now or ever, regardless of improvements in theory and training, is that science, by its very nature and in all of its conceptualizations, is the objective study of objects, while psychoanalysis attempts to know and transform persons in their subjectivities.

By "object" I mean anything that has no interiority, no intentionality, no experiences, no peculiar way of being the kind of thing it is, and no self-generated agency. By "objectively" studying something, I mean that one is not subjectively responding to the object in terms of values or empathy, but dispassionately observing its properties and behavior. Scientifically minded psychology students training rats to run a maze are not to empathically im-merse themselves in the rat's psyche but to observe what reinforcement schedules optimize the rat's ability to run the maze.

Objects are identified as having stable properties and as being located in a field of causes. They are available for public observation; that is, the proper-ties of objects are either empirical or have empirical correlates. When science studies any empirical phenomenon, it studies those features of the entity that are observable, have empirical correlates, and which behave in regular and predictable patterns. Science is the best method ever invented for the study of objects, for it lessens the possibility of subjective distortions more than any other discipline and has highly sophisticated ways for discovering regular-ities, coding correlations, and making predictions about how objects will behave.

In contrast, something is a subject if it has internal experiences that are unobservable to anyone else. These experiences have the character of inten-tionality—that is, there is a subjective awareness of something appearing to consciousness. A subject is also something that is capable of agency and spontaneous responsiveness in ways that are not fully predicable from the objective circumstances of the subject. One can know all the objective condi-tions affecting subjectivity and not be able to predict fully the outcome for the subject, for what the conditions *mean* to the subject will make a consider-able difference.

Also, subjectivity has a qualitative way of being a subject that cannot be understood by anyone who does not have that kind of subjectivity. Thomas Nagel captures the privacy of subjectivity when he asks us to consider what it is like to be a bat, for the bat experiences the world in a way that we can never comprehend, even if we know with great exactitude the structure of the bat's neuronal and perceptive equipment (1986). There is a "how" the bat experiences the world that is unavailable to anything but a bat. There is a how a subject experiences itself and the world that is simply not available to anyone who is not that kind of subject. Finally, all subjective events are private. They are not capable of being experienced by anyone else but the being having the experiences. A neuroscientist might be able to see electrical and chemical activity going on in my brain when I think of Aunt Sally, but they can never see my thought of Aunt Sally or what it means to me no matter how high powered their instruments are.

Another way of saying this is that objects simply are what they are. In Jean-Paul Sartre's terms, they are "in-itselfs" (1943). Subjectivity, on the other hand, is a "for-itself." Its essence is not to be anything, but to be in an internal relationship both to objects and to itself. This relational experience is not a field of energy but a field of meanings. This field of meanings is the essence of subjectivity and is not reducible to any set of physical events. It might be necessary for neurons to fire in order for a person to have a meaningful experience, but the neurons are not identical with, nor could they ever be proved to be identical with, the meanings of the experience.

Let me stay with Sartre for a moment: he says that consciousness—subjectivity—is in essence a radical freedom—a primordial power of choice that has no objective ground. No matter who or what we are, we can, according to Sartre, "choose" to change. I believe that Sartre is correct in saying that consciousness or subjectivity has a free activity at its core that objects do not. This is not to say that subjectivity cannot have genuinely obstinate structures that compel it into repetitions, but that it can never be reduced to these structures.

We can mine further riches concerning subjectivity from Sartre. He says that when subjects look at one another, they tend to objectify the other, tend to turn the other's subjectivity into an object. Others see me as having a certain set of defining objective characteristics—male, somewhat advanced in age, married, of moderate build, etc. They expect me to act today as I acted yesterday. That is, they treat me as an object. Sartre says that insofar as humans naturally tend to objectify the subjectivity of others, human sociality is a hell with no exit. I think that in locating the objectifying gaze, Sartre has articulated a prevalent structure of human sociality, but that this kind of sociality is not the only kind available to us. There is a way of relating in which a subject can affirm and deepen the authentic subjectivity of another rather than objectify it. More than any other discipline, psychoanalysis is the realm in which this form of sociality is being explored. We might say that the gaze of the scientist necessarily objectifies the world, while the gaze of the psychoanalyst subjectively affirms the subjective powers of the other to such an extent that creative transformation is ignited and a subjectivity that had been frozen in repetitive structures begins to break free. We can conclude that insofar as psychoanalysis is an activity that inquires into and hopes to transform the subjectivity of subjects—that inquires into coherencies or disruptions in a subject's field of meanings, her ability to be an agent, and her ability to respond creatively and spontaneously to the world, it would be incoherent to expect it to be a science that studies objects objectively.

Of course, there is one stunning complication to this tidy conclusion, namely, that all subjectivity is structured, and the structures of subjectivity can be objectively studied as objective features of it. It was Immanuel Kant who first discovered that subjectivity is always structured (1787). In order for consciousness to experience any kind of world, it cannot be, as Aristotle, Locke, and others proclaimed, a *tabula rasa*. It has to have a structure by which to organize the rather chaotic and overwhelming data of experience. Every form of subjectivity has a structure that organizes the data given by experience into a world. While Kant attempted to map the essential structures of an empirically knowing mind, a moral mind, and an aesthetic mind, post-Kantians have taken his basic idea and used it to explore all kinds of ways in which the structures of subjectivity produce not only different ways of experiencing the world but different worlds. We now think that nationalities, races, genders, sexual orientations, etc. deeply affect how persons subjectively structure and experience their worlds.

Freud adopted this Kantian orientation and took it into the realm of unconscious subjectivity. What each of the designated psychopathologies names is a certain way a subject has of organizing experience. A paranoid's structured subjectivity will find dangers in the world that ordinary people experience as safe. A narcissist is structured in such a way that he will experience the world as centered on himself where other people can recognize multiple centers of importance and being. Obsessive compulsives often structure their realities around seemingly meaningless rituals that require perfect compliance.

What is important for us is to see that these psychological structures are objective features of subjectivity that can be known in a more or less scientific way. They are like properties that are the bases for classifications in biology or chemistry. Types can be identified, symptoms linked, likely origins determined. In botany we can tell what a plant is by examining such features as the shape of its leaves, its height, the color of its flowers, and nature of its stamens, etc. Likewise, in psychoanalysis when we find someone who is highly self-referential, treats others as having worth only if they can give him important tribute, makes numerous entitled demands, and typically demands to be center stage, we can hypothesize that we are dealing with someone who suffers from a narcissistic pathology.

As with all classificatory schematisms in the sciences, the typologies of psychopathological structures will get more sophisticated with time and diagnosis will become more exact. Psychoanalysts and other mental health practitioners have over the past century greatly refined the categories of psychological illness and I imagine that this refinement will continue. It is because psychoanalytic theorists have mapped the contours of unconscious subjectivity with more precision and depth than ever before that they have thought psychoanalysis to be a science. Nevertheless, while scientific knowledge of subjective structures and the development of an objective ability to diagnose which structures are predominant in an individual are crucially important to the analytic field, they do not and can not represent the heart of what psychoanalysis is about, for psychoanalysis is, in essence, two subjects inquiring into the subjectivity of one of them without reducing that subject to an object.

It is the unremitting attending to subjectivity that lies at the essence of Lacanian psychoanalysis. Lacan wrote, "What must be understood about psychoanalytic experience is that it proceeds entirely in this subject-to-subject relationship, which means that it preserves a dimension that is irreducible to any psychology considered to be the objectification of certain of an individual's properties" (1966, p. 215). What appears wild and strange about Lacan's way of doing psychoanalysis can, I believe, be attributed to his unremitting insistence on attending to the subjectivity of his analysands and refusing to box them into objective psychological cages.

When Freud wrote in the *Introductory Lectures* that "knowledge is not always the same as knowledge" (1916–1917, vol. 16, p. 281), he was saying that the objective knowing of oneself could not be the kind of transformative knowledge needed in psychoanalysis. His renunciation of hypnosis as an adequate vehicle for doing psychoanalytic work was also due to his recognition of the difference between objectively knowing an objective truth of oneself and subjectively knowing what it means to be a person who is living that truth.

A passage from Jonathan Lear's *Therapeutic Action* (2004) makes it clear as to the difference between making an objective statement about an objective structure and the genuine work of psychoanalysis. Suppose, he writes, that at the end of a patient's first session the analyst says, "Your case is easy: you want to kill your mother and have your father to yourself. That will be $50,000 and we don't need to meet again" (p. 11). Discursive statements of objective facts, even surprising and hidden facts of unconscious intentions, simply is not what psychoanalysis is fundamentally about.

The question that looms before us is how we can understand the concepts of knowledge and truth in relation to a non-objectifying exploration and transformation of subjectivity.

PSYCHOANALYSIS AND THE KNOWLEDGE OF SUBJECTIVITY

Psychoanalysis was invented as a way to overcome psychological pathologies by a person's coming to know who she really is, renouncing infantile
wishes, and accepting truths about herself that at one point were so unbearable as not to be tolerable to consciousness. The key to the whole process is a
form of human interaction in which a human being with an unconscious
mind can come into a state of self-knowledge. As such, psychoanalysis falls
under the command that was written in stone over the portal at Delphi, *gnothi
sauton*—know thyself—a command that also provided the sacred ground for
both Socratic philosophy and Attic drama.

The Greeks realized that the gaining of self-knowledge was a different
kind of enterprise from the acquisition of other forms of knowledge. There
are a number of words for knowing in ancient Greek, but *gignosko*—from
which *gnothi* is derived—has more the sense of "coming into knowledge"
than the other verbs, indicating that the process of coming to know ourselves
might not result in a finished end product. Indeed, there is the sense with this
verb that the process of coming to know oneself is profoundly connected to
the process of becoming who one is.

That was certainly how Socrates understood the process of coming to
know who one is. That process involved the discovery that underlying one's
particularity was a realm of universal meanings that grounded and sustained
all human souls. The more we can, through dialectical questioning, come to
dwell in this realm, the more we can realize our immortal nature and not be
so terrified by our transience nor driven crazy by tyrannical urges that invade
us. For Socrates, the process of coming to know oneself has the power to
release persons from pathos—pathology—which he understood as any form
of passivity—and give them the possibility of self-determination. Since the
state of being fully self determining rather than being determined by external
forces is a state akin to the gods, the philosophical journey to self-knowledge
is seen by Socrates as nothing less than an apotheosis—a transformation to a
different realm of being.

The Greek tragedians did not think that the process of coming to self-
knowledge was always so felicitous. When Sophocles' Oedipus comes to
know who he is, it is so unbearably traumatic that he violently stabs out his
eyes. When Sophocles' Ajax comes to clarity after being in a state of delu-
sional madness in which he killed a herd of sheep thinking it to be an
opposing army, he commits suicide as the shame of this self-knowledge
makes living intolerable.

Psychoanalysis draws from each of these understandings of self-knowledge but is neither of them. Like Sophocles, psychoanalysis finds that under-
taking the path to self-knowledge is a courageous journey that often leads
one into a dark realm of agonizing truths about oneself, but unlike the So-

phoclean heroic descent into the shadows of the soul, psychoanalysis is a shared descent, and the sharing makes it far less likely that the journey to self-knowledge will end in tragedy.

Like the philosophical tradition, psychoanalysis believes in the possibility that self-knowledge can be genuinely transformative, but unlike philosophy it grasps this transformation as one solely within the realm of particularity or singularity. Psychoanalytic transformation is not a metaphysical or religious transformation from one state of being to another but from having a dysfunctional psyche unable to live fully in reality with openness to possibilities, especially possibilities of love and friendship—to one that is more open, creative, and capable of engaging in nourishing relations with others.

In that psychoanalysis draws on empirical evidence as in the sciences, grasps the fated darkness that intersects human lives as in tragedy, believes in the power of self-knowledge to be transformative as in philosophy, and understands that the journey into self-knowledge must be done in a guided way as in the great spiritual traditions, it gathers these most important ways of exploring what it means to be human but supersedes them by conceiving a new path into the mysterious world of self-knowledge, one that can do something none of the previous methods could do—delve into unconscious subjectivity. I believe that psychoanalysis has been able to produce this profound and transformative way of exploring human subjectivity because of three startling innovations it has made in understanding what is needed to achieve self-knowledge.

First, it redefines the process by which self-knowledge is gained from an individual journey to a shared voyage. The analyst's participation in the passage to self-knowledge is important not simply because humans are subject to massive delusions, denials, and over-idealizations of themselves, but because in gaining and accepting knowledge of who the analysand is, the analyst gives the safety and acceptance necessary for the analysand to proceed down the dangerous path into the horrors and glories of his own soul.

Second, it is crucial that the analyst have objective knowledge about the structures and dynamics of the human psyche, especially its unconscious dynamics. Without this kind of objective framework, the possibilities of falling into the trivialities of everyday psychological explanations or getting lost in a haze of indecipherable signifiers are too great. This is to say that the process of attaining self-knowledge must be a theoretically informed process. I believe that the great psychoanalytic theorists of the twentieth century have given us the most profound and effective maps of unconscious subjectivity that have ever been produced. Without these the unconscious depths of the human psyche could not be explored.

Third, the analyst is capable of knowing who the analysand is by empathically immersing herself in the subjectivity of the analysand. Kohut called empathy "vicarious introspection" and thought that knowledge gained through empathy defined the field of psychoanalysis (1959). He thought of empathy as a kind of sixth sense that could produce knowledge of the internal states of human beings the way that the other senses give us knowledge of the external states of the world. While he believed that empathy produced a kind of scientific knowledge, I think that this claim is misleading. While empathy can result in objective data about another subject's inner states, this is not the primary way in which empathy is an epistemological process. Because empathy involves a mimetic subjective response to the inner state of another subject, it affirms and accepts that state while knowing it. It is the one form of knowing that does not objectify another subject because it duplicates the subjectivity of the other in itself. Duplication is the most profound form of affirmation.

The mimetic replication of feeling that occurs in empathy is like, but falls short of, identification. Although I sadly feel your sadness, I am not sad. Although I depressively feel your depression, I am not depressed. While there is a direct transfer of the subjective state of one person into the subjective state of the other, it is received not as how I am feeling but as how another is feeling. If empathy were identification, then all that would happen would be a replication of reality; it would be an ontological event, not an epistemological one. On the other hand, what is known through empathy is not reduced to mere objective data, for it is kept in a form of subjective animation in the mimetic act. I know how you are feeling or what is motivating you in the most direct way possible, by finding it subjectively present in my own subjectivity.

I believe that empathic responsiveness might be the most powerful way we have of knowing reality—by taking it into ourselves without identifying with it. We see this kind of empathic knowing in the dances of original peoples in which they gain the strength of bears by mimicking bears, the soaring wisdom of eagles by mimicking eagles, or the creative energy of the earth by mimicking the rising up of plant life in the spring. Great thespians use empathic knowing in grasping how their characters feel, think, and orient toward the world without becoming identical with those characters. Empathy allows them to know their characters in a way that they could never get by reading intelligent literary criticism. Empathy is also crucial in the process by which we come to know the meaning of a work of art. When we find ourselves profoundly attuned to the meanings in a work of art, I believe we are empathically replicating the creative visioning of the artist in our aesthetic response. In sum, empathy gives us reality directly; discursive knowledge gives only an account of reality.

While empathic knowing often does not—and ought not—reach a level of linguistic articulation, it nonetheless constitutes a form of knowledge that can be further validated or falsified because it acts in a predictive way. If my empathy tells me that you are in a state of sorrow, I can predict how your eyes will look, how your limbs will be held, and how your voice will sound, and if you leap off the couch and start whistling a happy tune, then I know my empathic grasp was more than likely mistaken. The ability to self-correct what one learns in empathy is crucial for it to be thought of as a genuine way of gaining knowledge. The truth discovered in empathy needs to coherently resonate with other indicators of unconscious subjectivity. However, I need to emphasize that it is not propositional coherence that I am speaking of but the kind of coherence that occurs at a level of implicit knowing, a level that often does not reach explicit articulation in focused consciousness but which operates as an important background understanding to almost everything we do in life.

We now have one more question: how does the combination of an objective knowledge of psychological structures and empathically knowing subjective states produce transformation? This is, of course, the great mystery of therapeutic action. I believe that the objective mapping out of the psychological structures haunting a person's subjectivity not only gives a feeling of safety but allows the person to see what needs to be changed. It is hard to transform something without knowing what that something is. But objectively knowing facts about ourselves does not itself bring about transformation. Rather it is the empathic immersion that is the catalyst for transformation—but only if the patient can reach a point where she can empathically identify with the analyst's empathy. The problem with dissociated material is that patients cannot accept it as a truth of themselves. But in empathy, the analyst does. When patients are able to empathically experience and accept the analyst's empathic acceptance of their dissociated parts, then they can both start to accept themselves and change who they are (Bromberg, 1998).

The analysand is able to change because she now has a dual relationship to her psychological reality: she both is it and has an empathic knowledge of it. The parts of her subjectivity that are pathologically functioning operate by being fragmented off of the major center of subjectivity. They are being denied by a conscious subjectivity as being real or as representing a truth of who the subject is or what the subject experienced. The analyst in discovering them and empathically accepting them make them available to the analysand to know, accept, and integrate. The dual relation of the subject to her dissociated parts allows a dialectic to set up in which a rejecting and an accepting subjectivity can discourse with one another—with, of course, the help of the analyst.

Let me clarify the above. When subjectivity fragments, each fragment is itself a subjectivity. That is, each fragment acts as though it were a subject with intentions, a way of grasping the world with its own structures, and a characteristic way of being in the world. Phillip Bromberg calls these fragments, "self-states" (1998). While a split-off self-state might not be the full-blown personality that is found in multiple personality disorders, it might be given a name and be treated as an undeveloped subject. Psychoanalysts have tended to talk about split-off parts as though they were objects—repressed oedipal desires, frozen affects, traumatic memories, denied narcissistic rage, etc., not as mini-subjectivities. What I am claiming is that, for instance, the split-off oedipal desires belong to an immature five-year-old little self that has a whole way of being in the world and grasping the world and which can be communicated with by an empathic therapist.

Each dissociated subjectivity carries in it, by necessity, feelings of isolation, detachment, unworthiness, and despair. When the analyst empathizes with one of these subsidiary subjectivities, it stimulates the dissociated subjectivity to enter a relation with the more mature subjective core of the analysand and with this new relationship, the split-off part can become integrated and engage in a developmental trajectory. It is the analyst's empathic recognition and acceptance of these neglected or denied subjectivities that initiate the movement toward greater coherence, maturity, and self-knowledge.

Since subjectivity always tends to be fragmenting—either traumatically or just by having so many complex aspects to itself that it enters into contradictions with previous objective structures, to be a subject means always to be repairing and re-integrating ourselves. More than any other form of human interaction, the psychoanalytic relationship educates us in how to go about performing this essential human function of repairing and re-integrating. It reveals the path towards integrity. But it also reveals that with this view of the fragile and fragmenting subject, there can be no finality in self-knowledge, self-cohesion, or authentic self-expression.

This understanding of subjectivity gives rise to a very different view of what constitutes self-knowledge from the usual one of a person's being able to articulate in discursive language a number of true propositions about themselves. Such a view reduces subjectivity to a set of objectifying statements and does not capture the dynamic and inter-relational aspects of the self. It is not that discursively articulated knowledge is not important—it is—but self-knowledge is most completely expressed simply by being who one is. So long as persons are effectively actualizing their core values and talents in an integrated way, are empathically attuned to the different areas of subjectivity working in them, and have some idea about what is essential to them and what peripheral, I would say that they "know themselves."

Although Hegel did not grasp the crucial role of empathy in the development of the psyche, he was the philosopher who most brilliantly saw that the spirit's needs for integrating its divisions, achieving self-knowledge, and attaining freedom were all aspects of one and the same developmental journey (1807). Hegel describes subjectivity as taking on various objective forms, each of which implicitly claims to be a fully adequate way of being in the world and an adequate expression of subjectivity. However, every objective structure fails to deliver on its promise of adequately expressing subjectivity and making the world a home for the subject, and so the spirit must move on to more complex and encompassing ways of relating to the world and expressing itself. The final outcome of this dialectical progression is the realization that subjectivity is an active reality that can never be adequately expressed through any objective structure. Its proper way of being is developmental growth into an ever-expanding openness of possibilities. It has come to know itself as a primordial self-moving activity that must always be involved in developing ever more complex and self-actualized ways of experiencing the world and creating itself within those worlds.

Finally, I would like to draw some wider social implications of this understanding of psychoanalysis as that discipline that explores and enhances a self-knowing, authentic subjectivity. Above all the modern world is an economic one, dominated by market pressures to be successful in the exchange of goods and services. To make oneself successful in this economic world, one must first submit to institutions that legitimate one's skills and knowledge and then bring one's legitimated talents to a highly competitive market in which a person wanting to be recognized as a psychoanalyst must contend not only against other therapists but other options for persons' use of capital. These pressures for legitimation and competitive success tend to make us objectify not only others but also ourselves. We reduce ourselves to a set of properties that we think will be highly sought after in the market and evaluate others on what properties they have, especially what properties they have in relation to our needs.

Heidegger terms this kind of objectification "technology," a way of being in the world in which we tend to experience everything and everyone as having a use-function (1949). The tree is not something that simply is, present before me, but something that adds to the value of my property or something that could be used for firewood, lumber, a place to hang a swing, etc. Other persons carry meaning insofar as they are useful for me—for sexual pleasures, soothing companionship, professional opportunities, or just helping me to check out at a store. Most important of all, in a technological way of being in the world I become a use-object for myself. I develop certain skills and knowledge in order to make myself a desirable commodity in the marketplace, one whose skills and talents will command both respect and substantial remuneration.

While this economic technological kind of world is spectacular in producing increasingly better goods and services—far outdoing all other types of worlds in this area, it does come with a substantial price tag—the tendency to identify oneself and others with objective properties arranged in a hierarchical way. With this objectification, the essence of what it means to be human—the exploration and expression of one's deepest subjectivity and the empathic relation to others' subjectivities—has a propensity to get lost.

In a world in which there is tremendous pressure to convert ourselves and others into objects, in which we are constantly subject to social and economic forces that would make us passive vehicles of their power, psychoanalysis stands as one of the great bulwarks that proclaims the irreducible reality of the human subject. In a world in which philosophy is increasingly buying into the scientific paradigm, religion retreating into an untenable archaic fundamentalism, and the arts getting co-opted into the entertainment industry that panders to trivial desires, psychoanalysis stands almost alone in proclaiming the worth of a coherent self-knowing individual and the worth of empathy as the great virtue of human sociality. The modern world constantly pressures us to objectify ourselves and others—to judge them, rank them, use them, discard them, while psychoanalysis asks us to be empathic, to subjectively immerse ourselves both in others and our own fragile souls. Psychoanalysis might feel like a voice crying in the wilderness, but without it and other small voices, all turns to darkness. The theories and practices of psychoanalysis are needed to repair not just the health of those with injured souls; it is needed for the health of the whole modern world.[1]

NOTES

1. See Frank Summers' *The Psychoanalytic Vision* (2006) for a robust account of the forces of objectification at work in psychology and the modern world and a further validation of psychoanalysis as one of the few disciplines that embraces human subjectivity.

Chapter Two

The Life of the Soul

Heinz Kohut devoted his life to restoring liveliness to souls that somehow had lost their abilities to live fully. Sometimes the life had disappeared into a depressive dullness, sometimes it could be expressed only within painfully narrow compulsive limits, sometimes it blew itself up into a stupendous but empty grandiosity. In addressing the question of how the soul might be able to achieve its fullest life, Kohut was exploring what I think has been *the* question for Western culture since the middle of the nineteenth century, a question pursued with unremitting complexity in Henry James' novels, excavated with frightening depth in Nietzsche's philosophy, and exhibited with artistic intensity in Van Gogh's paintings. It lies behind the great cultural revolutions at the turn of the century, especially in Vienna, where Klimpt, Kokoschka, Otto Wagner, Robert Musil, Schoenberg, Berg, Freud, and others purposely disrupted an elegant, quite-pleased-with-itself Vienna in an attempt to make life more than one more variation of a waltz by Strauss.

For a number of the most profound thinkers of the past century and a half, happiness and pleasure do not hit the mark as the goal that life ought to be seeking, for these goals are too tame, too connected with the Crystal Palace and the banality of bourgeois existence. The goal of life, for these thinkers, can be nothing other than to live, to live as intensely and as fully as possible, even if that intensity entails destruction and suffering. Thoreau, Nietzsche, Dostoevsky, Charcot, Virginia Woolf, and their comrades courageously destroyed traditional cultural forms which they thought were not fully alive, opened the doors of darkness, and attempted to find deeper forms of life that might be hiding in the insane and possessed, the dispossessed and the desperate, the disordered and the wild.

Did they succeed in bringing our culture into a more profound liveliness? The deepest fear I have encountered in students over the past half century is that their lives in particular and life in general might turn out to be boring. The worst thing that can be said about a professor or a class is that they are boring. Students are hesitant about committing themselves in work or love, for long-term anything raises the specter of boredom.

Boredom is life that has lost its liveliness.[1] In having such a desperate fear of boredom, these students express the anxiety that our culture, which seems to be the liveliest ever invented, might be hovering over an abyss of deadliness, an abyss Nietzsche called "nihilism" (1968), and Kohut connected to the ever-growing presence of narcissism and its inner deadness (1977). One of the quintessential novels of our age, *Madame Bovary*, identifies modern life as so shallow and its privileged as so self-centered, that *ennui* is always lurking on the penumbra of the soul. Emma Bovary, like other modern souls, desperately tries to stave off becoming infected with boredom's deadly poison by doing anything that might give excitement. Indeed, the excitement industry—travel, entertainment, television, sports, etc. is by far the largest sector of the modern economy. When one adds that most of the upper classes shop not for things they need, but as a form of excitement, then I think we can see that today's economy is fundamentally about the production of excitement, or, more exactly, about the production of life understood as excitement. The shockingly high rates of infidelity, the cultural obsession with sex and seduction, and the massive use of illegal drugs can all be seen, in part, as desperate attempts to escape boredom and find life in the excitement of the forbidden.

But is excitement life? Might the overemphasis that our culture places on excitement be a flight from some form of cultural deadness? Might we be confusing vitality with pseudovitality, where pseudovitality involves a great deal of doing that has little meaning and gives no lasting satisfaction? What is real life? What sustains genuine vitality in the soul?

Kohut understood that the lack of genuine life in a soul was due to an injury to the self, where by "soul" is meant the field of experiencing and "self" that which gives unity, meaning, and continuity to experiencing over time. Kohut thought that if the self could be repaired, even restored, then the field of experience would once more have a zest and liveliness to it (1977). In claiming that the life of the soul requires a harmoniously structured self, Kohut places himself in a classical tradition that has its origins in the philosophies of Plato and Aristotle, but pits himself against the most thoughtful of the late modern thinkers who find that having a self limits the possibility of the soul's liveliness and spontaneous expression. Philosophers as diverse as Thoreau, Nietzsche, and Whitehead have connected the life of the soul not with structure but wildness and the wilderness (Thoreau), Dionysian chaos (Nietzsche), and adventure and creativity (Whitehead). Heidegger elucidates a concept of authentic living without reference to a self and Lacan goes so far as to see the self as a symptom of pathology. When the postmoderns declare the end of grand narratives, the grandest narrative of all that must die is, they proclaim, that of the self (Lyotard, 1979). They see the self as standing in the way of life, while Kohut sees the self as the *sine qua non* of soul life.

This conflict between soul life needing to be grounded in a structured self versus soul life flourishing in chaos, disruption and spontaneous originality is only one of the tensions between the classical philosophical bedrock that undergirds Western culture and the postmodern re-conception of human life. These conflicts constitute a primary reason why our culture seems so confused, indeed, disoriented about what it means to live most alively, a disorientation that makes us highly vulnerable to the market's dominant vision of life as the exciting pursuit of desire. It is thus crucial that we inquire into the questions of what most deeply nourishes the life of the soul and what gives it a sustained liveliness, for nothing less than how we think it best to live is at stake.

Let me begin this inquiry where I think it must begin: in the vision given to us by Plato and Aristotle, for this understanding of the soul's life grounded the West for two millennia and still compels much in how we go about living our lives.

THE CLASSICAL CONCEPTION OF THE SOUL'S LIFE

Socrates, the first Western psychologist and philosopher who inquired into the soul, made a remarkable, brilliant claim: "And again life? Shall we say *that* is the function of the soul?" (*Republic*, 353d). Simple, direct, and, perhaps, the most profound of all truths—the soul's proper activity is life. What the psyche most deeply yearns for is simply to live—to live as fully as it possibly can. Socrates then took a fateful step, perhaps the most fateful step ever taken in Western thought. He might have reveled in the myriad different ways that people find to bring life to the soul—adventure, love, art, friendship, having children, encountering danger, political maneuvering, gourmet appreciation, discussing philosophy, and so on, but he didn't. Rather he posed this question, "What kind of life is most alive?" as the most fundamental question that a human being can ask and thought that a life that didn't ask this question was not a life worth living. Life is not something that merely happens to one, but something we can actively pursue. One can not only be alive but have a life.[2] Not only do we each have a life, but a kind of a life, and it makes all the difference what kind of a life we live. Socrates then proposed a startling idea: the kind of life we lead is determined by the kind of soul we have. Not only does life come in kinds but so do souls.

What kind of soul is most alive? Socrates' and Plato's answer to this question is stunning. They proclaimed that the most alive soul is the soul of an ethical person. The most alive person is one who was just, courageous, self-controlled, and wise; someone who lives by principles rather than personal whims and desires.

Their reasoning for this stunning conclusion is equally stunning. First, Plato and Socrates equate life with activity, with a self-generating motion. As Plato says in the *Phaedrus:* "All soul is immortal, for that which is ever in motion is immortal. But that which while imparting motion is itself moved by something else can cease to be in motion, and therefore can cease to live . . . we shall feel no scruple in affirming that precisely *that* is the essence and definition of soul, to wit, self-motion" (245d-e).

From this one basic claim—that the essential activity of the soul is self-motion—we can derive all the major tenets of Plato's philosophy. If self-motion is the essence of the soul, then passivity, or being determined by exterior forces is the negation of this essence. Likewise, if the soul's proper function is life, then its most dreaded enemy, its ultimate violation, is death. Yet, passivity and death seem inevitable, for the soul must respond to objects and sooner or later will be done in by them. It seems then that tragedy offers the proper understanding of the life of the soul. But Plato, who was tempted by, but eschewed, becoming a tragedian, followed Socrates in thinking that the soul could establish its first principle as a self-generating motion and thereby come to discover its immortality. When it does, then all the anxiety and passivity that comes from fearing death is overcome and the soul, now secure in the knowledge that its life will never cease, is fully able to live.

To understand how the soul can properly enact its essential activity and achieve fullness of life, it is best to first look at the most tempting form of false life that attracts the soul, the form of life espoused by the Sophists: the life of desire. Desires, for Plato, are atomic, blind impulses that want immediate satisfaction without concern for the person as a whole. They arise not from the soul itself, but typically from the body or from social pressures. And they are ceaseless. As soon as one desire is satisfied another arises, and another, and another, like the hydra's head that simply seems to keep multiplying when one thinks it has been cut off. When we live out of our desires, we are, in Socrates' words, sieves, desperately trying to fill a bucket that is full of holes (*Gorgias,* 493b). We suffer desires and become enslaved to them. This is not life; it is passivity. It is bondage.

The soul properly engaged with its essential life is not the Desiring Soul but the Erotic Soul (*Symposium, Phaedrus*). Desire seeks to consume the world, to transform what is other into what is mine. Eros loves the world and reverences its beauty. It wants to merge or join with the beauty of its objects, not consume them. Like desire, eros begins in lack, but what it seeks is not this or that satisfaction but the completion of the soul itself. Indeed, the original act in originating the life of eros is the acknowledgment of the lack—the lack of grounded meaning, the lack of knowledge of what it means to be human, the lack of completeness, and the lack of immortality. These profound gaping holes in the soul are understood by Plato as a kind of originary ugliness that the soul longs to overcome. The proper activity of the soul then is to transform this chaos by seeking the beautiful and through its becoming itself beautiful by gaining structure, knowledge, meaning, and immortality.

However, all forms of beauty that are connected to the physical, changeable world are subject to disintegrating forces. That is, they are subject to external causes and can change. To have them as the soul's grounding objects is to endanger the soul, for when they change, the soul passively suffers and again becomes chaotic. The only object that can truly sustain the activity of the soul is an object that in no way participates in the passive and changeable, namely, the form of beauty itself—pure, eternal, unmoving, and immoveable Beauty.

The need for the soul to dwell on Beauty itself, or in the *Republic*, the Good, can be made clearer by understanding the fundamental principle of all ancient psychology: the soul becomes like the object it intends. If all it intends are the objects of this world—objects that change, come into being and pass out of being—then it retains a chaotic mortal nature. But should it dwell upon eternal, perfect objects, then it, too, cloaks itself in these characteristics and knows its nature for the first time—to be that which has eternal life. Anxiety leaves the soul and we attain a peacefulness that goes with the knowledge that "nothing can harm a good man in life or after death" (*Apology*, 41d). Paradoxically, the moment in which the self-movement of the soul most profoundly realizes itself is a moment of total stillness, of non-movement. Whatever else the life of the soul is for Plato, this paradox seems to be at its heart.

The most alive life, the most erotic life, then, is the life that seeks and discovers the eternal. But part of the eternal is the ethical. The ethical is the life of principle in which what is particular, that is to say mortal and changeable, is not recognized as compelling. Particularity—our gender, class, nationality, biological desire, and socially constructed desire are all ways in which we participate in passivity, in fields of causation. By rising above our particularity to universal principles that hold for all human beings, we escape the field of causation and gain a different kind of meaning for our lives, a meaning which supersedes the narrowness of constant self-reference that haunts the life of particularity. For Plato, the ethical is not a restriction on our life, but a way to break our bondage to passivity and free the self-motion of the soul.

Finally, that part of the soul that can locate and dwell with the universal and the eternal is, of course, reason (*Republic*). Desires and emotions are tied to the immediate world of change and particularity, but humans have another part of their souls, seemingly unique to them, that can do mathematics, ask about essential definitions, and contemplate essential forms. Reason, with the help of the moral virtues, also has the power to guide and control the desires and emotions. With this control we can have genuinely active, self-determining lives, rather than being at the mercy of the vicissitudes of existence.

Aristotle transforms the germ of Plato's ideas into a naturalist framework that emphasizes that the life of the soul, understood not as an eternal subjectivity but as lived experience, is essentially connected to a process of becoming. Life is growth, development, actualization. For Aristotle, all species of life involve growth from an initial immature state to a mature state. Each living thing has a natural *entelechy*, a potentiality, longing to reach a mature state. This concept of potentiality is like Plato's originary lack, but has more of a sense of an unactualized germ longing to achieve a definiteness proper to its species. The mature state for humans is that state that they alone in nature can attain, namely the state of being self-determining beings capable of choosing their own lives (*Ethics*, 1097b–1098a). But choosing a life is no easy matter—it requires first that we be able to moderate the power of the passions, for their demand for instant gratification is compulsive and takes away the possibility for choice. Second, we must be able to deliberate about the options and possibilities available to us and select the right one. The development of the moral virtues is what moderates the passions, and the development of the intellectual virtues is what allows us to think well. The moral virtues and reason transform blind impulses and worldly pressures from passive determinations of the soul into proper soul activity. The more we are capable of self-control—*sophrosyne*—and careful, complex reasoning, the more we are capable of being self-determining agents. Indeed, it is gaining the abilities to control the impulses in the human organism and choose how we want to live that define, in modern terms, what it means to have a self. I think Aristotle is the first theoretician to clearly make the claim that the kind of person capable of the most soul life is the person who develops the most self.

Add one other important Aristotelean doctrine to this picture of the alive soul. In order for the moral virtues to develop, a person needs to grow up in a polis in which the virtues are both modeled and reinforced. When a person develops the moral virtues, such as courage, moderation, justice, benevolence, and generosity, he not only gains a self but becomes the kind of person who can live in and sustain a well-functioning polis. That is, the intellectual and moral virtues not only allow individual agents to emerge, but they are also the traits that allow community to emerge, a community that in turn provides the arena in which the good person is able to enact the virtues.

Here we have the moral equations that have stood as the cornerstone on which Western culture was built. The most alive person is not passive—not thrown around by circumstances or irrational emotions, but is a self-determining agent, someone capable of choosing and enacting his own life. Such a person is also the most mature, most actualized, most morally virtuous, most rational, and most community-oriented of human beings. And we can add that this person is also the happiest, for happiness ensues when we develop our deepest human potentials for living a rational, self-directed life.

This classical paradigm for what constitutes the most alive soul can be seen as regnant for the West throughout its history. The emphasis on the life of the soul as rational activity rather than emotional passivity underlies the great Hellenistic ethical systems in which the Epircureans sought *ataraxia*— a cessation of disturbance—and the Stoics sought *apathia*—the overcoming of suffering due to exterior forces. Even Kant's ethics can be seen as merely purifying the classical system. Since the moral virtues must be inscribed by social agencies and the intellectual virtues learned from teachers, the classical model of the soul still has heteronomous forces working in it. The only fully active, free act of the soul is willing the categorical imperative, for this is the one act in which the soul wills only its own rational nature (1797). The classical paradigm's remnants are still with us in the emphasis we place on the development of reason, self-control, the grammatical abhorrence of the passive voice, and, above all, the active, assertive nature of individuality. But these terms waver in their meanings from those of the classical paradigm because an eruption of thought that began in the late eighteenth century has modified everything.

LATE MODERNITY'S CONCEPTION OF THE SOUL'S LIFE

With *Faust*, Goethe announces the death of the classical vision. The play opens with Faust as a great philosopher/scientist who has lived the life of the mind—precisely the ancient paradigm of the best life—about to commit suicide, the only act that can adequately express his inner deadness. Reason did not bring life to him but an empty, lonely existence. Rather than killing himself, Faust magically opens up the dark powers of the soul represented by Mephistopheles and proceeds to locate life in emotion, adventure, sex, love, the chaos of Walpurgis Nacht, and even capitalist land development. Along the way he seduces and leaves Margarita, kills her mother and brother, drives her to such insanity that she kills their child, has an affair with Helen of Troy, kills paradigmatically good persons in Baucis and Philemon to get their land for his development project, and for all of his destructiveness and compact with the forces of darkness, he is saved because he has strived. Faust—wild, chaotic, dark, emotional, immoral, disruptive Faust is the new hero of the modern age, the hero who proclaims that life must include the forces of darkness, irrationality, and chaos to be fully alive.

The shift from life understood as the outcome of rational deliberation and moral control of the passions to life as spontaneity, creativity, concrete particularity, and emotional intensity explodes upon the West at the end of the eighteenth century and is found in almost all aspects of the culture: in the shift from formal French gardens to the English natural garden with its surprise pagoda or secret pond; the shift from Alexander Pope's ordered couplets to Wordsworth's open verse recalling us to mysteries of nature; the shift from the serenely ordered canvases of David to the wild shapes and colors of Delacroix and Turner; and the shift from the divine harmonies of Bach to the driving dissonances of Mahler. Emerson called us to discover our own originality of experience by spontaneously responding to nature, and Thoreau wrote, "The most alive is the wildest . . . All good things are wild and free" (1861, pp. 645, 652). Whitehead asserted that life was a creative rather than repetitive response to the environment (1929). Life is, above all else, adventure. And in his *Happiness, Death, and the Remainder of Life* (2003), Jonathan Lear argues that life cannot be contained within any constructed system for the production of happiness. Life refuses to be captured in planned activity, for the unconscious is always disrupting our organized consciousness in swerves or breaks that occur for no good reason. Life is that which must disrupt itself in order to live. It is more connected to irrationality than rationality, more to be enacted than understood.

It is Nietzsche who finds the most compelling style to express this new vision of the alive soul. Aphorisms, metaphors, symbols, spontaneous outbursts of rage, delight, disgust, joy, night songs, and unremitting irreverence explode off his pages, bringing to life and making us believe in his vision of the fully alive soul, the overman or free spirit. The free spirit is forever being like a child, spontaneously creating new games to play and then not taking the games too seriously so that they trap it in a structure that then becomes *the* purpose of life (1883). The most alive soul must value nothing higher than life itself. All metaphysics, all morals, all higher goals are in essence life-destroying for they proclaim that life is worthwhile only if this value can be attained or only if some metaphysical being, such as God, exists. Nothing can be higher than life itself. Even if a structure of meaning is of our own making, it must be challenged and questioned and overcome, or else we become prisoners of our past decisions. Life is will-to-power; and all acts of genuine will destroy previous structures to create new horizons. For what purpose—for no purpose other than the sheer life joy of willing.

While Nietzsche's free spirit can been seen as another attempt to find what kind of soul is most alive, it is an ironic attempt, for it is the kind of soul that refuses to be a "kind of a soul." Free spirits enact their particularity and refuse to define themselves in universal terms.

Note that Nietzsche accepts the classical notion that life is in essence the self-movement of the soul, but rejects the notion that this activity is to be understood as rational choice. Reason is not capable of lifting us out of external determination, for all of its forms are polluted with social presuppositions. The only true motion of the soul is the will enacting itself—not for a purpose or rational goal, but out of its spontaneously creative particularity.

We are a long way from the classical vision of the life of the soul. For Plato, chaos is the worst enemy of the state and soul; now it is valorized as the proper breeding ground of life. For Aristotle the virtues are habits, reinforced and predicable responses to common human situations. As such the virtues seem to negate a readiness to be creative and spontaneous. Reason—the faculty most revered by the ancients—is now seen as controlling, abstract, impersonal, unspontaneous, and deadly in its effect on the intensity of emotional life. The happy, virtuous, rational person is not only not seen as the most alive kind of human being but is despised as a false paradigm luring us away from what really is most alive.

It is this emphasis on the spontaneous, creative, particular, and intense as the essence of the soul's life that puts into grave doubt whether some kind of substantial self is a necessary ground for its liveliness. Whatever else the self is, it is always seen to carry some kind of identity, some explanation for our felt sameness through time. But sameness is just the opposite of adventure, creativity, and spontaneity. How can something that is permanent, structured, and repetitive explain or ground the possibility for creative, original responses?

Late Modernity stands opposed to the classical vision of the life of the soul in another crucial way. When asked, "What is the greatest danger to the life of the soul?" modernity with almost a singular voice answers, "society." With the coming of mass democratic society, the harmony of self and society so eloquently espoused in Aristotle is shattered. John Stuart Mill was horrified by a new kind of tyranny, "the tyranny of the majority" (1859). Emerson and Thoreau would have us leave society for nature in order to find our natural vitality.

For these mid-nineteenth-century thinkers the dangers of society, such as the pressure to conform, could be consciously recognized and negotiated. What Nietzsche and Heidegger discovered in the next half century was that social forces infiltrated the soul beneath a level of conscious awareness. While these unconscious social forces impose themselves without noticeable trauma and can be uncovered without working through defenses or resistances, they are, nonetheless, deadly in their effect on the soul's original vitality.

Nietzsche located society's most life-negating force in the institution of morality (1887). Psychologically what moral ideals do is to constrict experience within a narrow range, repress individual expression, and demand a stifling conformity. When we impose moral judgments on others we not only demand that they conform to our standards for what human beings should be but also express our rancor and *resentment* for having had our own vitality reduced by moral judgments having been imposed on us.

Heidegger goes further. He claims the social collective can colonize subjectivity. "It could be the case that the who of everyday Da-sein is precisely not I myself. . . . The 'who' is the neuter, *the they*. In [its] inconspicuousness and unascertainability, the they unfolds its true dictatorship. We enjoy ourselves and have fun the way *they* enjoy themselves. We read, see, and judge literature and art the way *they* see and judge. But we also withdraw from the 'great mass' the way *they* withdraw, we find 'shocking' what *they* find shocking" (1927, pp. 108, 119).

When the *they* colonizes subjectivity, everyday life becomes characterized by idle talk, shallow curiosity, and a tranquilizing busyness. Life falls into an average everydayness, like a stream caught endlessly in an eddy. The subject is not even alive; rather the *they*, like a parasite, lives through its host body converting it into a token of the social type. Such socially colonized organisms lose awareness of their own being and the Being of beings as they live out the social agenda. The only way Da-sein can overcome this social dictatorship is not through reason or the virtues, but by experiencing Angst and being thrown toward its own mortality.

In short, if in the classical model the most alive person is the rational moral citizen, contemporary philosophers understand that both society and morality are infused with life-negating power. While they understand that we could not be human without society or some ethical system, they hold that in order to be fully alive, we must at some level rebel or retreat from the social order. Life involves a necessary alienation. Thus, the exquisite classical vision of the harmony of individual and society, of a coincident individual liveliness and social vitality is shattered in the modern world. The most alive soul can no longer be the beautifully socialized person, but is the alienated individual who must both affirm her social being and struggle against it.

Worse, not only do unconscious social forces enervate us, but we can have our souls controlled and diminished by unconscious personal forces. This is Freud's piece of the puzzle. Freud found that a soul could turn against itself, constrict its own liveliness, and never know consciously that it was engaged in undermining itself. Life lived through the psychic defenses is repetitive—that is, dulled, and constricted. Projections, transferences, and dissociations distort or distance us from reality, making us feel as if we were living "as if" lives rather than existing in the robustness of reality. The narcissistic defenses cocoon us into small solipsistic universes. The manic defenses make us feel ever-so energized, but it is a false liveliness, a great deal of motion in which nothing much matters except the motion itself.

Strangely the soul enacts these life-lessening defenses in order to protect its very life, for had the defenses not been erected the coherence of the ego might have been shattered by an intense conflict and the person become psychotic. The problem with the defenses is that they seem like a good bargain at first—to protect the ego from traumatic, coherence-shattering conflict and anxiety, but as repetitive structures, they then disallow emotional growth and connection to reality, even when the psyche eventually becomes strong enough to deal with the conflict that traumatized it.

Freud associates the life of the soul with the id. The more the id is able to directly discharge its drive energies, the more alive we feel (1930). This is somewhat complicated by the fact that one of drives is not for life, but death; yet, the act of discharging aggression is an act of life. But Freud understands that humans with unrestricted id drives cannot form the social communities necessary to sustain the existence of the species. Compromises must be made. The spontaneous discharge of the drives needs to be balanced by attending to reality and the values of the community. The best compromises seem to occur in psyches that have strong egos, or what I will term an ego grounded in self structure. The more self there is, the less the organism will experience anxiety and have to use defenses to control the id forces. Defensive structuring of psychic dynamics always results in less life than when an ego can sustain its coherence and find either sublimated activities or substitute objects for drives that have unacceptable consequences in social reality. This need for a structured ego to ground life dramatically contrasts with the direction taken by Nietzsche and Heidegger. Freud understood what the Romantics didn't—that irrationality at its extreme is not the height of life but its negation—psychosis. Without psychological organization of some kind there is no experiencing of a world that makes sense.

KOHUT'S CONCEPT OF THE SELF

The preceding history of ideas about the life of the soul from Plato through Heidegger and Freud prepares us to see why Kohut's concept of a soul organized around a nuclear self is so incredibly important. As we shall see, Kohut integrates Plato's notion that the most alive soul erotically seeks ideals, Aristotle's notion that the self must be developing its essential nature for the soul to be fully alive, and the existentialist notion that the alive soul expresses the creative singularity of the self above all else, a singularity that can provide agency against the power of social impositions. Since Kohut locates both the self and soul-pathology in unconscious dynamics, he brings into play all the rich understanding we have gained about the psyche in the psychoanalytic tradition. The key to understanding how Kohut's theory can perform these integrations is his differentiation of self functions from ego functions. (see ch. 4 for a full elaboration of this distinction).

The ancient and Enlightenment philosophers were right: the development of the rational powers of the ego are crucial in order for us to negotiate our existences in the precarious natural and social environments we occupy. The development of a core unconscious self, however, is what gives zest, coherence, and meaningfulness to life. While the Western tradition in philosophy has superbly grasped how to develop the rational powers of the ego, it has not understood clearly the nature of the self, largely because the self is unconscious and its exploration needed to await the coming of psychoanalysis. Thus, to see how we can bring together the ancient wisdom concerning the life of the soul with that of modernity, we need to comprehend Kohut's notion of the self.

Kohut claims that we all start our psychological lives in a state of narcissistic grandiosity (1966). I believe that Kohutian grandiosity is the exuberant, wild, dynamic, chaotic spontaneity cherished in modern thought. It reverberates with Plato's self-moving soul, Freud's libido, Bergson's élan vital, and Thoreau's wildness. It is akin to Lacan's *jouissance*, or, as psychoanalyst Michael Eigen writes, "In the beginning is *Jouissance,* and *Jouissance* in delirium sings, dances, creates the Word. Aliveness is ecstasy." (1998, p. 135) This original grandiosity is the kind of energy that Nietzsche has in mind when he images the highest metamorphosis of the soul as being a child, "a new beginning, a game, a self-propelled wheel, a first movement, a sacred 'Yes'" (1883, p. 27). Grandiose energy lives in the chaos of a soul that has, as yet, no self to structure it.

But this grandiosity is also without form and, hence, is only a potentiality or in Aristotle's terms, an *entelechy.* It is energy that is in a divine state, a state of perfection. It has not yet incarnated. It is also narcissistic energy— energy that has no concern for others, no concern for the necessary conditions that make life possible. In order to actualize and live, it must incarnate. The primal energy must transform into a self, a self that retains the exuberance of primary grandiosity but organizes it in productive, life-affirming ways.

Kohut claims the development of the self follows two paths (1966).[3] First, the grandiose child soon realizes that it is not the master of the world; indeed, it is the world's most vulnerable entity. This helplessness causes great anxiety and in response the child takes a portion of its perfection and projects it onto its parents or caretakers, idealizing them as gods whose fundamental concern is, of course, to care for and protect the child. If parents can carry this idealization well, then later the child will be able to re-integrate this projected perfection back into itself, but now in terms of having its own ideals rather than as a characteristic of the self, for reality won't easily allow that. These ideals form a teleological part of the self, a part that lures the organism to develop by providing the hope of re-experiencing its own perfection through realizing its ideals. When the idealizing function of the self is healthy, life is alive with purpose, for there is a meaning to be achieved, and as it is achieved the psyche glows in its perfection—just as Plato said.

The second path of transformation sees the grandiose energy converting into what Kohut calls ambitions or what I would term a person's ability to be assertive and active in the real world without undue guilt or sadistic aggression. This pole of the self is our particularity—the concrete vitality we have available for doing and living. It makes us want to accomplish, to stand out, to shine like a Homeric warrior. In contrast, the idealized pole concerns meanings to be realized—it says that what is important is not so much me, but the values I represent in my actions.

In order to intersect the real world and be effective, the grandiose pole must undergo a developmental maturation through what Kohut calls optimal frustration. In optimally frustrating experiences the child replaces infantile greatness with the sense of worth that comes through accomplishment. For instance, when the young child receives the command that it must give up its infantile defecation habits and use a toilet, it is deflating to its infantile grandiosity. But, if the toilet can be mastered, the sense of greatness that accompanies this triumph will replace the original infantile grandiosity. This replacement of infantile grandiosity with self-esteem that comes through accomplishment gives a person the impetus to be an active self-determining agent capable of living in reality.

The remainder of the grandiose energy, what is left over after portions of it have been transformed into ideals and ambitions, is a sheer exuberance of being alive. It sometimes expresses itself in aesthetic delight, sometimes it comes forth as playfulness, and sometimes as the spark of creative imagination. It is this part of life that classical philosophy left out, and which Nietzsche, Thoreau, and the Romantics remind us is essential.

When the idealized pole and sense of ambitious agency unite with the idiosyncratic predispositions and talents of a person, a nuclear self is formed. This self harbors the original liveliness of the organism, gives it disciplined energy for action, and generates a strong sense of meaningfulness in its ideals. It is a self that embodies the ideals of Plato, the developmental path toward self-determination of Aristotle, and the creative verve of Nietzsche. By balancing these three senses of life, Kohut avoids the infantilism and lack of development that haunts Nietzsche's free spirit, the over-control of Aristotle's virtuous agent, and the negation of particularity that mars Plato's thought.

What is crucial is that the three strands of the original energy be well-balanced. Too much energy in the idealized pole with concomitant injuries to the grandiose side of the self leads to attempting to live out an idealized version of who one is, without ever feeling real or grounded in one's particularity. Since one can never be equal to an ideal, such a person can fill with unconscious guilt and self-loathing. On the other hand, if the grandiose pole is intact but the idealizing function is injured, then one can engage in a great deal of accomplishment, but lack a sense that it is meaningful. Life is full of action, but it has an internal "so-whatness" to it. Also, if too much of the grandiosity is devoted to accomplishment, one can lose a sense of the joy, creativity, and playfulness of life. Life becomes a bit too much of a serious business. Finally, if too much of the grandiose energy is left in its original narcissistic state—unorganized and ready for spontaneous involvement, then a kind of shallowness of experience ensues. An overemphasis on life as exuberant playfulness entails that one can be fully alive without development, without the attempt to forge oneself through difficult choices, without deepening one's aesthetic awareness or complexifying one's ideals. This kind of narcissistic energy is overemphasized in our pop culture that valorizes youth, adventure, and non-commitment. Many young people dread the thought of growing up, seeing adulthood as a set of burdens and responsibilities that make life a bit less alive. However, as we will see, the self can fully be engaged with realizing its ideals and ambitions only if the person can construct commitments to realizing these deep values.

Add one more important part of Kohutian theory to this picture of the soul's life. Kohut discovered that the self could not sustain its vitality and coherence without the aid of others assuming its functions, almost totally in infancy but also in less needy ways throughout life. He found that the grandiose energy of the self needed to be empathically mirrored and soothed in order to remain vital and that the sense of meaningfulness could not be sustained unless early caretakers were comfortable being idealized and did not violate that idealization. As such, he thought the key to sustaining the liveliness of the soul was having others close to one who are capable of empathic mirroring, holding idealization, and, later, forming twinship relationships. Those who play these roles for us Kohut entitled selfobjects, because they function as part of ourselves. He went so far as to say that selfobjects are as crucial to psychological life as oxygen is to biological life (1984). By including this strong notion of interdependency as part of the self, Kohut breaks with the value of self-sufficiency that runs from Plato through Nietzsche and sides with the strongest value of feminist philosophy. Plato's truth that the soul is a self-moving principle must be balanced by an opposing equal truth: the soul cannot live without the care of others. Parents, friends, and beloveds are as vital to the life of the soul as any internal principle of self-motion it develops.

We need to add that the self is the most dynamic of all the psychological structures. The self must be, in Nietzsche's terms, always overcoming itself—always expanding beyond itself. This is because both ideals and ambitions must stand over us as that which we are not yet. Once we fully achieve them, they die. This is not to say that I need to give up being a professor of philosophy because I am already accomplished in this activity, for I can always expand my horizons and abilities. Indeed, I must if I am not going to become dead wood. In many ways this notion of self corresponds with Heidegger's notion in *Being and Time* that who we are more than anything else is not a set identity but "our ownmost possibilities" (1927). The self always remains that which is both realized and unfinished.

In order for persons to engage in this lifelong developmental journey of the self, they need to form commitments to those activities in which they experience their souls becoming most alive. We can commit only to those activities in which we can both remain stable and grow beyond ourselves, for this is what the self needs to feel alive. Once possibilities in an activity are exhausted, then it can no longer be a realm of full life for the soul. For example, when a form of art or music becomes so explored that only repetitions seem possible, that form of human expression dies and must be replaced. Conservatism hates this fundamental law of the human psyche, but to be alive demands that we be in adventure—not chaotic adventure, but development growth.

The above is Kohut's theory of the self in a nutshell. It is a theory that reveals how the classical emphasis on ideals and agency achieved through development can fit with the existentialist emphasis on exuberant spontaneity and the expression of singularity. It ties together both the need for individual expression of life and the social element of interdependency with others. It gives us a psychoanalytic theory of how the source of psychopathology is trauma to the self and also gives us a new clinical theory for how best to work with injuries to the self. However, as stunning as this theory is, it is not a complete theory for understanding and enhancing the life of the soul, for it lacks several crucial philosophical inquiries into its basic concepts in order for it to be a full ontology for how to occupy and live our humanity.

For one, Kohut rarely addresses the problems of sustaining one's self while living in contemporary society. He should not be chided for this lack, as he is a psychoanalyst who was deeply concerned about psychological injuries to the self and their repair, not a sociologist worried about issues of a generalized social conformity. However, the self can be lost as readily to social pressures as it can to psychological injuries. What we have learned from recent post-structuralist theory is how powerful and pervasive socio-discursive systems are in the construction of persons. Indeed, a common theme in this literature is that, given the power of disciplinary systems, there is no such thing as a self that is capable of spontaneous uniqueness or agency. Our language(s) and social constructs invade the very core of our mentality, embed their meanings, and dictate how we are to think and act. In order to address this problem, we need to develop an understanding of how the ego in alignment with the self might be powerful enough to assert its unique presence and values. To see how this might be true, we need to develop a new metapsychology in which the roles of the ego, self, body, and social investiture are mapped out. This is the task of the next chapter and will remain a theme throughout the book.

Second, Kohut does not explore the nature of the narcissistic energy that forms the vitalizing factor of the self. This is important because while the structure of the self at any given time is its constellation of ideals and ambitions, there is something that "has" the ideals and ambitions—namely, some kind of core energy that is the self. I will argue (in chapter 4) that this narcissistic energy ought to be understood as *eros*. Eros is not the same as sexual libido (as Freud himself said), but is, as Plato said, a kind of primal psychological energy that seeks wholeness, is capable of development, and can be structured by ideals. In these ways it is different from usual desires that tend to seek immediate satisfaction without concern for the wider interests of the organism. By seeing eros as the psychic energy of the self, we can more easily differentiate self-motivation from the motivations of other parts of the psyche. We are most ourselves when we are feeling erotic.

Third, for Kohut the self is multidimensional and can express itself in a number of different ways. Hence, the question arises as to why posit that there is one primary self rather than many interconnected self-states? Such a position is favored in postmodernism that strongly veers towards multiplicity rather than singularity and oneness. I will offer an argument in chapter 5 for why we need to consider the self as a singularity, but in so doing must face the important criticisms that have arisen against "oneness" in metaphysics, theology, and psychology. Once we have determined why the nuclear self needs to be singular (although with multiple values) and how eros provides the unifying force for the self, we will have completed our initial understanding of Kohut's concept of the self and how it grants life to the soul. However, we will still need to discuss two further important aspects of the self that Kohut does not address.

The first of these absences concerns the role of nature in the formation and sustenance of the self. For Kohut, who is thinking primarily about how to bring psychologically injured souls back to life, it is other human beings—especially analysts—who have the power to help construct and re-construct the self. However, what I have found in my own experience is that nature has had a powerful effect on my ability to both generate and sustain a self. Hence, I think we need to supplement Kohut's notion of the self with the wisdom of America's first great self psychologists: Emerson and Thoreau (chapter 6).

Finally, while Kohut does produce a wonderful set of characteristics for a person who has transformed narcissism into a mature state, namely, humor, empathy, creativity, the acceptance of transience, and wisdom in which we devote ourselves to wider ideals, he never specifies that part of these wider ideals needs to be the ideal of becoming an ethical person. I think that becoming someone who has matured their narcissism into a strong, vitalized self, by necessity, needs to become an ethical person—someone who develops the moral virtues as described by Aristotle and the willingness to extend empathy and care to all human beings. Further, I will try to show that humans who do not develop coherent selves will be prone to act unethically, such as cheating, and that therefore it is of extreme importance for society to develop a set of social practices that help children develop nuclear selves and adults to sustain them. The first three chapters of part II will develop these crucial ideas.

Here then is a portrait of a soul capable of living as alively as possible. At its nucleus is a coherent self with ideals and ambitions that arise out of cherished traits that express the singularity of the person. The person's well-developed ego has not only found activities, places, and relations in which the self can be expressed, but located a matrix of selfobjects to help sustain the self through its perilous journey. While coded social pressures are irrevocably present in the soul, they are not crushing but are transformed by the self from being impositions to being opportunities. The bodily desires do not tyrannize the ego but become integrated into a lifestyle in which the self is being realized.

When persons are engaged in activities or relations in which the self is being actualized and sustained, they are not bored, mechanical, or aimless. They feel vitalized in their very cores. Hence, the ever-present anxiety in contemporary culture that life might turn out to be boring reveals that this is not a society that produces strong selves and that we need to uncover and alter those social practices and concepts that are injurious to the production of vitalized selves (see chapter 9). Indeed, nothing less than the life of the soul is at stake in the transformation of an untenable economic society into a psychologically astute one.

NOTES

1. For interesting psychological accounts of boredom, see Bernstein's *Being Human: The Art of Feeeling Alive* (1990) and Fenichel's "On the psychology of boredom" (1951).

2. See Lear's *Happiness, Death, and the Remainder of Life* (2003) for an elaboration of this discovery of Socrates that humans "have lives."

3. For a fine description of the development of Kohut's theory of the self, see Allen Siegel's *Heinz Kohut and the Psychology of the Self* (1996).

Chapter Three

Subjectivity, the Ego, and the Self

Understanding the nature of subjectivity is, to me, the most essential of all philosophical tasks, and one that never admits of certainty.[1] While we often tend to fuse self and subjectivity, it is of utmost importance to distinguish them. I am in agreement with Kohut in thinking of the self as a largely unconscious set of psychological functions which, when they are intact, give subjective experience a depth of meaningfulness, coherence, and organized energy for accomplishment in the world. While there is always a subjective element to the self—it seems to experience the world especially in relation to whether it is being affirmed or negated, strengthened or depleted, accepted or rejected, etc.—it is not what we think of as subjectivity, which is more connected to a set of conscious ego functions than self functions. Or, more properly, subjectivity is the set of experiences of a subject, where a subject is understood as a person who is organizing experiences such that they are capable of both having a world and acting in that world. Unless we make this distinction between "being a subject" and "having a self" we cannot make sense of a subject's very important experiences of "losing one's self," "finding one's self," "being one's self," or "not feeling like one's self." As Kant discovered, the sense of "I" or subjectivity must accompany all experiences, but only a subset of those experiences are ones in which we feel our selves to be present.

Part of the brilliance of self psychology has been to show that when subjectivities are haunted by a chronic sense of inner deadness, incoherence, depletion, drivenness, or just a sense of not living one's own life, it is because the self has suffered traumas and needs repair. However, self psychologists tend to have the attitude of "if things are well with the self, then they are well with the subject," and this might not be true. That is, there are certain kinds of subjectivities that allow selves to flourish and other kinds that dismiss the needs of the self and do not acknowledge its presence, even when it is healthy.

A subjectivity is what Heidegger calls "Da-sein"—it is a being that has awareness both of its own being and that of being a being in the world (1927). As such, subjectivity is intentional experiencing, for there is the appearing of objects to subjects who are aware not only of experiencing something but also that they are subjects experiencing something. Since subjectivity is that form of being in which other beings can appear (in distinction from an opaque object that is just what it is), it is variously defined as an openness (Heidegger), a nothingness (Sartre), or a being-for-itself rather than a being-in-itself (Hegel and Sartre). It is an interiority in which experiencing happens rather than an exteriority governed by causal forces.

However, it is not enough for subjectivity merely to allow objects to appear, for the objects need to be organized into a world in order for human subjects to have experience. While many processes need to go into the construction of a world, they all focus on giving meaning to the objects and events of experience. Hence, the essence of human subjectivity is the production of meanings. That is, if the external world of objects is defined by their position in space/time and material forces working on them, the internal realm of subjectivity is defined by the production of meanings. When we cannot determine the meaning of our experiences, we feel lost, for the world makes no sense. When we change interpretations of our experience—perhaps through psychoanalysis—and give it a different set of meanings, a whole new world appears to us. The world is not just there awaiting our entrance into it; it needs to come into existence through our granting it meanings.

Subjectivity and the realm of meanings seem to belong to a subject. I say "seem" because the subject who is having subjective experiences never appears. We have an inescapable sense that there is a subject—an "I"—having experiences, but whenever we attempt to experience the experiencer, we fail to discover it. As David Hume remarked, "For my part, when I enter most intimately into what I call *myself,* I always stumble on some particular perception or other, of heat or cold, light or shade, love or hatred, pain or pleasure. I never can catch *myself* at any time without a perception and never can observe anything but the perception" (1740, p. 252). Kant held that a necessary condition for the possibility of coherent experience is the presence of a singular subject connecting the moments of experience, but because such an experiencer could not also be a moment of experience, it could not be an object of experience. Hence, he called the subject a "transcendental unity of apperception,"—a necessary condition for the possibility of experiencing, but one which always transcends our ability to apperceive it (1787).

The problem, of course, is that the objects of experience are objects, and subjectivity is that which is experiencing objects. While we can be aware of our experiencing, we can never know who the subject of the experiencing really is, for to do so would be to find an object and, hence, negate the subjectivity of the subject. I believe that this mystery of the subject can never be penetrated. We can finally never know who we really are.

However, this is not to say that we cannot know a great deal about subjectivity. What the continental philosophers starting with Kant discovered is that subjectivity is not a *tabula raza* ready to be written on by an already organized world, but an activity structuring received data into a world. To have a world is an achievement of mind. For Kant, of course, the achievement was the application of a priori categories to sense data in order to turn them into objects connected by causal patterns. Since Kant, a number of different answers have been given to what the necessary conditions are for someone to be a subject having a world. For Freud, one had to convert narcissistic libido into object libido in order not to be stuck in a paraphrenic existence without a world. For Heidegger, the world appears only insofar as one cares for it. For Wittgenstein and many postmoderns the world and subjectivity are given through language, while for Kohut, enough self structure must develop in order for a person to have some semblance of a world and not fall into one of the psychoses.

All of the above seem true—that to become a subject who has a world, one needs some kind of innate structuring abilities, love or care for the world, language, and a minimal amount of self structure so as not to be psychotic. Now, to be clear, selves do not have worlds and do not act in worlds; subjects do. In short, having some self structure is a necessary condition for becoming a subject; conversely, being a subject is a necessary condition for the ambitions and ideals of the self to be realized in the world.

The analysis of subjectivity is essentially the analysis of the structures by which humans organize their worlds, themselves, and their relations to the world. Now while there might possibly be general ontological structures that are present in all instances of organized subjectivity as Kant thought, what is most important is that subjectivity can be—will be—structured very differently depending on which sector of the psyche becomes predominant in motivating its actions. To understand this notion that experience is structured differently depending on which sector of the psyche is uppermost in the pressures it is exerting on the ego, we need to construct a phenomenological map of the motivational sectors of the psyche, as Freud did in his *Ego and the Id.* Our map will be close to his, but it will revolve around the ego and the self rather than the ego and the id.

Producing such a map is the essential task of philosophical psychology, for, as Plato found, how we live our lives is fundamentally dependent upon how we organize the motivational centers of our psyches. Plato's famous three centers are reason, spiritedness, and the desires/cravings. Those who live well use reason to direct the desires according to what it finds to be good, using the spirit's energy to enforce its aims over those of the desires/

emotions, for the latter typically pressure us to do their bidding in the moment with little regard for the future or the concept of a well-lived life. It is reason that can discover the nature of a fitting/good life for humans and use this knowledge to construct a life freely chosen rather than one tossed this way and that by the tyrannical and insistent desires.

While the models of optimal psychological organization developed in the Enlightenment tended to be variations of the Platonic soul, Romanticism and Existentialism came to see the reason-dominated soul as dry, arid, and lifeless, and Freud discovered the unconscious—a realm of desire and emotion that was not available for either rational inspection or control. A new model of the mind was called for, but it could not be simply a reversal of the Platonic soul, for the emotions and desires really are too chaotic and drawn to immediate satisfactions rather than long-term life goals to be the organizing force for psychic life. Freud, of course, said that what psychoanalysis wanted was to have the ego descend into the id and integrate its forces and meanings into the ego's wider field of meanings and activities. This can appear to be a re-instatement of the Platonic model in having the rational, scientific ego gain dominance over the irrational id, but Freud could not have meant this, for he knew that unconscious material would simply not submit to such rational tyranny. Freud found that simple knowledge of unconscious material gained either through hypnosis or an accurate interpretation given by an analyst had little effect on psychological illness, for patients have to "own" their rejected experiences in order for transformation to occur, not just rationally know them.

However, Freud was never clear on what agency it was that was doing the owning. In his later work, he transformed libido into eros in order to find some force that wanted to integrate the parts of the psyche that had been dissociated.[2] However, when you look at the unifying, teleological language that Freud uses to describe this psychic agency, it looks a great deal like Kohut's self. And this leads us to ask what a model of the mind and its motivational centers would look like if we tried to make the self rather than the ego the fulcrum of psychological functioning.

I think that such a new psychological map based on self psychology is crucial for contemporary persons, because we find ourselves constantly assaulted by pressures demanding that we take care of this and that, buy this, travel there, change websites every three minutes, and so on. If we do not know where these pressures are coming from in our psyches, then we don't have a means of knowing how much to validate each of them. Without such ability we find ourselves always and already overwhelmed by pressures, treating each with a kind of equal, democratic importance. If we could know whether pressures were coming from internalized social forces, momentary desires, or from our core selves, then we could better establish importance and know how much to attend to the assaulting pressures. If we don't know what in our psyche is pressuring us, we are likely to feel as though we are being psychologically assaulted, oversaturated, and inundated with things we must do with never enough time to do them all. This busyness which characterizes so much of modern life, offering a simulacra of liveliness, is often experienced as rather meaningless and empty, and we end up depleted and exhausted. Unless we know how to locate what our selves need in distinction from other motivational directives, we will be doomed to live in this exhausting busyness. However, when we locate what the self needs, it is fairly easy to reject social pressures in order to concentrate our energies on self-activities, and involvement in them is always meaningful and fulfilling rather than depleting. In short, we cannot really be free to direct our lives unless we can learn to discern whether we are being pressured by society, our bodies, our ego's need for power and control, repressed infantile needs, or our selves.

A PHENOMENOLOGICAL MAP OF PSYCHIC MOTIVATION

First, we will use the term "ego" to designate a subject's conscious and self-conscious experiencing. The ego's activity is primarily what we mean by the term subjectivity and the person whose ego is consciously or self-consciously experiencing is the subject. The essence of this experiencing is the negotiation of the subject with its social and natural environments. As such, the ego has as its primary values gaining power and control over both internal stimuli and external circumstances. In order to gain this control, the ego needs to distance itself from both internal and external impingements, and develop rational strategies for solving the problems that these environments present.

Given the task of achieving satisfactory resolutions to the problems presented by a person's shifting internal and external environments, the ego must value freedom—the ability to be self-determining rather than determined by forces outside of its control. Note that the motivational center which carries the codes of the culture doesn't have the urge to free itself from those codes, the id just is what it is, and the self doesn't wish to free itself from its sustaining self-object relations and self-sustaining rituals. It is subjectivity—the ego—that is built to value freedom. From Plato through Nietzsche and Sartre, from the origins of democracy in ancient Athens to all those today fighting for their freedom from tyranny or the impositions of fate, freedom has been esteemed as the highest goal for all human beings. Indeed, it might be said of Western culture that its fundamental values have revolved around the ego and its quests for freedom, power, and control. Even the religious age, which appears to be a strange bondage to God and church, can be seen as an attempt to fully free the soul from the demands of bodily existence.

Indeed, we can see much of Western cultural history as centering on the development of the ego and its needs for freedom, power, and control. Plato discovered that the key to the ego's gaining power and freedom was the development of its rational capacities and these, in turn, could best be developed through education. From the ancient Greeks through contemporary culture, westerners have valued education as the vehicle for transforming somewhat chaotic dis-organized human beings into persons who can direct not only their personal lives but the great social, economic, and political institutions of nations. Education almost always concerns the production of the rational ego—an ego that can distance itself from bodily and emotional pressures in order to rationally solve whatever problems might arise.

As much as the ego seeks its own freedom and self-determination, it always finds itself under pressure from other sectors of psychic motivation and must respond to them. We can think of these sources of psychic pressure as voices. Each "voice" is an organized set of meanings/values (quality) that comes with a certain amount of psychic energy or felt pressure (Freud's quantitative factor). For instance, it is not unusual for me, after an intensive morning of teaching, to hear a voice in the early afternoon telling me to take a short re-vitalizing nap. However, depending on the circumstances of the day, the voice will pressure me with more or less sleepiness, sometimes almost forcing me to rest, sometimes merely suggesting it. Hence, phenomenologically we experience both a set of meanings (take a rest) and a quantitative impetus. The crucial voices pressuring the ego are first of all its own voice (freedom, power, control), the social unconscious, the body, character, the self, and repressed self-states with their sets of defenses and resistances. Let me give sketches of these powerful voices, each of which is distinct and each of which represents a crucial part of our psychological lives.

The social unconscious: The social unconscious is that sector of the psyche that includes all the social concepts, values, rules, and codes that we have ingressed so thoroughly that they unconsciously inform our way of being in the world. Unlike the dynamic unconscious that harbors repressed material, the social unconscious can usually be uncovered without working through resistances and defenses.[3] To be human is to be a member of society and, as Heidegger, Foucault, and countless social theorists have taught us, we are built in such a way as to unconsciously adopt the primary values, orientations, and codes of our societies. We are thoroughly situated and can never fully escape our situatedness. My way of being an adult male is thoroughly scripted by twentieth/twenty-first-century American culture. I would think, look, and act differently not only if I belonged to another culture, but if I were a member of American culture a century earlier or was a member of a different race or class. The imposition of the codes of the social unconscious is typically painless and non-traumatic. They quietly invade us and colonize our psyches such that, in most cases, we always and already find ourselves doing what we are socially supposed to be doing. As Heidegger says, the subject of everyday experience is not an "I" but "the they" (das Mann). We find ourselves liking what "they" like; abhorring what "they" abhor, rebelling the way "they" rebel, and so on (1927, sec. 27).

If we understand the world which we occupy as being organized in large part by our way of giving it meaning, then we can see that our introjected social codes play a massive role in determining what constitutes a pressure from the world and what doesn't. For instance, if I belong to a stratum of society in which a good college education is seen as mandatory for a decent life, I will respond to pressures to do homework from my teachers in a way that differs greatly from a young person coming from a social world in which education is not valued. I might feel no pressure to join a gang because my codes do not recognize gang existence as a viable way to be human, but persons from other social environments might organize their whole lives around such a pressure.

Despite the fact that great nineteenth-century thinkers such as John Stuart Mill, Nietzsche, Emerson, and Thoreau commanded us to free ourselves from social impositions, Heidegger more accurately discovered that full freedom from social existence is not a possibility. We can achieve authenticity but it is a modification of social inauthenticity (1927, sec. 27). We can locate ourselves and act from them, but the actions always take place in a coded arena. I can't even rebel against the codes unless what I do is socially recognizable as a rebellion.

Wittgenstein would put it this way: there is no such thing as a private language, for language is always socially constructed (1958). We cannot have purely private meanings because we would never be able to tell whether we were getting the meanings right or only seeming to get them right. When we come to form meanings for ourselves, we find that we are already in a realm of meanings, a realm of social discourse and understanding. In short, there is no escaping the social unconscious, nor is there a need to, unless this sector of the psyche becomes so predominant that the voices of the body and the self cannot be heard.

When the social unconscious is the primary voice determining the ego's orientation towards the world, experience has the feeling of "average everydayness," to use Heidegger's poignant phrase (1927). We do what we are supposed to do but feel as though the impetus for our actions is imposed from outside of ourselves. The impositions sometimes are direct, as in being commanded by one's parent to clean up your room; but most of the times, they are simply ingrained values. We find ourselves doing what we need to be doing to get along in the world without questioning it.

While it is true that when we find ourselves living our lives out of social codes and pressures, there tends to be resentment, dullness, and an urge to rebel or escape, there is another way of seeing the modern social world and that is as a field of opportunity for realizing our selves. That is, the realization of the self's ideals and ambitions typically needs a social setting in order for our actualizations to have a sense of reality. To mirror Wittgenstein's critique of "private language," we cannot really accomplish an ideal or ambition unless there is some social recognition of that accomplishment. If all we had were private events of accomplishment, then we could not tell the difference between whether we had actually achieved a value or only thought we had. We could not tell the difference between a somewhat psychotic self-perception and one based in reality, unless our accomplishments had a social setting and social affirmation. I might think in my head that I am a philosophical genius, but it is only when there are social venues in the world for realizing philosophy that I can have an adequate notion of myself as a philosopher. Yes, getting a recognized Ph.D. is a pain, but it is also the path not only to becoming a more able thinker but also the path in which one receives confirmation that one is, indeed, a philosopher. There were other paths in Confucian China or Hindu India, but there must be some socially articulated way of expressing and accomplishing one's personal values in order for them to be fully realized. The social world is not simply the world of the "they" pressuring us to conform to its ways of being human; it is also the world in which our singular ownmost selves can find actualization. It is not only alienation that expresses authenticity, but active participation in the institutions of the culture. Aristotle and Nietzsche are both correct. [4]

The id: let us define this sector of motivational life as all the wants, needs, desires, and emotions that we are biologically hardwired to feel. [5] When the ego is being motivated by biological needs/affects it feels embodied, real, singular, and often intensely pressured to respond immediately. Intensely feeling our affects and desires is often what fills us with the most life—at least in the moment, and without strong emotions and desires, life often feels a bit lifeless. Realizing the self may be the key to a sustained liveliness of life, but we would lack a fullness of life without the presence of vibrant emotions and forceful desires.

However, while the drives, desires, and affects make us feel alive, they also constitute a danger. Freud calls this motivational input "the it" for a good reason—it is impersonal; it exists beneath the level of the "I" and often forces upon the ego pressures which, were they followed, would be disastrous for the person. That is, the drives and affects originate from an evolutionary set of responses to our internal and external environments and can, if strong or un-integrated, force the ego to do their bidding sometimes in negation of the ego, the self, and the social order. It is not by chance that the first work of literature in the West—*The Iliad*—commences by telling how the rage of Achilles destroyed a civilized world. From Paris abducting Helen of Troy and igniting the Trojan War to a myriad of contemporary politicians having to resign because of sexual boundary violations, un-integrated sexual desire has ruined countless lives and disrupted social orders. While the desires and emotions of the id grant intense liveliness to the life of the soul, they must be modulated and integrated by the ego to not be, as they were for the Stoics, our direst enemies.

It was Aristotle who discovered that the key to retaining the liveliness of the *epithumia* (id) while avoiding its dangers is to develop character traits that moderate the power of the passions without repressing them. He thought that these traits were so important that he called them the "moral virtues" and claimed that achieving human happiness depended more on the acquisition of these traits than any other factor in human life, even more than good luck, wealth, or honor. He described the moral virtues as "means between the extremes" with which we respond to our desires and emotions that arise in common human situations (1962). These traits allow us to feel our emotions and appetites without being overwhelmed by them. For instance, if we have developed courage, we can feel fear without having to immediately and blindly respond to the danger it indicates is present. Courage delays response long enough for us to be able to rationally assess the danger and determine the best course of action in response to it. Further, the virtues predispose us to find the right action—the courageous action, the temperate action, the generous action, the just action. With these character traits we can allow the intensity of experience that arises from the affects and desires to appear, grant us life and information about our relation to our problematic environments, but not destroy our personal and social paths.

These traits allow us to respond with the right amount of emotion to each situation—the right amount of anger when we have been injured, the right amount of fear when we are in danger, the right amount of desire when food, drink, or sexual opportunity appears. Hence, when I speak of being motivated by this sector of the psyche, I assume that the desires and emotions that appear have been modulated by the moral virtues so that they can give us crucial information about our worlds and ourselves and enliven us with the intensity they provide.

However, it is not only character which helps moderate the affects, it is also the self. Indeed, most self psychologists see the self as crucial in affect regulation, such that if the self is fragmented or otherwise unable to function, there tends to be difficulty in soothing powerful emotions. I think that Kohut and Aristotle are probably right in respectively claiming that the self and character are crucial for affect regulation. Since the process by which the moral virtues are formed is the same as the process by which the mature grandiose sector of the self is formed, namely, optimal frustration, we can see how both the self and the moderating character traits can each play a role in affect/desire regulation. These dual systems are important, for it means that all is not lost in terms of being able to be a functional, decent human being if the self is injured. Acting from moral character and developed intelligence can make for a very good life even if the self is traumatized. However, we will always feel as though something—a core—is lacking in such a life.

THE SELF[6]

We are not born with selves; we are born with a swirling mass of narcissistic, erotic energy that has the potentiality for being transformed into a self. The characteristics exhibited by infants who are infused with this primordial mass of narcissistic libido/eros are perfection, grandiosity, and a sense of omnipotence (when the infant is hungry and cries, the breast magically appears, as though the baby has complete control over it). However, sooner or later traumatic failures to respond adequately on the part of the infant's social environment will occur, and when this happens the infant's sense of perfection, greatness, and power is shattered and replaced by one of the most unendurable of all human emotions, hopelessness. But luckily the psyche has built-in mechanisms with which to deal with such traumas, and one is used immediately: projection. The infant knows now that it is not perfect but a helpless, immobile creature and so it projects its perfection into its caretakers, making them gods whose primary concern is, of course, the infant. This projection explains the glow of specialness we feel our parents to have in childhood—a glow that can continue for a lifetime.

If all goes well—the caretakers hold the idealization and give the child good enough care, then the child will be able to merge with their idealized strength in times of hopelessness and failure and feel supported and sustained. Again, if all goes well, the child will discover over time and non-traumatically that the parents are not perfect and will re-introject the perfection it granted the parents not now as its own characteristic (reality won't tolerate that easily), but as the characteristic of ideals it is forming, ideals which the child can love as it once loved its caretakers and from which the person will be able to gain strength and sustenance in times of difficulty. The idealized pole of the self will contain those values that teleologically motivate us to live into the future. They make the self dynamic—more a set of potentials to be realized than set identity to be repeated.

Society, of course, also gives a person ideals and meanings—indeed, a slew of them. These, however, are not the same as the self's ideals, for they get ingressed into the social unconscious and pressure us as though from outside of ourselves. We feel burdened and obligated by them. They are oughts, not loves. Typically my students have introjected social ideals to be fine students and for the most part realize this ideal. However, when they approach the assignments they must do to be good students, they tend to go a bit depressed and mechanical. They try to get through them as fast as possible and when they are completed, they feel free and energized. How different it is with one's self's ideals, for when we are achieving a value that comes from our core selves, it fills us with life and vitality, feels deeply meaningful, and we could keep doing it forever. When the idealized pole of the self is injured, we often feel a sense that our lives are meaningless and that all of our doings are "a tale told by an idiot, signifying nothing." This feeling is so painful, that we defend against it by rushing to social ideals and losing ourselves in their demands.

Kohut called the other major sector of the self "the grandiose self" or "the pole of ambitions." This sector of the self harbors the energy of the self for accomplishment, for being vitally active in the world. It's the energy we have to perform in hopes of achieving recognition. This sector of the self is also dynamic, for when it is strong we want to go beyond our past achievements, always looking for the next mountain to conquer. When this sector is injured, we have low self-esteem and can feel hesitant about asserting our "worthless selves" into the world, lose ourselves in diversions, or defend against these unbearable feelings by constructing a narcissistic false self with an overblown sense of importance and entitlement.

This sector of the self also has a developmental path, one different from that of perfection and ideals. According to Kohut, we originally feel narcissistically grandiose—the greatest thing in the world, and if all goes well, our caretakers feel exactly that way—the gift of a new child—my son, my daughter! This is the sector of the self that harbors the all-important sense of self-esteem. While we always want to keep a deep feeling of being wonderful in our sheer particularity, we also need to transform most of this original grandiosity away from "I am great because I am" to a more mature "I am great because of what I have accomplished."

The path to achieving a mature sense of agency with a strong but modulated sense of self-esteem involves a steady diet of empathic mirroring along with a continuum of situations in which one is asked to achieve, but not traumatically so. From any number of sectors, especially studies of microsecond responses between mothers and their infants, we have learned the vital importance of empathic mirroring for the creation and sustenance of self-esteem and a continuous sense of secure attachment (Beebe & Lachmann, 2014). When an infant—or anyone—has their inner feelings mirrored by another, there seems to be the sense of "I am important enough for this other person to become just like me." There is nothing like having steady secure sources of empathic mirroring to make one feel like a strong, vitalized self.

Along with empathic mirroring, children need to be placed in situations of "optimal frustration" in order to mature and modulate their sense of narcissistic grandiosity. Optimally frustrating situations challenge a person/child to stretch their capacities and knowledge in order to solve the problem with which the situation confronts them. For a long time, parents need to tie the shoes of their children, but sooner or later—and, hopefully just at the right age—children will be asked to master this task. It requires a lot of hand co-ordination, the application of theory to reality, and, of course, lots of practic-ing. If the process goes well with no shaming for failures, then not only will a skill be learned but esteem will be built. "Look at me, I can tie my shoes!" With many instances like the above, a great deal of the original narcissistic grandiosity can be converted into grounded self-esteem and a strong impetus to be active in the world. Kohut called this side of the self "the pole of ambitions" because he found that people with well-consolidated selves had a strong sense of agency and energy available for accomplishment in the world while those with injured grandiose poles tended to shy away from the world, being afraid that they will reveal their un-modulated infantile grandiosity and be shamed.

There is one other important dimension to Kohut's notion of the self, namely, that each person has singular propensities, predispositions, skills, or other traits which, when active, make us feel most ourselves. For instance, I have a natural felicity with concepts and a theatrical bent that make thinking and teaching philosophy a joy. On the other hand, I was not granted mathe-matical gifts and have a propensity to get extremely anxious when in a scientific laboratory. Hence, although being a physician is a highly valued profession in the general society, it is not a value for me. It does not fit. And while I like history and other social sciences, I do not love them and have no interest in generating new ideas in these fields. They are good subjects, but not my subjects. Although New York City might be a cherished place to live for millions of people, it is not where I would choose to live. These idiosyn-cratic traits are crucially important in giving our lives the specificity of desire that make us feel singular and real, rather than just generalized variations of the social codes.

To put the above picture together: when our ideals incorporate our idio-syncratic traits and our ambitious energy is directed toward realizing the ideals, we then have a coherent self. It is possible to have ambitions that aren't connected to ideals, in which case our successes have a feeling of emptiness to them. It is possible to have strong ideals that are disconnected from ambitious energy, but they feel like abstractions. It is only when the two poles of the self are aligned with favored idiosyncratic traits and propensities that we feel like a full singular, vitalized, coherent, harmonious self.

Two additions need to be made. First, since the self is unconscious, it does not appear. Rather, it is the increase in erotic attraction and sense of liveliness that announces that whatever the person is doing, the self is present and is being either nourished or activated. I walk into an art museum and like almost all of what I see; but then a Cezanne landscape appears and my eyes freshen, my heart quickens, and I am drawn to the painting, standing motionless in a kind of timeless way, drawn into the painting as if into the depths of myself. I am in love; for some reason Cezanne calls to my self. When the self is active in self-activities, relationships, or special spaces (for me, the classroom, a mountain trail, a ballroom dance floor), we are filled with eros not only for them, but for life itself.

There are other signs besides a heightening of an erotic liveliness that tell us when the self is motivating the ego. For one, the activities, things, or persons just seem to seamlessly fit who we are. It is like finding a piece of clothing and saying "This is just me." We feel most like ourselves when we are engaged in activities that realize the values of the self or are with friends whom we trust enough to just be ourselves. Finally, one of the core markers of the presence of the self is a feeling of spontaneity. What we are doing is not contrived or the outcome of a scheme but just naturally erupts from our selves. Thoreau associated this with "being wild" (1861) by which he did not mean being chaotic and disorganized, but being who one naturally is. The wild animals are not disorganized, they simply are themselves, and this is what it feels like when we are being our selves.

Finally, we need to add that the self is especially vulnerable to psychological injury. For Freud, psychopathology arises when our drives are aroused and then blocked from discharging their energies. For Kohut, psychopathology arises when the self is injured and this can happen when our selfobject needs for empathic mirroring or merger with an idealized presence are thwarted or our self-esteem is crushed. These injuries can occur in a number of ways, including abuse, shaming, neglect, failure to empathize, forced compliance to a parent's needs rather than living out of one's own, failure of caretakers to hold idealization, failure of caretakers to empathically respond with affirmation, failure of caretakers to optimally frustrate, and so on. In short, the self is, by far, the most vulnerable of our psychological faculties. Slights to our self-esteem are everyday affairs—someone fails to acknowledge our greeting, our friends are so self-absorbed that they have no empathy for our little wounds of the day, our favorite team just lost, the weather destroys a hoped-for picnic, the car is scratched in the parking lot, and so on, endlessly. Since the self is always vulnerable to injury, it is always in need of refueling and repair.

The most important source of this refueling/repair is, of course, other persons. Kohut claimed that others who were willing to play self functions (soothing, self-esteem regulation, support of ideals, mirroring, optimal challenging) were literally as important to psychological life as oxygen is to biological life (1984). Hence, it is paradoxically true that one's self is located not simply in a personal psyche but in the psyches of one's selfobjects. This is a relational theory of the self in which the self both has a nucleus in a single psyche but also has part of its atomic structure located in selfobject orbits surrounding it. This theory, surprisingly, mirrors the indeterminacy principle in physics in which any existing thing can be seen as a particle located in one place or a wave located throughout space. The relational self psychologists emphasize the wave interpretation and see the self as fundamentally composed of selfobject relations, while the more classical self psychologists concentrate on the nuclear self with its ideals and ambitions. Both are part of the truth of the self.

It is because having a matrix of persons willing to be selfobjects for one is so important that I can make the argument that the best way to construct oneself as a human is an ethical way, for ethical people are most able to form and sustain reciprocal relationships with other persons. It is ethical persons, as Aristotle so brilliantly shows, who alone can have deeply sustaining, affirming friendships with others and—and this is crucial—with themselves (1962, books 8 and 9). Unless we think well of ourselves at the deepest (even unconscious) levels of our psychic life, we cannot be friends with ourselves. Hannah Arendt writes that the one person we are condemned to live with is ourselves and if we are fragmented, repressed, or just unlikeable, then we cannot be or have a self, for we will lack the necessary grounds to form a genuine dialogue within ourselves (2003). As we will see, the inner dialogue between the ego and the self—the I and the me—is crucial for having a coherent psyche capable of living with psychological depth and the fullness of life.

AN ECOLOGICAL CONCEPTION OF THE PSYCHE

The positive centers of psychic motivation—the ego, id, social unconscious, and the self—all have crucial roles to play in psychic life, and it is wrong to proclaim, as a number of theorists have, that we need to free ourselves from one part or the other of this psychic landscape. Some, like Nietzsche, would have us get rid of the social unconscious, yet without it we might lose out on opportunities for self–realization and, worse, might become somewhat sociopathic. Some religious theologians would have us deny our bodies and all the aliveness they bring to life. Others find the ego's search for power and control to be nasty, but without these aims, we could not be agents in the world. One can even read most ethical philosophy as saying the singular self needs to be ignored so that we can follow universal principles. Obviously, all of the motivational regions of the psyche are important and each voice needs to have a say in an integrated, ecologically organized soul (Riker, 1991).

The optimal organization of the motivating centers of the psyche is clear. The self ought to be strong and vital in giving the person meaningful values and robust energy for realizing them. The ego ought to be educated, perceptive, far-thinking, and skilled at negotiating with the world in order for the self's values to be realized. Our relation to the social world ought to be one in which we locate socioeconomic roles in which we can realize our selves' values and find social structures to help stabilize crucial relationships. And we should have a relation to our bodies such that we can feel their desires, emotions, pleasures, and pains without being overwhelmed by their insistences or underwhelmed by mediocre intensities.

The key, obviously, to a strong, healthy psyche is the alliance between the ego and the self. When the self infuses the ego's subjectivity with its presence, then our experiences feel zestfully alive, real, and integral. We brim with esteem and feel that our lives are meaningful. We feel ourselves, and others feel us, to have psychological depth. As Kohut says: "The psychological question is not whether the psychic structure under consideration is in a state of conflict or of peace with the rest of the personality, but whether it is shallow or deep. The analytic examination of the nuclear self—in contrast to the examination of peripheral selves—leads always into the psychological depth, and, as the deeper layers are gradually penetrated, to the discovery of a dynamically and genetically meaningful pattern" (1985a, p. 30). When the ego is grounded in the self, we feel as though our lives have a rich depth of meaning, for the self participates in every level of psychic life. "The nuclear self is thus that unconscious, preconscious and conscious sector in id, ego, and superego which contains not only the individual's most enduring values and ideals but also his most deeply anchored goals, purposes, and ambitions" (1985a, pp. 10–11). That is, when the voice of the self is being heard, it reverberates through every sector of the psyche.

Persons who have well-consolidated selves do not need to be doing self-activities all of the time. So long as some portion of our lives is devoted to self-activities and we have formed a strong network of self-object relationships, we can feel a continuous sense of vitality and well-being, even when accomplishing such typically non-self-activities as running errands, paying bills, or washing dishes. Since all of these activities are in support of a life that is meaningful and valued, they, too, gain meaning rather than being mere drudgery. In living this life we are, of course, immersed in social existence, and the codes/mores/practices that are embedded in us tend to generalize us. Contra Nietzsche, this is all right if we also have a core singular self that can stand in tension with the socializing pressures—utilize them when they offer opportunities and confront them when they violate essential self-values—or values of empathy and care. To enact a self is to be "natural," but such enactment is not real unless it has social meaning that can be recognized by others.

In addition to having a strong self infuse the ego with its poetic idiom, we also need to develop the moral virtues, as elaborated by Aristotle, for these character traits moderate the passions and allow us to respond in a mature way to the needs and emotions of our bodies. When the bodily passions are fused with the values of the self, then they are transformed and given deeper meanings. For instance, hunger being sated at a family meal of camaraderie and mutual recognition is a very different experience than just wolfing down food while alone. Sexual experiences with a partner in a committed relationship and about whom one cares deeply are very different from those with a moderately anonymous hook-up partner. Rather than being a mere genital release, sex with a beloved partner can profoundly affirm one's self and reverberate through the entire realm of meanings that constitute the person and their being in the world.

This ecological vision of the well-functioning psyche is an ideal, rarely achieved, because the self is so easily lost or damaged. Even if the self is intact and has not suffered severe trauma, it can still be ignored completely by the ego when its values conflict with those of the social order or the ego's need for power. Indeed, Kohut says "the majority of adults" disavow the self in order to "quickly and opportunistically adjust their convictions under the influence of external pressures" (1985a, p. 11). Heidegger would certainly support this claim, as he finds that the they (the indefinite social pressure) to be so powerful as to convert all humans into variations of its codes. The self, however, can call through the silent voice of conscience for us to return to the singularity of our being from its lostness in the they (1927). While coming out of such lostness is difficult, a person's strong willful resolve can restore the self's presence.

Heidegger dealt only with selves that had been lost to social pressures; he did not recognize the complex, tenuous psychological conditions necessary for selves to be developed and sustained. That is, he did not grasp the power of trauma to injure the self, fragment it into pieces, and cause distorting obdurate defenses and resistances to come into play. This coagulation of a fragmented self, defenses, and resistances constitutes another source of motivation that can pressure the ego to do its bidding in ways that override or distort motivation from the other sectors of the psyche. When this state exists the psyche cannot be a fully coherent ecosystem.

THE TRAUMATIZED SELF

When the self is significantly injured or traumatized, the ego typically engages in various forms of dissociation both to protect the self from further injury and itself from the anxiety, incoherence, rage, and pain now located at the site of the self. Dissociation can include the classical notions of repression, defense, and resistance but can also involve what Kohut terms vertical splitting (indeed, his elaboration of this concept is one of his great contributions to psychoanalysis). Vertical splitting occurs when someone is conscious of what they are doing, but refuse to own its meaning and relevance to their identity. For example, an upright citizen in most contexts of life can also be a "flasher," revealing his genitals to innocent children. He is consciously aware of what he is doing when he is doing it, but does not associate it with his main concept of who he is. He does not "own" that he is a person who does this kind of thing. He might even sincerely preach against perverts. He does not know why he is doing it or what it means that he is doing it (since the motivation is an unconscious set of meanings that come out of trauma). We also see vertical splitting at work in the addictions and other compulsive behavior in which persons at the same time know and do not know what they are doing. When a person's psyche constructs vertical splits, it obviously fragments itself. We now no longer have integrity of psychological functioning, for part of our motivations are not under our control and their meanings are neither understood nor integrated.

When the self is largely excluded from motivating psychological functioning because of injury, there results both a sense of inner depletion or emptiness and a developmental arrest. Because the self is now cocooned behind defenses, it is not in a significant relation with the environment and cannot grow. Hence, the injured self not only is full of narcissistic rage for being violated, but often harbors infantile needs for grandiose displays and omnipotent control over objects. As these desires are shameful, they cause the ego anxiety and must remain repressed.

There are further negative outcomes of trauma to the self, including a loss of vitalized energy (depressiveness) and a loss of a sense of being fully real (since important real events are being denied). While there are a number of different ways in which the ego can defend against the intolerable inner deadness, depressiveness, murderous rage, and a catastrophic loss either of meaningful ideals and/or self-esteem, one of them is to develop a narcissistic personality in which we feel (a false) overblown sense of greatness, act with entitlement, and treat others as mere appendages to our being. There are, however, less drastic ways to protect the self than developing a full-blown narcissistic personality disorder. If the self has been injured due to a lack of responsiveness (neglect)—the most common injury in today's busy world—then there is a tendency to over-stimulate oneself with addictions to drugs, alcohol, gambling, sex, shopping, etc. That is, one finds a substance or activity which when addictively engaged in prevents one from feeling the inner emptiness and enacts the rage by being self-destructive (Kohut and Wolf, 1978). One can also be injured by being over-stimulated—told constantly that they are the greatest thing ever. "Since these people are subject to being flooded by unrealistic, archaic greatness fantasies which produce painful tension and anxiety, they will try to avoid situations in which they could become the centre of attention. . . . The creative-productive potential will be diminished because their intense ambitions which had remained tied to unmodified grandiose fantasies will frighten them" (Kohut and Wolf, 1978, pp. 186–87). If idealized others were not available to lend strength to the developing self and the idealized pole never adequately develops, one might feel overburdened, and long to find idealized others on whom to lean rather than developing a core set of meanings for themselves.

Finally, one of the major ways in which one can defend against an injured nuclear self is by developing what Winnicott calls "a false self" (1960). It is not uncommon for narcissistic caretakers to demand that their children take care of their needs rather than attending to the child's needs. The nascent selves of children are ignored, punished for being selfish, or disapproved of by such caretakers. The caretakers insist on "compliance" to their needs, forcing children into what Bernard Brandchaft terms "pathological accommodation" (2007). In these instances the self is then buried as a motivational source that causes the child difficulty, punishment, loss of love, etc. and, hence, anxiety. It is displaced by a persona, typically one bent on being pleasing and helpful to others, for it is these traits that are praised rather than an expression of a singular self. Such persons—and they are very common—do not know how to access their selves, nor do they want to, since their selves stopped developing and harbor a Pandora's box of rage, pain, and infantile needs. Rather than attend to the voice of the self, compliant persons become very sophisticated in reading the needs of others and attending to those needs. Although such persons are always nice and get a lot of praise for being "such good people," they never feel as though they are quite real, for they lack their selves. Often they are fighting inner depression and are highly deficient in feeling anger, as it is likely to set off the timebomb of rage they harbor within.

This is the bad news. There are very few people, as far as I can tell, who have not suffered some injury to the self and/or pushed it aside for pragmatic reasons, and, thus, most persons suffer from some narcissistic symptoms. The good news is that for persons with traumatized selves, the self can, at crucial moments, still appear, proclaim its values, and ground choice. To be personal: I had a profoundly shattered self that had suffered both too much of the wrong kind of attention (sexual and physical abuse) and too little of the right kind of attention (empathic mirroring). I had to develop a keen sense of when my mother's explosive rage was about to break out, learn how to constantly soothe her to reduce such dangerous occurrences from happening, and learn how to seduce her into a state of loving attention. I developed all kinds of symptoms, including a false self. Yet, at crucial moments in my life an authentic self has appeared and let its deepest values appear, as when it lured me to sign up for a philosophy course and then proclaimed that I had found my life's work. This voice of the self spoke through my symptoms and fragmentations not only then, but later in telling me to choose a position at a moderately unknown liberal arts college rather than at more prestigious institutions from which it might have been easier to launch a substantial career. It also told me very clearly that marrying my first spouse was wrong, but I did not have the courage to call off the wedding and have my false self suffer enormous shame. It spoke, I heard, but did not act, and thereby caused much suffering for myself, my spouse, and our children.

However, even with such moments of self clarity, there is no doubt that having traumatized selves compromises our abilities to live well and freely, for even if we make the right basic decisions about work, intimate partner, and where to live, devastations to the self still must be worked through, for we will tend to undermine our relationships, make narcissistic blunders in our workplace, or get destroyed by addictions unless they are tended to.

In sum, the self is fragile and needs selfobject support. A great matrix of empathic friends can help a lot with injuries, but, alas, for many, a thoughtful self-psychological therapy is needed to shore up the self so that the defensive behaviors and personality structures can either be given up or transformed into structures which work for the self rather than against it. Such a suggestion, of course, goes against the grain of modern culture that believes the ego can conquer all of its problems without the help of professional others. Yet, the very ego that is supposed to restore the self is the ego that has unconsciously cocooned it and erected defenses against its trauma and rage. How is such a protective ego going to shift into one that will allow the injured self to appear and be repaired unless it has some trusted help? It is one of the great shortcomings of the individualistic everyone-can-take-care-of-themselves culture that it does not encourage help for injured souls nor make such help more available.

The greatest joy in the world is an integrated well-functioning psyche, one that has an active, vitalized self structured by meaningful ideals that can motivate a well-educated, thoughtful ego, one which can utilize social opportunities for the self and integrate the body with the needs of the self. An ideal self-psychological society would recognize the needs of the self and do everything it can to set up institutions and practices to foster the development and sustenance of persons' selves. Alas, such is not economic society, and so it is up to individuals to manage as best they can. [7]

In this chapter I have tried to delineate the nature of subjectivity by differentiating the ego from motivational pressures that can structure and infuse it—the self, the social unconscious, character, the id, and the repressed/defenses. I have also attempted to describe the optimal ways for the psyche to ecologically interrelate all of its motivational centers. However, we need to further inquire into the nature of the self that has nuclear ideals and ambitions. What is *it* that "has" ideals and ambitions? This question will be explored in the next chapter on the erotic self. The subsequent chapter will confront a question that arises from a postmodern temperament: why think of the self as one rather than many? Why not see ourselves as having many selves over time or as having the ability to be structured by any number of self-states? Hence, it is onward to eros and beauty; the singular self, monotheism, and the need for but dangers of unity.

NOTES

1. Much of the material in this chapter is paralleled in chapter 3 of *Why It Is Good to Be Good* (2010).

2. See chapter 4.

3. The exception to this principle is when racist or sexist prejudices have been internalized and denied. Uncovering this material can take some difficult psychological work. See, for example: A. Johnson, "In the Gaze of the Other" (2002); L. Layton, "Racial Identities, Racial Enactments, and Normative Unconscious Processes" (2006); and M. Suchet, "A Relational Encounter with Race" (2004).

4. Mari Ruti's *Reinventing the Soul* (2006) makes a similar claim that socio-discursive disciplinary structures can offer opportunities for creativity, agency, and self-assertion. She critiques contemporary constructivists for seeing only the negative, oppressive, agency-denying side of social pressures that turn us into conformal passive beings.

5. See my *Human Excellence and an Ecological Conception of the Psyche* (1991) for a full elaboration of the hardwired basic needs and emotions. Also see J. Panksepp's *The Archaeology of Mind: Neuroevolutionary Origins of Human Emotions* (2012).

6. Kohut's concept of the self was discussed in the last chapter; this section is a condensed review.

7. See chapter 9 for a full account of self psychology and economic society.

Chapter Four

The Erotic Self

Plato, Freud, and Kohut

Ever since Kohut declared that the development, maintenance, and flourishing of a core self is the chief psychological task for humans, there has been a fracas in America between classically oriented analysts who see the theory of self as breaking from Freud's scientific Darwinism and analysts who find that the theory of self is a far more effective theoretical orientation for understanding and treating their clients. Kohut's self is not the same as Freud's ego, as the ego is largely a set of conscious functions for establishing psychic coherence and dealing with reality and whose character is developed mainly through oedipal identifications and social education, while for Kohut the self is largely unconscious and is developed before the oedipal stage by early caretakers empathically helping the child transform early narcissism into a structured self. Further, Kohut created a picture of psychic dynamics, including the production of symptoms, that did not revolve around drives but rather around the development of the self, while Freud's whole theory of psychic dynamics and psychoanalytic intervention is based on the notion that the fundamental motivators in life are the drives and all of psychic life revolves around their management. It appears as though the gap between drive theory and self theory simply cannot be bridged and that the destructive divisiveness that has entered the field will not easily go away.

What I hope to do in this chapter is to show how we can bring Freud's late theory of eros and thanatos into harmony with Kohut's notion of the self by showing how the energy of the self needs to be conceived of as an erotic energy. This will be a difficult project as Kohut does not write about eros at all and eschews drive theory, while Freud does little to explicate what he means by eros. However, Kohut's theory desperately needs an understanding of what the binding energy of the self is, and Freud did not realize that when he shifted his theory from libido and survival to eros and thanatos in his later works, he abandoned his drive theory and began developing a theory that can be seen as a clear forerunner of Kohut's concept of the psyche as revolving around a self. That is, I think that for Freud eros seems to behave much like Kohut's notion of the self and that thanatos captures much about the psychological dynamics of what happens when selves are injured.

Here are some of Freud's key statements about eros: "The main purpose of Eros [is] that of uniting and binding" (1923, p. 45); Eros "aims at complicating life and at the same time, of course, preserving it" (1923, p. 40); "Eros operates from the beginning of life and appears as a 'life instinct'" (1919, p. 61n); and

> I may now add that civilization is a process in the service of Eros, whose purpose is to combine single human individuals, and after that families, then races, peoples and nations, into one great unity, the unity of mankind. Why this has to happen, we do not know; the work of Eros is precisely this. (1930, p. 122)

However, most tellingly, he says that to understand what eros means, we need to go back to Plato:

> What psychoanalysis calls sexuality was by no means identical with the impulsion towards a union of the two sexes or towards producing a pleasurable sensation in the genitals; it had far more resemblance to the all-inclusive and all-embracing love of Plato's *Symposium*. (1925, p. 218)[1]

Now, whatever else eros might be, it does not look like a drive. In his earlier works, especially his *Three Essays on the Theory of Sexuality,* Freud says that drives originate from identifiable parts of the body, such as the lips, anus, or genitals for libido and the stomach for hunger. But where in the body is an impetus for "uniting and binding," or "complicating life" located? He even says that eros is not to be identified with an impetus "towards producing a pleasurable sensation in the genitals." Further, drives build up tension and need to discharge; but eros seems to be a much more constant presence— while a sexual urge certainly seems to desire discharge, a motivation for unifying disparate elements or seeking life does not seem to operate in this way at all.[2]

If eros is not a drive, then what is it? Freud says that to find out what eros is we need to turn to "the divine Plato" and his *Symposium.* However, when we do so, we find that in the *Symposium* Plato himself goes back to Hesiod and Empedocles, and so I would like to initiate our inquiry into eros with Hesiod's seminal statement that "First of all the Void came into being, next broad-bosomed Earth, the world and the eternal home of all, and Eros, the most beautiful of the immortal gods, who in every man and every god softens the sinews and overpowers the prudent purpose of the mind" (1953, p. 56). Here we have succinctly stated that the ontological ground of everything is the void, the earth, and beautiful eros. From these three all else will come. Hence, from the beginning, we have a concept of eros as connected to the void and to the beautiful, as a primal force of generation, and as being disruptive of rational order—themes which will never be relinquished in our discussion of both eros and the self. Empedocles, whom Freud also claims to be a predecessor of his theory, says that there are two elemental forces: love and hate. Hate breaks things into pieces and sends the universe into an entropic chaos of unconnected parts while eros lures them back together into a harmonic whole. That is, the aim of eros is to overcome dissonant multiplicity and create, as Freud says, ever more inclusive structures of coherence. Again, this concept of eros as a unifying or binding power will remain throughout our discussion.

There is another important background to Plato's concept of eros in the *Symposium*. In previous dialogues, Plato has severely critiqued the Sophist ethic of basing life on the satisfaction of desires, claiming that desires are chaotic little tyrants that pressure the psyche to do their bidding often at the expense of what is good for the person and community. While reason can determine what is good, it does not have sufficient motivational force to bring it into being. Hence, Plato turns toward the strongest, most captivating motivational force in the human psyche—eros—and claims that it is not like desires, for rather than dissipating the psyche it longs to bring it to wholeness and the good. It is capable of doing this because eros always seeks beauty, and beauty is simply the aesthetic face of the good, for the good, in the final analysis, is harmonious order. Hesiod got it right that eros and beauty are intrinsically connected but did not see that eros is not itself the beautiful but is that which is awakened by beauty, longs to possess beauty, and finally is fully satisfied only when it generates beauty. While it looks as though yoking eros to a harmonious order is in contradiction to Hesiod's statement that eros "overpowers the prudent purpose of the mind," we can bring the two into coherence if we see that all structures of order need to open up to that which, according to them, is the irrational, but which in a wider vision represents a more inclusive form of order or beauty. To stay alive, eros must always be opening up to new, more complex forms of harmony.

The erotic desire for the beautiful occurs, according to the *Symposium*, because the soul in its very nature of self-consciousness lacks wholeness, harmony, and groundedness. Here we recall Hesiod's connection of eros with the void and look forward to Hegel's correlation of self-consciousness with negativity and Sartre's description of consciousness as "nothingness." That is, human subjectivity must be conceived of as an openness—as a negativity—in order for a world and ourselves to appear. If it were dense, then we would be material objects, not subjects. Hesiod is right to say that first there is a void and then a world, for the void is the necessary precondition for the appearance of a world. However, the void of self-consciousness haunts us with two further nothingnesses at the core of our human existence: that we are mortal and that we lack sufficient ways to make sense of ourselves and the world—in Heidegger's terms, we experience ourselves as "thrown" (1927). Because the void of self-consciousness opens up not only space but also the horizon of time, we can anticipate our deaths, our coming to be nothing. Further, we are the kind of being that must have meaning in order to live in a world; however, meaning is not given and must always be generated. Hence, we live always with the possibility that our systems of meaning will dissolve. Eros is birthed out of this womb of emptiness and propels us to discover forms of beauty and connectedness sufficient to triumph over our pervasive lacks.

Plato continues by saying that we don't really want to simply possess the beautiful, the object of our eros, for eros is "a longing not for the beautiful itself, but the conception and generation that the beautiful effects" (*Symposium,* 206e). Obviously, the operative paradigm here is eros in the form of heterosexual coupling for the sake of reproduction; however, just as Freud in his later work refuses to collapse the erotic into the sexual, so does Plato refuse this equation, as he sees the erotic urge to reproduce as part of a deeper yearning to overcome our voids by erotically birthing the beautiful—not occasionally, but essentially. To be human is always to be adventuring beyond our selves to fashion new, more inclusive structures of meaning, new ways of inhabiting our humanity and the earth. In the widest sense, this theory that eros seeks to give birth is, of course, present in Hesiod and Empedocles and lies beneath the Kantian perspective that the worlds we experience are not just there, ready-made for us, but must be generated and organized by acts of the psyche.

Freud, would agree, for he says in "On Narcissism" that in order to live in a world, our eros must relinquish its original narcissistic orientation and go out to objects (1914). If it doesn't, "we will fall ill"—we will become psychotics without worlds. That is, a world does not exist for us unless we love it, and, perhaps, it comes into being only to the extent that we can overcome our narcissism and love what is other than ourselves.[3] While I feel there is a profound truth in this claim, I reject Freud's further contention that eros works in a hydraulic zero-sum game, such that the more love we give the world the less we have for ourselves and vice versa. Rather, I think that when we find ourselves erotically loving the world, we feel most like ourselves. That is, not only does the presence of eros give us a world, it also gives us our selves.

Let us now add one more platonic doctrine, namely, that eros is a dynamic inner force, one that cannot and will not cease until the void at the heart of human subjectivity is filled. Hence, for Plato eros propels us to climb a ladder of increasingly abstract objects until we locate a set of meanings that in their universality and permanence can both ground human existence and allow it to participate in an immortal realm beyond the sufferings of change and death. I will not follow Plato into this august place that appears to be more of an unchanging death rather than the zenith of life, for when the void is fully erased, so is birthplace of the erotic, the birthplace of life itself. We need to deal with death and the fragility of meaning not by immersion in some kind of fantasy of permanence but by embracing or accepting them as the necessary conditions for the possibility of living our lives with a fullness of life, for the possibility of living erotically. Eros is Faustian—it must forever strive or it will plunge into a Mephistophelean darkness; eros is Nietzschean—it is that which must always be overcoming itself. That is, eros is a primal developmental force but there is no teleological endpoint at which it can stop and say, as Faust never can, "this is so beautiful, let me rest here."

Hence, while erotic adventure might commence with a spontaneous, irrational eruption, we must then develop this erotic moment by exploring how it needs to unfold. That is, we must be committed to developing the depths of our loves. My eros for philosophy stays alive only insofar as I keep exploring ever further what it means to be a philosopher.

When Plato attempts to identify what kind of being this dynamic, creative, beauty-seeking force is, he calls it a *daemon,* which he says is a kind of spirit that is neither the unchanging immortal divine nor the ordinary personality structure of the human mortal (*Symposium,* 202e). Earlier, Heraclitus had pronounced *"Ethos Daemon,"* which can be taken to mean that a person's *daemon* is his fate or destiny (Wheelwright, 1966, p. 74). That is, both Heraclitus and Plato intuited that there is a singular erotic spirit which more than anything else is who we are. Unfortunately, Plato did not pursue his insights into the erotic inner *daemon* he discovered in the *Symposium* because he became so concerned with the need for the psyche to become rationally ordered, that he declared in the *Republic* that eros is a tyrant and that the best soul is the un-erotic soul ruled dictatorially by the faculty of reason. We needed to wait almost two and a half millennia until the rise of psychoanalysis and Kohut's discovery of the self in order to resume our exploration of this erotic inner *daemon.*

Let me highlight and expand the key themes we have encountered in this whirlwind tour of the ancients. First, eros has a primordial sense to it—it is that which explains why the world or psyche comes into being but nothing further can explain its presence. Eros is like a Freudian drive in that it is psychological bedrock, but it is a different kind of bedrock than a drive, for it is a developmental force. The primordiality of eros that we find in Hesiod, Plato, and Empedocles also means that eros must be a source of spontaneity—that which causes without itself being caused. What we are erotic about is not the outcome of a rational project or a series of organized steps, for eros comes upon us, unbidden, spontaneously, like being struck by a mysterious arrow. That is, what we are erotic about spontaneously expresses our most profound singularity of being. That which an individual's eros seeks as the beautiful seems to be fated, embedded, destined, daemonic. The primordial spontaneity and singularity of eros also means that it is not open to rational explanation. We cannot tell adequate stories about why we fall in love with what we do, or why we must become what we must become. We can add that since eros is experienced as spontaneous and primal, it is also experienced as a fully embodied arousal. Eros is not *agape* or *philia*—gentle, somewhat intellectual forms of love which we often adopt out of moral duty. Rather, eros rivets our whole beings, not just a part of us, and in its arousal of the whole of our bodies, calls us to wholeness.

Second, eros involves a longing, a desire for something that feels as though it could complete one and take one out of emptiness and disharmony with oneself and the world. This unifying force of eros is deeply associated with its being aroused by beauty, but encountering beauty is not enough, for this is a passive act. When eros is aroused it longs to create and unite with what it loves and in so doing to produce a new way of being oneself in the world. Once eros spontaneously erupts, it is up to the subject to explore what this eruption might mean and this sends eros on a developmental trajectory that will attempt to actualize the subject's ownmost potentialities. At one time I had the potentiality to be a lawyer and perhaps a business executive, but while I had the skills to do well at these professions, I had no eros for them. They are good professions but not my professions. When eros sets out on its developmental trajectory to actualize a person's deepest possibilities, it sets out on a road that has no final completion. To be erotic one must be in full adventure.

You might now be asking, why did we need to take this rather long excursion into ancient Greek literature and philosophy? It is not simply that we needed to flesh out what Freud meant by eros, but to engage a significant question for self psychology—namely, what is the self? Kohut says that it has two poles, but what is it that binds these poles into something that feels like a self, that feels like me? In a weak attempt to answer this question Kohut proclaims in the *Restoration of the Self* that the self is a tension gradient between the poles of ideals and ambitions (1977, p. 180). This sounds a bit as though the self is some kind of electromagnetic field holding structures of meaning together. While the concept of a tension gradient attempts to capture the sense that something dynamic must be holding the poles of the self together, it is an inadequate concept because it does not help us phenomenologically to distinguish between self experiences and experiences motivated by other psychic pressures. It is an experience-distant concept that comes from a mechanical vocabulary rather than a psychological one. But what concept can account for the force that more than anything else binds the poles of the self into a self? I propose that it is the psychological impetus that Freud was attempting to grasp when it shifted from libido to eros and that Plato originally described in his *Symposium*. The binding energy of the self is eros—daemonic, longing, beauty-seeking, creative, spontaneous eros.

Here is a contemporary psychoanalytic re-telling of the *Symposium:* both Freud and Kohut thought that human life begins in a state of primary narcissism, which we can now think of as eros directed toward one's self, or, since there really is no self for eros to love, it must be conceived of as a pool of static or potential eros swirling around itself. In this state of erotic narcissistic bliss the baby feels itself to be perfect, omnipotent, and grand, and acts, as Freud says, as though he were "his majesty, the baby." There is a feeling of oneness, especially with the mother, whose liquids flow into the baby as though there were a shared body. In a real sense the child is not yet object-seeking because it has not fully differentiated itself from the mother or its world. But sooner or later caretakers will fail to respond adequately to the child's needs and reality reveals to the baby that far from being omnipotent, perfect, and great, it is the most helpless of all creatures. Its early narcissism had been a great protection against this traumatic realization, but now its wholeness is shattered and it must face the void, the emptiness, the loneliness of being a separate being. It is at this moment that eros is born as a transformation of the initial narcissistic libido and we begin our lifelong erotic journey to once again be whole with ourselves and the world.

According to Kohut, if the child has adequate responses from its selfobjects, it will over time re-integrate its sense of perfection into ideals, which it will *love* as it once loved its caretakers and convert its grandiosity into ambitions that it *longs* to accomplish. In sum, the self that "has" the ideals and ambitions is our erotic love/longing for them. We can now see how fusing the ancient theory of eros with Kohut's concept of the development and structure of the self allows us to see that it is eros that constitutes the selfness of the self, the *daemonic* oneness of the self. In short, we are most ourselves when we are erotically loving. The phenomenological benefit of associating the self with eros is that eros is not a theoretically inferred psychological structure like "the self" but an immediately felt experiential presence, and one which is somewhat easy to place on a continuum for how much or little eros one is feeling. To go back to Freud's equation of eros with a life force; we can say that the more we feel alive in any experience is the extent to which our selves are present. Here phenomenology and ontology come together, for eros is nothing other than the presencing of the being of the self. There is no going behind eros to find something deeper.

This fusion of the ancient theory of eros with Kohut's notion of the self also deepens our awareness of the relation of eros to the void, for both ideals and ambitions must stand over us as that which we are not, but that which we long to be. Like Plato's eros, the self must always keep developing beyond itself into ever more complex and mature instantiations of its ideals and ambitions, because ideals and ambitions die once they are reached. In short, Kohut's self is not defined by an identity structure, but by a dynamic structure of values that evolves over time.

While neither psychoanalysis nor self psychology has a theory of beauty as that which lures eros into being and represents its goal, it is easy to see that the concept of psychic health as the integration and harmonization of the disparate motivational sectors of the psyche is in fact a theory of what constitutes a beautiful soul. That is, we respond so powerfully to beauty because psychological life is so often chaotic or stale, and we need to be lured either by some great exemplar of harmony or by an adventurous extension of ourselves beyond our stabilized patterns of life. The aesthetics embedded in self psychology then involves both Classical and Romantic conceptualizations of beauty. The searching for coherence or harmony is Classical, while the need to spontaneously adventure beyond any achieved stability is Romantic.

In short, I think that the ancient theory of eros was the first attempt to capture what it means to have and develop a self. What Kohut adds to the ancient theory is a very important understanding of how the self develops out of early narcissism, how it becomes structuralized in terms of ideals, ambitions, and traits, how this structure explains the dynamic/developmental character of the erotic self, and how the self is incredibly vulnerable to injury and trauma and thus why it essentially needs others to play self functions when one's self is unable to.

The erotic presencing of the self is extraordinarily important, because, as we have seen in the last chapter, the self is only one of a number of motivational sectors in the psyche and must compete with these for the ego's attention. That is, the self is not the subject of experience—the ego is, and the ego needs to attend not only to the needs of the self but to pressures arising from the necessities of reality, internalized social norms and values, biological urges, and the ego's own need for power and status. In this matrix of motivational pressures, the self's need to have its singularity recognized and actualized is often foregone, as reality, society, and biology are accommodated. This plurality of motivational pressures explains the common of experience of feeling that one has lost oneself or never really found oneself. The self tends to get buried beneath all the other needs that the ego must attend to, and like the last thing on one's "to do" list, often never gets heard. Eros is the self's way of calling out to the ego that something of profound importance has appeared and needs to be tended to. Unfortunately, the self loses so often to other motivational priorities that the general kind of life lived by adults is one of "average everydayness," to use Heidegger's poignant phrase (1927), rather than one of vitalized self-actualization. In order for us to live lives that are erotically alive, we—our egos—must make commitments to the values announced by our erotic selves.

Note that with this theory of the energy of the self as eros, we can have a deeper understanding of why and how empathy is so effective in forming and healing the self. Empathy is a form of eros because it seeks to unite with the object but not destroy, consume, or control it. Like eros, empathy allows the object to be itself. That is, empathy seeks to paradoxically become one with the object but to insist on differentiation. Identification, on the other hand, seeks to eliminate difference, and, hence, is a form of desire, not eros. In erotic empathy, we love deeply, so deeply that we mirror the other; but we do not desire. If empathy is a form of eros, then we can understand why Freud called psychoanalysis a cure through love. It needs also to be noted that eros and desire can both arise at the same time in a fully fused way and that this leads to so many of the delights and problems with sexual love.

Before we bring this lovely discourse on the erotic life to closure, we need to confront a titanic hurdle, namely, that history and literature are replete with persons—Dido, Anna Karenina, Don Juan, and scores of politicians— whose erotic adventures rather than actualizing their selves, injured them. Such cases have been so powerful that they have led many philosophers, including Plato of the *Republic* and *Laws*, Augustine, and Schopenhauer, to proclaim that the fundamental task of human life is to free ourselves from the irrational eros which drives us mad with its intoxications and ruins our life's rational plans.

In his *Open-Minded: Working Out the Logic of the Soul* (2000, chs. 6 and 7) Jonathan Lear gives an interpretation of the *Symposium* as saying that eros, rather than being a developmental force as I have described it, is a regressive force that resists development. After all, the aim at achieving wholeness can be seen not as a developmental task but as a regressive long-ing to restore a primitive state of being.

My equation of eros with the self, I think, can explain why eros can be both developmental and regressive and even demonic in the negative sense of that term. When early childhood is felicitous, eros takes on the structure of what Kohut called a self, with a set of deep values and organized energy for achieving those values. But if eros does not become structured into a self but is thwarted by inadequate or hostile social responses to the emerging self's needs, then eros can become regressive and long for an earlier undeveloped state of wholeness—a return to the state of pure potentiality—rather than seek ever more inclusive forms of wholeness. Indeed, it is not unusual for there to be both a developmental and a regressive form of eros in a person with a deep struggle as to which form of eros will predominate—one which longs to be a self or one which wants to retreat back to an undifferentiated bliss. However, worse can happen, for if injuries to the self are severe enough, some of the original erotic energy can transform into narcissistic rage and then the urge to love is fused with the urge for revenge and destruction. My supposition is that it is not unusual for a person to harbor all three forms of eros: developmental, regressive, and destructive. These are often fused in transference in which the analysand erotically loves the therapist as the vehicle for restoring the self's developmental trajectory, longs to regress to a blissful stage by so idealizing the analyst that she feels entirely safe and does not want to leave this space, and also wants to destroy the therapist as unconsciously fused with earlier harmful love objects. It is the task of psychoanalytic therapy to heal erotic wounds such that the developmental eros—the self—can predominate over the distortions of eros. Marion Tolpin called this "finding the forward edge" (2002), and Frank Summers termed it "transcendent empathy"—empathy for developmental possibilities that had not yet awakened in the analysand (2005).

Hence, we need to complexify our phenomenological approach to the erotic self, for it is only eros in its developmental form that fully expresses the self, and we can often be fooled by an erotic longing for regressive objects or objects which eros seeks eventually to destroy because they are unconsciously identified with those who earlier injured the nascent self. The phenomenological difference between what we might call "good eros" and these distortions of the erotic is that when the doppelgängers are motivating us we have the sense that we are being manically driven. While eros and drivenness are both high intensity, intoxicating, riveting kinds of experience, eros is felt as grounded in who we are and has a firm sense of rightness about it, despite the fact that it is spontaneous and irrational; drivenness, on the other hand, is an ungrounded manic kind of energy that tyrannically pressures us without our ever feeling that this is who we are. That is, when we are in a state of drivenness, we are likely to be destructive to ourselves, to others, and violate what we know is right. One of the reasons that we get captured by our regressive or destructive eros is because these are so close to the self—indeed, they might be authentic expressions of a deeply injured self.

Surprisingly, eros' doppelgängers—the longing for an earlier state of existence and an aggressive impulse to destroy— look a great deal like Freud's death drive, thanatos, and this brings us finally back to our original problem of showing how Freud's late theory is not so far apart from Kohut's self theory. When Freud wrote "On Narcissism" his entire psychoanalytic theory had to change, for the drive for survival had collapsed into narcissistic libido and so the conflictual basis for the dynamic understanding of the psyche also collapsed, as there was now only one drive, libido. When Freud re-conceived his understanding of the basic psychic forces as eros and thanatos, he radically altered his whole notion of drive and psychic life in a way he did not grasp, for eros and thanatos are not the reproductive and survival drives which Darwin posited as fundamental for animal life, but the basis for a decidedly un-mammalian human psychology. I suggest that what Freud intuited in his shift from libido to eros was that the psyche had within it as one of its primal motivating structures something that had to dynamically develop beyond itself, always needing to expand into ever-widening realms of meaning, connectedness, and complexity, and which, when it was able to motivate the ego to pursue its needs, filled the psyche with a sense of aliveness. According to Jonathan Lear (2004), Freud shifted from libido to eros because he needed some kind of basic motivation to explain therapeutic action—to explain what motivates persons to try to become whole in analysis. Rather than calling this motivation for wholeness a drive, which has more of a biological than psychological sense to it, I want to equate this primordial urge with Kohut's theory that the most basic of all psychological motivations is the need to develop and sustain self structure. This is not to say that we are not wired sexually and for survival—we obviously are; but that there is also a more fundamental motivation: the need to develop a psyche organized around a core self.

What Freud was intuiting in the death drive is the ego's need to maintain a psychological homeostasis that has a tension with the eruptive, spontaneous, and often disrupting impetus of the erotic self. However, the most psychologically disruptive events of all are traumas to the self and the fragmenting forces these traumas release. When Freud says in *The Ego and the Id* that the task of the death drive is "to lead organic life back into the inanimate state" (1923, p. 40), I think that he is explicating the ego's need to deal with the fragmentation of the self by (1) regressing to an earlier state in which the self was more coherent (regressive eros), (2) dissociating the fragmenting pieces in order to de-cathect the trauma (breaking the organic whole into parts), and (3) grasping that a highly destructive force (narcissistic rage) emerges from traumas to the self. All of these notions appear in various of Freud's descriptions of the death drive and they dovetail beautifully with Kohut's understanding of the psychological dynamics that occur when the self is injured. This convergence of Freud and Kohut is of extreme importance, for Freud was a brilliant observer of psychological processes. He described them in the late-nineteenth-century terms of "drives," while Kohut looked at much the same phenomena and used the language of self. We can now see how Kohut's theory of the dynamics surrounding the creation of the self and its possible injuries can be seen as an interpretation of Freud's theory of eros and thanatos.

In sum, I have tried to show that the ancient theory of eros both anticipates the Kohutian contemporary theory of the self and significantly enhances it by answering the question of what binds the separate aspects of the self into a self and by giving persons a phenomenological marker by which to recognize the presence of the self. I have also tried to show that in Freud's shift from Darwinian libido to the eros of "the divine Plato," he was intuiting that his dynamic psychology of the unconscious needed another agency besides those he had already found—the ego, id, and superego. It needed a concept of the erotic self.

NOTES

1. Quoted by J. Lear (2005), p. 196.

2. According to Jonathan Lear, the shift from libido to eros is more important than the addition of thanatos, which seems to be only a variation of the constancy principle, namely, the psyche's need to discharge tension by getting rid of what is disturbing to it; however, the switch from libido to eros is nothing less than a change from a mammalian psychology of sexual reproduction to a human psychology of striving for wholeness and creative development (2003).

3. I am indebted to Jonathan Lear's *Love and Its Place in Nature* (1990) for this interpretation.

Chapter Five

Ancient Theology and Contemporary Self Psychology

Monotheism, Mono-Selfism, and the Transgressions of Omnipotence

In this ancient land of Israel[1] which birthed monotheism in the midst of dominant polytheistic cultures, it is opportune to inquire into how the primordial divide of the one and the many is now playing itself out in contemporary psychoanalysis in the battle between those who hold that having a singular self is the fulcrum for healthy psychological functioning and those who hold that there is no singular self but an indefinite number of self-states or as many selves as there are relationships. William James considered the problem of the one vs. the many "the most central of all philosophic problems, central because so pregnant. I mean by this that if you know whether a man is a decided monist or a decided pluralist, you perhaps know more about the rest of his opinions than if you give him any other name ending in *ist*" (2000, p. 59).

This issue of the one vs. the many is crucial to the problem of what it means to belong—to oneself, to a community, to a land, to a universe. When Socrates attempts to find out from Euthyphro what piety is and Euthyphro answers that it is "doing what is pleasing to the gods" (*Euthyphro,* 7a*),* Socrates retorts that if there are many gods, then one and the same act might be pleasing to some and unpleasing to others, and hence be both pious and impious at the same time. Insofar as we need our worlds to make sense in order to belong to them, Socrates said that our world needs a singular divine presence, and, if we are to belong to ourselves, we must organize the multiplicity that plagues the human psyche into an integrity. This connection between oneness and belonging was concomitantly explored in the Hebraic tradition in the conviction that worship of a singular deity is the ground for creating a unified community. Were the Hebrews and Socrates right? Must we be monophilists in order to have a sense of belonging?

THE ONE AND THE MANY

Those who favor oneness tend to like order—organized lives, organized states, organized universes, and complete explanations; they tend to see arbitrariness, anarchy, unpredictability, and chaos as destructive of the good. In metaphysics, these monophilists favor either an orderly universe governed by a single God or a world completely explainable by the laws of science. In psychoanalysis, they like to find a fulcrum, such as the self, in terms of which psychological functioning can both be organized and explained. On the other side are those who favor chaos and multiplicity and link these states to creative possibilities, openness, and the liveliness that comes from engagement with difference and the other. These polyphilists tend to dislike overly ordered psyches, political states, and universes, thinking that any unifying agency, be it God, the self, or the ruler, is likely to be tyrannically limiting of possibilities and freedom or denying the unbounded multiplicity of reality.

For the most part, the monophilists have dominated the conceptual history of the West. From Plato's remarkable statement about the unifying power of The Good in his *Republic*, to Aristotle's Unmoved Mover, to the reign of Judeo/Christianity with its one God for over a millennium, order centered on oneness has dominated metaphysical accounts of human existence, while the ideal of an organized, self-controlled psyche so brilliantly proclaimed by both the Hebrew prophets and Greek philosophers, has prevailed almost without opposition. Even the concept of psychological illness as fragmentation, splitting, or repression points to psychological health as being identified with unified coherence and pathology with psychic multiplicity.

However, the supporters of multiplicity, chaos, and multi-centeredness have gained the current day with the rise, and, I would say, dominance, of the postmodern perspective. It is from this perspective that self psychology has been most challenged. Many postmodernists, especially academics, dismiss self psychology (without ever reading it) as hopelessly old-fashioned because it still seeks a unified organizational ground for experience in proclaiming that we need to have a self rather than multiple sources of free-flowing motivation. If we are to talk about selves, then it is best to talk, as Phillip Bromberg does, of a multiplicity of self-states that can be in connection with one another but not organized around a central dominant self (1998). These negative appraisals are joined by an in-house critique from self-psychologists Stolorow and Atwood, who claim that Kohut created a reified notion of the self and that this stultifying concept has acted as a defense against the teeming multiplicity and tragic becomingness of existence. "The theoretical language of self psychology with its noun, 'the self,' reifies the experiencing of selfhood and transforms it into a metaphysical entity with thinglike properties. . . . The objectification of the experiencing of selfhood serves to render stable and solid a sense of personal identity otherwise subject to discontinuity, uncertainty, and fragmentation. A phenomenological-contextualist viewpoint, by contrast, embraces the unbearable vulnerability and context-dependence of human existence" (2013, pp. 416–17).

Is Kohut's concept of the self a reified fiction blinding us to the irresolvable chaotic flow of life, or, worse, limiting our creative possibilities? Does it make more sense to speak of a multiplicity of self-states with only "spaces" inbetween them rather than a unifying self? Do we really not need to belong to ourselves or to some kind of home base?

In response to these questions I want to show that the concepts of oneness, self, and belonging are crucial for human beings and that it is not these concepts that are the problem either in metaphysics or psychology, but a hidden notion that has snuck into these concepts and infected them with a mortal disease, namely, omnipotence.

THE TRANSGRESSIONS OF OMNIPOTENCE

Let us begin with the central problem that human beings have faced since time immemorial, namely, that their natural and social environments are unstable and precarious and, hence, dangerous. That chaos is toxic to the human psyche is revealed in its tendency to produce anxiety, the most debilitating of our emotional responses. It is, thus, crucial for humans to establish order in our psychological, social, natural, and political environments if we are to survive and attain emotional stability. When the chaotic and unpredictable are transformed into a predictable order, a habitation comes into being, a place, whether in the world or in oneself, where one can belong.

However, if there were more than one principle of organization—in the state, psyche, or universe—then there is always the possibility of conflict and disorder. Hence, it seems that we need a singular highest agency for instilling order. As soon as political entities come into existence, we get singular pharaohs, kings, or emperors as rulers; the metaphysicians develop a monotheistic cosmology; and the prophets and philosophers preach the importance of personal integrity. But now a further problem arises. If the one agency that is supposed to grant order does not have the power to do so, then the hope of overcoming the precariousness and instability of life cannot be sustained. Hence, the concepts of order and oneness lead directly to granting omnipotence to the powers that are supposed to produce order. God must be all-powerful, the emperor must have unlimited dominance, and, in Greek philosophy, reason is granted unlimited authority to govern the rest of the psychic elements. In short, the inherent need for order leads directly to the quest for omnipotence.

As psychoanalysts know, the fantasy of omnipotence has its psychological origin in early narcissism, a fantasy likely to persist if there have been traumas to the self or some kind of failed growth. As Jessica Benjamin has shown (1988), the failure to relinquish narcissistic omnipotence (typical of men) or the projection of omnipotence onto others (typical of women), has resulted in domination/submission structures throughout human social life, especially in sexual relations, resulting in a lack of mutual recognition that we all need to feel human and to belong to human communities.

The quest for omnipotence also lies behind the debilitating Western ideal of the autonomous, independent self who needs nothing other than himself to sustain himself and who has attained a perfect control over his emotions and desires. This ideal has driven us away from life-sustaining sources of selfobject supplies, made intimate love almost impossible, and turned a rich inner world into one that Thoreau likened to self-slavery (1854).

Furthermore, the West's conceptualization of God as an omnipotent being has led, in the end, to the death of God, for such a God was incompatible with the presence of evil and denied humans the right to self-generativity. If God is all-good and omnipotent, then it makes no sense that he would allow evil to occur. Countless persons who have suffered senseless losses have lost their faith because God did not intervene when he clearly should have, being conceived of as good and omnipotent. Further, there is Nietzsche's powerful critique of God. If there is an ultimate omnipotent authority in the universe, then our primary orientation must be one of obedience and subservience to this authority. To be free, creative, self-generating beings, we must rid ourselves of the notion of an omnipotent authority. It is only in a universe without such a being that we can experience life as creativity and spontaneity to the fullest. God had to die in order for humans to live. In short, because the sense of a divine presence fell into the conceptual entanglement of oneness, organization, and omnipotence, the culture had to undergo a devastating loss of faith and meaningfulness. While there have been some brilliant theologies proposing a non-omnipotent god—such as those of Whitehead, Buber, and Tillich[2] —the conceptual affiliation of god with omnipotence is still so strong that it is almost a moral fault to have faith after the Holocaust.

In short, the narcissistic fantasy and projections of omnipotence have been devastating. When applied to divinity, they lead to the negation of the sacred. When applied to political entities, they lead to autocracy and servility. When applied to social relations, they lead to domination/submission structures. When applied to moral psychology, they lead to a repressive rational ego attempting to control all psychic activity; and when they infiltrate ethics, they lead to a false ideal of autonomy and refusal to accept the reality of human dependency. That is, the projection of the fantasy of omnipotence has led to conceptual incoherence, massive social and political suffering, and constricted personal lives. It is without surprise that when the Absolute Monarch gets dethroned at the end of the eighteenth century, the traditional concept of an omnipotent God is getting challenged, and the anti-slavery and women's movements are commencing.

We now can see why the postmoderns are so in favor of chaos, spontaneity, multi-centeredness, diversity, recognizing the other rather than dominating her, play, creativity, accepting the void, and rejecting unifying narratives or any theory that smacks of oneness, organization, and omnipotence. If that old unholy trinity led to deadly, stifling, repressive gods, rulers, and egos, then let the opposites reign. I believe it is this conceptual background that has made many contemporary thinkers shy away from self psychology, for the singleness of Kohut's self raises the specter of the over-control, repression, and narrowness of life from which we have just begun to free ourselves.

Self psychology can, and must, offer two responses, if it is to survive as a viable framework through which to understand human experience. First, it must retort that disorganization is as deadly as organization. Corpses are disorganized bodies; anarchy typically leads to lawlessness and an anxiety-ridden social existence; and a fully disorganized psyche is that of the psychotic—not the freest of human beings but a sad loss of the possibility of a human life. The healthy corrective to the old hierarchical and dominating way of achieving organization is to envision new models of organization, ones that eschew omnipotence and allow for difference, non-conformity, and a healthy amount of chaos—that is, ones in which we accept much more exposure to precariousness and vulnerability than under the old model, but without falling into the nihilistic void in which no values or forms of life can be substantiated. The question is whether Kohut's concept of human beings as having singular selves at the core of psychological functioning is a regression to the old oppressive types or organization or a vision of a new way to think about human life. Is the "oneness" of the self to be connected with an omnipotent organizational task or is it to be inherently open to multiplicity and difference?

SELF-STATES VS. HAVING A SINGULAR SELF

Let us suppose for the sake of argument that there is no central singular self, but a multiplicity of what Phillip Bromberg (1998) and other postmodern theorists call self-states connected to an ego. Each of these self-states is a configuration of self/other patterns of meaning, affects, memories, and a way of being a self in the world. In a healthy psyche they are all connected to one another and to a reflective ego; in psychopathology they are dissociated from one another. In this theory it is the ego that is responsible for bringing coherence to the psyche, not a configuration of a nuclear self in alignment with the ego. What Bromberg doesn't address is the question of what structure the ego uses or should use to unify the self-states and orient them to the world, for the ego cannot accomplish any work unless it is structuralized. If there is no such psychological structure as "the self" for the ego to align with, then the ego will probably be structured mainly around the social values and codes that have been internalized. In the vocabulary of Christopher Bollas, the subject has to arrange herself either normotically—that is to say, according to the norms of the social order—or according to its destiny drive —the self (2011).

In the contemporary world these social codes tend to form persons into economic subjects, persons who are structured to optimize their abilities to engage in market activities—buying low, selling high, being keenly aware of options and opportunities to enhance their market maneuverability, and developing a keen cost-benefit rationality and a drive to be competitively successful. That is, such persons seek to become as omnipotent as possible— over themselves, others, and any conditions that might thwart them. That is, they develop egos that are likely to avoid the needs and vulnerabilities harbored in the self. However, in order for such ego-driven persons to successfully position themselves in the market, they typically have to make themselves useful to the world by offering goods and or services that it wants, rather than asking themselves who they most essentially are and what they must do to realize their selves. Hence, there is a tendency to turn ourselves into market variables—identifying with both that which makes us useful and the desires we can get satisfied by being useful. That is, in Heidegger's terms, we convert everything, including ourselves, into "standing reserve," into structures of use functionality (1949). Such subjectivities lack what Heidegger calls "authenticity," Nietzsche terms "self creativity," and Emerson calls "self-reliance." That is, there is no singularity, no integrity, no "authentically being yourself" for such a subject. In a great paradox, the omnipotent subject becomes a slave to society.

In short, if there were no such psychological structure as the self, there would be no way to articulate what it means to be authentic, what it means to be singularly yourself rather than a variable of the social codes. If "being true to oneself" is the definition of integrity, then there is no way for those who do not believe in something like a self to define integrity except as some kind of arid rational consistency. For there to be any possibility of ballast against the intrusive invasiveness of modern society, there must be a singular self, which, like Dostoevsky's underground man, stands up in its irrational singularity as not being able to fit into a hedonistic calculus. Without positing such a self there is little way to explain those experiences that stand out as "this really is me." I have many ideals and ambitions, but most of them have been adopted from the social world. I have a lovely socioeconomic status, dress the part, pay my bills dutifully, am decidedly punctual, and always try to be nice. While satisfying such ideals gives me pleasure, the realization of them does not make my life meaningful or alive. However, when I live up to my self's ideal to teach a great philosophy class or dance a terrific waltz with my beloved spouse, I am in a state of joy. I can live off of those experiences, for these values stem from my self.

THE ONENESS OF THE SELF

But why say that the self that is present while ballroom dancing is the same as the self in the philosophy classroom? There is very little in common between these activities and other activities in which I feel most like myself, such as hiking in the mountains, playing with our dogs, gazing on terrific art and architecture, etc. Why not say that each of these sides of me is a self-state rather than trying to tie them up nicely in something called a self?[3] If the self consists of a multiplicity of ideals, ambitions, and talents, what unites them together into a self? Why not just say that within our psychic economies some values (ideals, ambitions, talents) are more cherished than others? The ones I value most highly I will call self-values, meaning by this nothing more than the fact that my subjectivity has elevated them in importance. Why posit a "self" behind these values that somehow gathers them and infuses them with a special meaning? Isn't all the talk about "the self" a reification of the processes of valuing, selecting, liking, feeling energized by, etc.?

First, there is the evidence from the clinic. What Kohut found was that he had a number of patients who were quite successful and had highly developed valuing functions, but were missing something—missing something so crucial that amid a great deal of success, wealth, and fame, they felt their lives to be empty. What was missing was not a drive or a repressed part of experience; what was missing was their very selves. That is, it is hard to account for the depth and pervasiveness of the feelings of emptiness and despair in these people without positing something like an essential self that is missing from the core of experience.

Second, I find that there is something common to all the activities I call "self-activities"—namely, I love them erotically. As we found in the last chapter, eros is the core of the self. It is not like biological desires or social pressures; for there seems to be something inherently "me" in what I erotically love. Kierkegaard expresses this insight by calling the self a "singular passion" (1846); while Nietzsche proclaims that we become free spirits only when we love our singular particular fates, when we become an *amor fati* (1882). For these existentialist thinkers, eros is that psychic urge propelling us not only to bond with what is strikingly meaningful to us, but in so doing to always be going beyond ourselves—to always be developing. Goethe's Faust cannot descend into perdition so long as he is erotically striving. Freud also came to grasp that eros was only secondarily about sex and primarily about "making ever greater wholes"—that is, striving to be more than we are. For these thinkers eros propels the process of self-realization, but always somewhat tragically, for there can be no final completion, no absolute resting place of final accomplishment. Hence, eros—the unifying singularity of the self is a paradox, for it is both the oneness of the self and that which is incomplete and longing to be more than itself. As Plato said, if our eros lacked nothing and stopped longing, it—the self—would die. I must add that whatever else this dynamic erotic core is, it is also personal—that is, it is not just a kind of objective energy, it is "me;" it is me in my singular, spontaneous exuberance. If asked to go further as to the origin of the "me," I must agree with Emerson when he says that the self is "that deep force, the last fact behind which analysis cannot go" (1982, p. 187).

In short, we are most our selves when we are passionately loving. However, if dynamic loving is the core of the self, it must be sustained by the ego's making commitments to those activities, persons, and places that lure forth our love. When I commit, I belong—to a place, a person, a community, or an activity. To belong through commitment means that one is committed to a loving exploration of the relations one has to what is beloved. Such exploration must develop to be vital, and this fits with Kohut's understanding that lying at the core of the self are ideals and ambitions, for no value can be an ideal or an ambition if it is fully realized; in order for a value to be an ideal or an ambition it must stand beyond us, luring us into further self-realization. To be a self is to be becoming a self.

There is a further complication: there is no self without selfobjects and this means that one's self is located in multiple other psyches. It is both singular—located at the psychological core of a subject—and multiple, located in important selfobject others. It is both a core set of functions providing a sense of sameness through time and space but also exists on a spatio/temporal continuum extending into important others. That is, Kohut is best understood as a dialectical thinker in the tradition of Hegel. The self is both one and many. It is both a unique core of a person and a set of relationships.

In sum the self must always be a many and a one. Without multiple ideals, ambitions, and propensities there would be no tensions, and without tensions there would be no dynamic energy or a developmental thrust to resolve and realize them. But without an erotic oneness to the self, we are left without a me. But what is this "me" without its web of selfobjects? What is any organism without its ecological environment? In sum both the monophilists and polyphilists are right—the self must be both many and one, both multiple values in a tension and a singularity holding them together.

Belonging to Oneself

We have already seen why it is difficult for an ego to form a strong alliance with the self. To do so limits options, makes us more vulnerable, and opens up the psychological site where we are most likely to harbor trauma and least likely to feel the power of omnipotence. On the other hand, when the self is present, experience becomes radiantly vitalized, meaningful, and coherent. We experience more life, more ourselves, and more connected with others, and this, in the end, is why the ego is lured to bond with the self. When it does so, we feel perhaps the most important of feelings—that we belong to ourselves. The singleness of subjectivity fuses with the singleness of the self and in so doing balances the primordial lack that so haunts self-consciousness with a solid ground for choice.

When we ask, what kind of subjectivity is best able to form an alliance with the self and care for its needs, we get a surprising answer: it is a subjectivity which has been constructed ethically (see chapter 7 for a full elaboration of this thematic). Kohut's most important revelation about the self is that it birthed from acts of the love and care of others and needs such others to sustain and vitalize it for the entirety of its existence. The best way for adults to create and live within a matrix of selfobject care is to be able to offer such care in a reciprocal way to others. But one cannot do this unless one also develops the traits of empathy, concern for others, and the other moral virtues that, as Aristotle has shown, are needed to sustain friendships. That is, in order to care for our selves, we must be able to care for others, and in caring for others, we care for our selves. To realize our selves we must become good.

There is another reason for why persons need to become moral. For the self to be erotically striving in adventure, persons need to extend themselves beyond an environment of mirroring sameness, the usual tribal cocoons we establish to affirm us. It is encounter with the other in the otherness of the other that challenges us to grow beyond ourselves. I suggest that the kind of subjectivity that can best do this is, once again, an ethical subjectivity, for such a subjectivity knows that all other subjects have intrinsic worth and will not negate them just because they are missing a piece of what mirrors him—the same color skin, the same gender, the same nationality, the same religion. It is the ethical viewpoint that respects and responds to the intrinsic worth in others that lets otherness fully appear.

There is yet another path by which to understand why individuals striving to realize themselves must become ethical. For Ranaan Kulka (2012), persons need to "dissolve" their narrow, self-involved selves and merge with a wider sea of meaning and human value. Without this wider set of meanings, our personal strivings have the character of being small, restless, and without final fruit. Such a dissolving of the self into a wider realm of meaning at the same time the self keeps its emergent adventure into singularity is what grants a person the joy of being a coherent Hegelian contradiction: singular, yet universal; forever striving and yet at peace. Or, as Emerson said, when we most realize our particularity, we are also most universal, most human.

But always the piper must be paid. To belong to our selves, our communities, and a universe of higher values, we must be willing to encounter our selves at our least omnipotent place, the place of greatest vulnerability. We cannot do this unless we also find ourselves capable of relating to the vulnerabilities of others. That is, we need to be responsive to the suffering of others to be truly responsive to the suffering the self always undergoes. This also is what it means to be ethical, but not an ethics of the superego—that is, an ethics of law, but an ethics of character, care, and love.

THE SELF AND THE DIVINE: BELONGING TO THE UNIVERSE

Self psychology holds that when we are actively expressing and actualizing ourselves, we fill with a radiant vitality, a glowing sense of purpose, wholeness, agency, integrity, and concern for others—precisely the gifts which in the Hebrew Bible were granted by God to those who acknowledged His presence. With self psychology we do not need a God with the power of reward and punishment to have adequate reasons for becoming moral human beings who care and are concerned for one another; an understanding of the self and its inherent need for others is reason enough.

So is belonging to the self an adequate substitute for the old Hebraic belonging to God? Is there still a need to feel oneself in a universe infused with a divine, caring Being? If there is, we cannot conceive of this Being as omnipotent, for there is no evidence that such an omnipotent power exists. If we think of the divine in the way Emerson and Hegel did, as Spirit, and understand that Spirit is fundamentally the same as creativity, then the sense of belonging to God or the Spirit is allowing ourselves to be open to creative possibilities. What the Hebrew Bible and other creation myths grasp is that there is always something divine and transcendent in acts of creativity. The more we take responsibility for generating the worlds in which we live rather than accepting what appears to be inevitable in them, the more we participate in the divine act of creation. Alfred North Whitehead locates the divine fundamentally as a realm of potentialities for creative possibilities. He sees evidence for a divine force not in the order of the world, but in the creative possibilities that have emerged and which cannot be explained by structures of causation in which all that happens is simply a re-arrangement of the past. For Whitehead, God is "a fellow traveler," who suffers with us, and offers poetic possibilities for new ways of being (1929). Whenever we are, in our small ways, creating a world, creating a good world, we participate in this ultimate mystery, the mystery of creation.

If the old god and the modern subject are obsessed with power and omnipotence, and in that obsession want to control worlds and obliterate difference, the new human being, the one announced in self psychology and reverberated with in the theologies of Whitehead and Buber, is a being who is open to difference, cares for the self and others, and in her singular creativity attempts to fashion a new world, a good world in which others can singularly be themselves. In this world of teeming manyness, of singular individuals creating themselves and respecting others who do the same, there resides a oneness, a profound spiritual oneness located in the self and in the world, the mystery of creativity. In self psychology, the one and the many come out of their ancient divisiveness and are resolved into a world in which difference—the many—is celebrated and greeted with empathy, but rather than being organized into a hierarchy ruled by an omnipotent power, they are affirmed by a singular self tolerating its fragility and vulnerability in acts of care.

There is one final problem that a discourse on God, the self, and omnipotence must confront, namely, the most profound of all human concerns, death. One of the reasons humans have posited an omnipotent God is that they would like a force strong enough to overcome death and grant us eternal life. If there is such a thing as eternal life, it is truly a mystery, for in order for anything to be alive in our world means that it must have limited existence. Protons and electrons are immortal; cells are not. Perhaps there is such a thing as immortal life and a God who has enough power to arrange for such a thing. But such metaphysical speculations are beyond what anyone can know, and what I hope to have shown, are not anything that we need to know in order to know how to live well as human beings. And that, of course, is the great question, perhaps the greatest question, and I think that self psychology gives us profound reasons for why it is best to live as a good person, caring for one's self and others, in a world in which we are all vulnerable, we all need others, we all need to belong to deeper meanings than those of individual self-actualization. It is a world that does not exist, partly because of a false valuation of omnipotence, but one, which we, with the help of the insights of self psychology, can help create. Strangely, beautifully, the world we might best belong to is one which calls to us to bring it into being—in our small encounters in the consulting room, in our daily interactions with our friends and family, and in the concern and care we extend to those who are different, even to those who hate and despise us, for this is the only way we can truly stay close to our selves. Belonging is, in the end, simple. We belong to ourselves, to others, to the world, and to our ideal of what humanity might be when we care with the very depths of our fragile, vulnerable beings.

NOTES

1. An earlier version of this chapter was delivered as a paper in Jerusalem at the International Conference on Psychoanalytic Self Psychology in October of 2014. The theme of the conference was "Where do we feel at home?"

2. Whitehead posits an interactive omnipresent but not omnipotent God who poetically suggests possibilities to the world, but who cannot control how they are received (1929). Buber locates God in the relation between two human beings treating one another as mortal, vulnerable subjects (1923), while Paul Tillich redefines God as the "ground of being" (1952).

3. Kohut himself theorized that the psyche contained many selves and that the nuclear self was selected out of this multiplicity (1985a). Charles Strozier, the editor of that book and Kohut's biographer, informed me in a personal communication that Kohut gave up the idea of multiple selves after 1974.

Chapter Six

Emerson and Thoreau

The Self in Relation to Nature

Kohut is not the first American thinker to identify and champion the singular self, for he was preceded by the magnificent Ralph Waldo Emerson and his friend Henry David Thoreau. Emerson's writings are still the most passionate and compelling statement for living out of a core self rather than a conformal socialized persona. While there are many differences between psychoanalytic self psychology and the kind of self preached by Emerson and practiced by Thoreau, the most crucial difference between them is that Emerson and Thoreau held that the essential agency for establishing one's self was a deep relationship not to other human beings but to nature. Can the experience of nature grant us the ability to develop and be ourselves? Can nature be an abiding source of nourishment for the self? Can nature restore an injured self? Does self psychology need a theory of self in relation not just to others but to nature?

I am drawn to these questions by my own psychological history. While I have had many years of therapy, some of my most important therapeutic moments were not with human beings but with nature. I grew up in Chatham, New Jersey, a small suburb of New York, which in the late 1940s was a village set in surrounding forests. My earliest memory is not of some delicious moment with my mother, but of seeing sunlight magically illuminating the silky fronds of a fern at the edge of the forest. The memory has stayed with me, vividly, for seventy years.

My next grounding nature experience occurred when I was around seven years of age. I wandered into the woods and, like a young Thoreau, poked my nose into this and that, including a dead tree trunk in which a screech owl was sleeping. The tree was so rotten and the owl so passed out—it must have had a wild night—that I was able to break the trunk from its stump and with a friend carry it back home to a shed. I had captured an owl without weapon or net. That I would become a philosopher was indeed fated. Thankfully, my father freed the owl that night for fear it would break its wings in the shed. These are some of the few memories I have retained from childhood. Despite years of therapy I still cannot recall what the inside of our home we lived in for the first seven years of my life looked like –not a room, nook, or mother-smell—nothing. But I do remember the owl and the fern.

My early childhood, as far as I have been able to recall it, was full of trauma, pain, loneliness, and despair. Although I reaped the benefits of being my mother's favorite, she was overwhelmed with her three children and often exploded in fits of violent rage in which she spanked me so hard with a wooden spoon that it once broke over my butt. Her violence would alternate with a hopeless depression in which she simply disappeared for long periods. Food often did not materialize at meal times. I also suffered severe sexual abuse from my father.

It was in this traumatized, barely sane state that I entered my eighth year of life and the late spring months of the second grade with Mrs Belcher. Mrs Belcher, an archetype of the battle-axe grammar school teacher who had undoubtedly been teaching second grade since the turn of the century, vehemently hated me and endlessly shamed me for picking my nose and other gross little boy habits I practiced. It did not help that my speech was so difficult to understand that I had to have speech lessons from kindergarten through the second grade. My mother always explained my speech deficit as due to the fact that I was left-handed in a right-handed world, but I think it was more due to the fact that what I had to say was unspeakable.

All the pain of early childhood came to a climactic moment on a fine spring day during lunch recess. The township school was situated in a swampy woods with nothing else around. All the other boys were involved in playing sports to which I was not invited, nor coordinated enough to play, and the girls had paired off into lovely dyads or triads that clearly excluded boys. My despair deepened and I felt utterly hopeless. Then, I looked around at the woods and decided that I would walk so far into them that no one could find me and I could not find my way back. I had decided in my confused little eight-year-old mind to commit suicide.

So I started walking. The dark thick woods beautifully mirrored my anguished despairing mood. The light was growing dimmer and I was determined to descend into the final darkness. Then, suddenly, a shaft of sunlight broke through the thick canopy of leaves and landed on a single yellow ladyslipper growing at the base of a magnificently tall tree. I was stunned, thrown into an eternal moment of wonder, and held captive by the sight. I then turned around and went back to the school, and that turning around was the turning around of my life. I had chosen, for all time, life over death. The despair did not, of course, disappear; it kept periodically ravaging my soul, but the ladyslipper, which still radiantly exists in the depths of my memory, has always prevailed and I have found myself able to love life with a far greater intensity than I would have been able to had I not been taken to the brink of death and then been saved by a radiant flower. Before this event I was a poor student without any promise; within two years I would become an A student, class president, and a fine athlete. It was the therapeutic moment that transformed my life.

A decade and a half later, as I was finishing up my PhD and looking for a job, I chose a somewhat unknown liberal arts college in Colorado over more prestigious universities in fine cities. I have never for a moment regretted the choice, as the mountains then and now have always seemed crucial to my sense of well-being. Upon waking at the first light of the morning, I gather our Shetland sheepdogs and go out to greet Pikes Peak, which stands to the West as the giant bulwark signaling the end of the great plains and the gateway to a mountainous land of mystery, danger, and adventure. We walk through the wondrous Garden of the Gods with its red rocks mysteriously shooting out of the earth, like some kind of ancient Titans. Up and down hills we walk in the newly dawned morning air, full of openness and possibility. Often deer motionlessly look on as we pass by, not wanting to attract the attention of the dogs, but I return their gaze in thankfulness for their presence. In the spring, a tempest of birdsong fills the air and my soul awakens in delight. In the summer we hike into glorious high mountain valleys with teeming waterfalls, fields upon fields of brilliantly hued wildflowers, and craggy peaks soaring into the sky. For years I climbed to the very top of the world on many of Colorado's 14,000-foot-high mountains, the journeys so difficult that my mind collapsed into my body and I was there, really there, at one with the mountain and the weather and the heroic adventures that humans have undertaken since their inception. And when the land was covered in its virginal white snow, we glided on cross-country skis through towering spruce trees and silent aspen groves, occasionally spotting a snowshoe rabbit.

These experiences with nature have saved my self and sustained it for a lifetime. Kohut does not talk about nature and self, nor does he inquire into the great question of what the self must be in order for it to be not only sustained by a relation to nature but brought into being by it. And, yet, it is clear that our selves are deeply connected to nature. When nature is disturbed we are disturbed. Hurricanes, tornadoes, global warming, wind blowing down a favorite tree, and sudden unseasonable shifts in temperature tend to upset our sense of self-equilibrium.[1] There is a wilderness-therapy business that is booming, especially organizations that take inner-city kids out into nature.[2]

How are we to understand nature as perhaps the first and most significant of all selfobjects? While Kohut is silent on this question, his great predecessor in self psychology, Ralph Waldo Emerson, does speak, and does so with the kind of brilliant writing which itself enlivens the soul in a way that Kohut's writing rarely does.

RALPH WALDO EMERSON

Emerson's first great work, *Nature*, begins with the following passage

> Our age is retrospective. It builds the sepulchers of the fathers. It writes biographies, histories, and criticism. The foregoing generations beheld God and nature face to face; we, through their eyes. Why should not we also enjoy an original relation to the universe? Why should not we have a poetry and philosophy of insight and not of tradition, and a religion by revelation to us, and not a history of theirs? Embosomed for a season in nature, whose floods of life stream around and through us, and invite us, by the powers they supply, to action proportioned to nature, why should we grope among the dry bones of the past, or put the living generation into masquerade out of its faded wardrobe. The sun shines today also. (1836, p. 9)

Here Emerson identifies the crucial phenomenological characteristic of experiencing oneself as having a self, namely, that one's experience feels originary rather than derivative, canned, or socially dictated, and as such, aligns with Kohut's definition of the self as "an independent center of initiative and perception" (1977, p. 177). However, for Emerson, the ability to have originary experiences and achieve independence in perception, action, and thought, one must leave other human beings and go into nature. "In the woods, too, a man casts off his years, as the snake his slough, and at what period soever of life is always a child. In the woods is perpetual youth. . . . In the woods . . . nothing can befall me in life,—no disgrace, no calamity (leaving me my eyes), which nature cannot repair" (1836, p. 15).

I believe that Emerson is right that when one is acting out of the self, one does feel the vitality of youth, regardless of age, and fills with a sense of both restoration and agency. But why should we feel like ourselves most when we go out to nature, when we walk in the woods? Why do Boston analysts flee to Wellfleet to restore themselves? Why are summer workshops for therapists held on Cape Cod or other places of natural beauty?

Kohut says that the self's basic needs are to be empathically mirrored, optimally challenged, and sustained by ideals or idealized others. Can nature mirror? Can it provide the strength of ideals? The psalmist certainly thinks so: "I will lift up mine eyes unto the hills, from whence cometh my help" (Psalm 121, KJV). How do the hills give help?

Emerson knew that there were two ways to lose one's self—to traumatic tragedy and social conformity. He lost his first beloved wife to illness shortly after they were married and he lost a son, Waldo, when he was only five. He both witnessed the power of the rising middle class to assert what John Stuart Mill called the "tyranny of the majority" over persons and turn them into mere variables of the social codes, and knew the traumatic pain of loss when he fell into a prolonged despair with the death of Waldo. His cure for both kinds of loss of self was to engage, alone, with nature. Obviously, nature does not impose social codes the way interactions with others always do, but how can it help us get in touch with ourselves? How can it help overcome traumatic tragedy? The exploring of these questions might open self psychology up in expansive directions—directions that will raise questions about the nature of the unconscious, whether nature can speak to the self in a way that humans can't, and whether self psychology might need to develop more aesthetic, poetic, and even woodsy dimensions to be a full psychology of the self.

First, I think that we learn from both Emerson and Thoreau that there is a natural element to the self, a primal singularity that is what it means to be just this person, this self. While we know from self psychology that selves cannot come into being without social responsiveness, they are not mere social constructions, the way some social constructivist theorists seem to hold. This natural element reveals itself when a person feels spontaneous and genuinely singular. When we are being ourselves, we feel natural—spontaneous, alive, individuated, present, rather than artificial, derivative, contrived—like the phonies Holden Caulfield railed against in Salinger's *Catcher in the Rye*. I think this is why Kohut decided to add our idiosyncratic talents and propensities to ideals and ambitions to form the core of the self. What he was trying to say is that we singularly and naturally really are something unique and this element needs to infuse the self's ideals and ambitions. There is something in us that is resistant to social conditioning—it is our natural selves resisting. When we are in nature, we feel surrounded by beings just being themselves and not constructing themselves to be the right kind of tree or cloud or brook. "These roses under my window make no reference to former roses or to better ones; they are for what they are . . . There is simply the rose; it is perfect in every moment of its existence" (1841, p. 67).

The second way in which nature can sustain and enliven the self according to Emerson is that we naturally experience nature not simply as being what it is, but also as offering us deep meanings through metaphor and analogy. That is, our minds are constructed in such a way as to unconsciously convert nature into meaning. When Freud explored the nature of unconscious experiencing, he found that three of its most fundamental processes were condensation, displacement, and symbolization (1915). All of these primary processes are based on the notion of "likeness." We condense two things that are "alike" one another; we can displace one thing onto another only if they have something in common, and the same is true for symbolization. Likeness seems also to be crucial in empathy, for we feel empathized with when we experience another feeling like we do, mirroring how we feel. Empathy could not be as powerful a process as it is unless we had as one of our primal abilities the ability to experience "likeness" or "sameness," which is the key property of metaphor. In short, the fundamental a priori structure of the mind is to locate likenesses and through these associations and our affective responses to them start to develop a world of meaning and significance.

What is crucial for Emerson is that we are built in such a way that nature naturally provides us with metaphorical meanings. In that life-changing incident with the ladyslipper, I did not consciously think, "Just as there is a delicate radiant presence in the darkness of the forest, so my deep inner self is a radiant presence that can break through the gloom of my personal darkness." Rather, the sight of the sunlight illuminating the yellow ladyslipper went to the depths of my soul and I knew inherently, spontaneously, and affectively what it meant and I turned around.

> Every natural fact is a symbol of some spiritual fact. Every appearance in nature corresponds to some state of the mind, and that state of the mind can only be described by presenting that natural appearance as its picture. An enraged man is a lion, a cunning man is a fox, a firm man is a rock, a learned man is a torch. A lamb is innocence; a snake is subtle spite; flowers express to us the delicate affections. Light and darkness are our familiar expression for knowledge and ignorance; and heat for love. Visible distance behind and before us, is respectively our image of memory and hope. (1836, p. 32)

In short, for Emerson nature is the soul externalized. We can understand our inner subjective states by locating them in natural events. I am sure that my attraction to the mountains, along with the attraction of millions of others, is that they mirror my longing to rise up and soar, to be great, to have an elevated life rather than one flattened like the plains into a dull sameness. Indeed, when I am climbing or hiking in the mountains, I have an elevated spirit and feel that I am rising above the everyday.

When Emerson writes, "The health of the eye seems to demand a horizon. We are never tired so long as we can see far enough" (1836, p. 22), he is speaking both about an experience of our eyes and our psyches. After being dulled by narrow confines, both our eyes and souls awaken when we come to a horizon. The eyes, once again, feel alive and ready to see; the mind, once again, opens to new possibilities. To stand on a mountaintop and gaze for as far as the eye can see in all directions is to fill with exuberant life, for one is actually and metaphorically on top of the world, rather than under the commands and codes that so lower us in ordinary life. When the eye is unrestrained the self regains its sense of freedom. Perhaps one doesn't climb a mountain but dives into the depths of a lake or ocean, to swim once again in life's boundless waters, to once again immerse oneself in the great sea of life so that one can once again tolerate the dailyness of everyday routine.

If it is true that self structure is largely unconscious and that throughout this level of subjectivity we are constantly working with metaphor and analogy, then nature can, indeed, speak to the self, give it meanings that revive it, nourish it. Did I realize somewhere deep in my soul that my capturing of an owl demanded that I become a lover of wisdom and also realize that wisdom, like the owl, can never be caged? If analogy and metaphor nourish meaning and connectedness at the most profound level of psychic process, then it raises the question as to whether the therapist need be in part a poet, a poet who is connected with nature and myth. If so, then the psychoanalytic therapist is a new kind of person—a poet-scientist, an integration of one of the deepest divides of our culture, that between the Humanities and Sciences, and in being such a union, is able to help others, and perhaps the whole culture, heal their splits. How many transforming clinical moments have been produced when just the right analogy, just the right image, just the right metaphor, or just the right dream came forth? I suspect, indeed, a lot, if not most.

The third way nature sustains the self is through its beauty. For Emerson, we have a natural innate responsiveness to the beauty of nature: "The world exists to the soul to satisfy the desire of beauty. This element I call an ultimate end. No reason can be asked or given why the soul seeks beauty" (1836, pp. 29–30). Here I replace soul with self and I think that we have come to a fundamental truth: that the self has a primordial longing for beauty. Beauty, especially natural beauty, inspires us—brings the spirit back to our all-too-often overburdened or dulled minds. This is another way of saying that the self seeks its own health, its own well-being, for in both beauty and health there is harmony, wholeness, connectedness. The harmonies can be simple or complex, for dissonance is not disconnectedness. A soul full of complex dissonances that are connected is a deep, beautiful soul. Our profound and natural responsiveness to beauty is a primal psychic force that calls us not only to create but long to become whole persons. What is this force? Emerson often calls it Spirit or Oversoul, but he also identifies it with love.

> The problem of restoring to the world original and eternal beauty is solved by the redemption of the soul. . . . The reason why the world lacks unity, and lies broken and in heaps, is because man is disunited within himself. He cannot be a naturalist until he satisfies all the demands of the spirit. Love is as much a demand as perception. (1836, p. 77)

If by "love" Emerson means eros, then we are transported back to Plato's *Symposium* and forward to Kohut's concept of the self, as we found in chapter 4. Most important is the profound connection Emerson draws between nature's lying "broken and in heaps" and the fragmentation of the soul.

If we interpret the shattering Emerson finds in nature with the pathology that permeates the modern soul, we can understand the cause of both as the replacement of the erotic loving self with the ego and its quest for power and status, both of which are granted by wealth in an economic society. The economic society is both desecrating nature in its ravenous exploitation of natural resources and desecrating the soul in its demand for the dominance of ego motivation. In succumbing to the forces of middle-class society, we lose both our love of nature and our core erotic selves. The quest to re-discover nature is the same as the quest to find ourselves is the same as opening up our eros so that we can once again love nature and work for her wholeness.

Emerson can further help us understand how to recognize when our selves are present in experience and what kind of character we need to sustain them. One of Kohut's deficits is his failure to develop strong phenomenological markers for those experiences which distinguish between when we are being motivated by our selves and when by introjected social codes or ego values. He rarely goes beyond saying that self experiences are ones of "joy" rather than mere pleasure. He also rarely tells us what we need, aside from courage, in order to live from our selves rather than other sources of psychic motivation. But Emerson's writings overflow with both the experiential markers of the self's presence and the qualities needed to assert one's self in the world.

"In the presence of nature a wild delight runs through the man, in spite of real sorrows" (1836, p. 15). Although I was full of the most dreadful, real sorrows when I came across the ladyslipper, I was overcome by such a "wild delight" that I had to go on living. I find that "delight"—especially "wild delight"—is almost always a marker that the self is being engaged and responding. We cannot plan to be delighted—it comes almost always by surprise, and when we find ourselves in the state of delight, I think we always have an erotic bond to what is delighting us—a connection in which we feel delightfully enlivened. The response of delight always feels genuine rather than contrived, as opposed to many positive responses that we feel because we are supposed to feel them.

Famously, in "Self Reliance" Emerson tells us:

> Whosoever would be a man, must be a non-conformist. . . . Nothing is more sacred but the integrity of your own mind. . . . No law can be sacred to me but that of my own nature. . . . I shun father and mother and wife and brother when my genius calls me. I would write on the lintels of the door-post Whim. I hope it is somewhat better than whim at last, but we cannot spend the day in explanation. Expect me not to show cause why I seek or why I exclude company. Then again, do not tell me, as a good man did today, of my obligation to put all men in good situations. Are they my poor? I tell thee, thou foolish philanthropist, that I grudge the dollar, the dime, the cent I give to such men as do not belong to me and to whom I do not belong. (1841, pp. 51–53)

What Emerson proclaims in these passages is that when one is being motivated by the self, one feels singular, unique, spontaneous and speaks and acts
with a voice that is not subject to rational scrutiny. One does not govern her
activity by general maxims such as "Help the needy" or "Always be kind"
for when one is acting from the self, one is not a general human being, but a
singular self. Non-conformity, integrity, genius, whim (spontaneity), inexpli-
cability, a profound sense of what belongs to one and what doesn't—all of
these are signs that the self has a strong integrating presence in a person.
Genius is, of course, not to be confused with extraordinary brilliance, but
with its original meaning of having a source within oneself that is one's own,
that is not simply offering another verse of the social song, but a voice which
articulates how one actually in fact feels, thinks, delights, or mourns. The
opposite of integrity, genius, spontaneity, and self-assertion is acting according to "oughts," the thousands of oughts that descend on us all of the time—
this is how we ought to behave, this is what we ought to be doing, this is what
makes sense and so we ought to do it, this is the right kind of person to love,
this is a Rembrandt, you ought to love it, and so on, endlessly. To have the
courage of one's own experience, of judging for oneself, of listening to an
inner voice that is one's own voice rather than all the other voices that are
constantly calling to one—this is what it means to have a self, to be a genius.
One must have the courage to tie oneself to the mast of one's own ship and
sail by the beautiful Sirens who are always luring one to the grave. "Trust
thyself: every heart vibrates to that iron string" (1841, p. 49).

The self, for Kohut, is both the source of a feeling of sameness through
time but also a dynamic urge to always go beyond any temporary realization
of the self's intrinsic values. Sameness and change are fused in the notion of
development, for in development we complexify and extend our steady
ideals and ambitions or else they become stale and repetitive. Here is how
Emerson brilliantly puts it:

> The life of man is a self-evolving circle, which, from a ring imperceptibly
> small, rushes on all sides outwards to new and larger circles, and that without
> end. The extent to which this generation of circles, wheel without wheel, will
> go, depends on the force or truth of the individual soul. For it is the inert effort
> of each thought, having formed itself into a circular wave of circumstance,—
> as for instance an empire, rules of an art, a local usage, a religious rite,—to
> heap itself on that ridge and to solidify and hem in the life. But if the soul is
> quick and strong it bursts over that boundary on all sides and expands another
> orbit on the great deep, which also runs up into a high wave, with attempt
> again to stop and to bind. But the heart refuses to be imprisoned; in its first and
> narrowest pulses it already tends outward with a vast force and to immense
> and innumerable expansions. (1841a, p. 283–84)

Here is a perfect description of what it means to live from one's erotic natural self—to be a "self-evolving circle" forever creating new forms of life and then refusing to be imprisoned by them.

THOREAU

Before leaving Emerson to return to the present, we need to hear Thoreau's reverberations with these Emersonian themes. His most famous statement is, of course, *"The mass of men lead lives of quiet desperation"* (1854, p. 8) by which he means that humans do not act from their selves but from social impositions, especially those of economic society. It is not by chance that the first chapter of *Walden* is entitled "Economy" and reveals how alively one can live with little labor and almost no money. *"I found that by working about six weeks in a year, I could meet all the expenses of living"* (1854, pp. 65–66).

Thoreau went to Walden with the question that is at the heart of this book: how can one attain the greatest amount of life in one's soul. "I went to the woods to live deliberately, to front only the essential facts of life, and see if I could not learn what it had to teach, and not, when I came to die, discover that I had not lived . . . I wanted to live deep and suck out all the marrow of life. . . . Our life is frittered away by detail. . . . Simplicity, simplicity, simplicity!" (1854, p. 86).

I think that living from the self is what it means to live deeply, for it is the marrow of who we are, the core, the final ground. When we live out of the self, life becomes simpler and we are not so tempted by the myriads of distractions that our contemporary world provides. How easy it is to lose ourselves in distractions which are always multiple while the erotic loves of the self tend to be few.

And, finally in *Walking*, Thoreau says, "Life consists with wildness. The most alive is the wildest . . . in Wildness is the preservation of the World" (1861, pp. 644–45). The young often interpret the wild as the anti-social, the anti-sober, or the unpredictable, but the wild for Thoreau is simply each individual being being itself and not trying to be something else. To live from one's spontaneous erotic self rather than social codes or economic pressures is to be wild. One of the great critiques of classical psychoanalysis is that its aim is to normalize persons. This is not true of self psychology, whose aim is to release the "wild" singularity of a person. In self psychology is the preservation of the world.

EPILOGUE

Nature is a great sustainer and enlivener of the self. It is a crucial environment in the attempt to free our selves from the pressures of social codes. But can it heal traumatic injuries suffered by the self? Can it restore a fullness of self-functioning? Here I must return to my own story. Although I was scaling the mountains of Colorado and achieving remarkable success within the classroom, my life fell apart when the sham of my first marriage fell apart. Nature couldn't take me out of my fragmentation or depression. I entered a psychoanalytic psychotherapy and some eighteen years of therapy later felt as though I had a genuine self. I never could have made it to therapy without nature; but nature by itself was not the cure.

In the end, there are a number of ways we can lose our selves. Self psychology focuses on traumas that undermine necessary selfobject relations and fragment, deplete, and arrest the self. But selves can also be lost to the conformal pressures of society or just the repetitions of everyday life. It is confronting this kind of self loss where Emerson and Thoreau are so brilliant and eloquent. But, further, I do believe that for those who, like me, suffered devastating psychological injures, nature can be sustaining of the self until the moment is opportune for engaging in a therapeutic process. My encounter with the ladyslipper saved my life and allowed for crucial moments in which my self could speak its truth, but nature could not overcome my early traumas or my tendencies to fall into dissociative states or narcissistic defenses. My encounter with a self-psychological therapy gave me myself and opened up possibilities for intimacy, thought, and feeling real that I never thought possible before.

Finally, this chapter presents a problem for self psychologists. Is discovering your patients' relation to nature important? Is your relation to nature important for your self-sustenance? If it is, how can self psychology better utilize our experiences in nature to help restore selves who have become lost and are wandering in a dark forest looking for that mysterious beam of light that will once again restore them to wholeness?

NOTES

1. See Joe Shaleen's "When the Wind Comes Sweeping Down the Plain: Embracing Atmospheric Interrelatedness" (2015) for a wonderful article on how weather, especially tornadoes, can deeply affect the human psyche.

2. See Gass, Gillis, and Russell's *Adventure Therapy: Theory, Research, and Practice* (2012) for a comprehensive overview of what is happening in contemporary nature therapy.

Part II

Self Psychology, Culture, and Society

Chapter Seven

Ethics, Modern Society, and Self Psychology

I wish to place psychoanalysis in a wider set of cultural meanings, one which will give this discipline a far greater importance than it currently has as simply one of the ways, and certainly not the most favored, of enhancing mental health. Indeed, what I hope to show is that unless modern culture adopts a psychoanalytic way of understanding human beings in general—that is, as beings who have an unconscious form of mentality—and a self-psychological point of view in particular, it can provide no reason, other than fear, for persons' adopting a moral way of being in the world. Since there is no greater conceptual need in a culture than a way of explaining why it is good for people to be good, modern culture, on my view, must come to accept psychoanalytic self psychology as its primary way of understanding humans or collapse into the internal contradiction of needing people to be moral but not being able to tell them why they should be.[1]

ETHICS IN MODERN CULTURE

The question "how is it best to live as a human being?" is so essential to human life that Socrates thought a life in which it remained unasked or was pushed aside as not worth living (*Apology*, 38a). Socrates not only asked this question, but offered an answer to it, an answer with which almost all of his philosophical successors agreed: the best way to live is as a good person. Philosophers might have disagreed about what is means to be a good person but they almost unanimously have proclaimed that it is personally good to be morally good. However, with the coming of modernity and its emphasis on the freedom of individuals to pursue their own satisfactions, the felicitous equation of personal good with a general or universal good has been radically called into question. Many modern persons seem to be asking whether it might be better to appear to be morally good while really being out solely for their own perceived interests.

By modernity, I mean that time period that has emerged since the seventeenth century in the West and which is currently spreading over the globe. It began as a rebellion against an entrenched religious authority and as an attempt to establish the freedom of individuals to pursue their personal well-being as the highest social and political value. It is a form of human life which values individuals over community, pleasures in this life over well-being that might occur in some afterlife, and the achievement of socioeconomic success rather than the salvation or purity of soul. It validates empirical and/or mathematical reasoning as the ground for knowledge and distrusts persons or institutions that claim to be authorities because they have had divine revelations or some non-empirical access to final realities. Obviously, not all persons—or even the majority of persons—living in modern times are modern persons, but it is modern persons with their values of individualism, naturalism, democracy, and science that have been the driving force of cultural history in the West for the past three hundred years. It is this kind of person who needs an answer for why it is good to be good.

When modern persons look to contemporary society for reasons as to why they should want to be good persons, they can locate none that are compelling. Modern society is principally an economic world in which persons are supposed to pursue their own individual satisfactions by doing as well for themselves as they can in market interactions. In this world of individuals pursuing personal pleasures in a highly competitive setting, morality is seen as a set of limits to what one can do to achieve those satisfactions. The question then arises as to why persons should constrain their quests by adopting these ethical limits. [2]

Since modern society was founded on the rejection of religious and metaphysical authorities, it cannot offer as a good reason for being good the rewards one will receive from a divine being either in this life or an afterlife. The only reasons that can be compelling for a modern person are ones that relate to this life, its satisfactions and necessities.

Given that modern society is fundamentally an economic one, can an economic reason be given for why persons should be moral? Why should economic persons who are encouraged by society to seek their own best market interests limit their pursuits by adopting a moral way of being? While it is true that economic society could not function unless people in general were honest, private property safe, and the pursuit of satisfactions not personally dangerous, this constitutes a compelling reason only for why a market society needs to generate moral persons. It does not constitute a compelling reason as to why I, as an individual, should be ethical if I can get more satisfactions by not being good and not getting caught.

Nor can modern society's newest legitimating vehicle, neuroscience, help. While recent neuroscientific studies have shown that the pleasure centers of the brain activate when persons act altruistically, this does not constitute a good reason for being good. Pleasure centers can also activate while one is cheating, being cruel, etc. If we never received any feeling of well-being for acting in empathic, altruistic ways, I doubt we would have any possibility for being moral beings. But ethics is a way of being that must compete with other ways of being, such as being unprincipled or unconcerned for the well-being of others. What happens if we feel more pleasure by getting away with something than we do when we are altruistic? We need to know why it is best to be moral and neuroscience's reports that we feel pleasure when we are moral cannot tell us this. This critique can be generalized to all of science. Science is constructed to determine what is the case—the facts of reality, but ethics is about what ought to be the case, about values. As Hume showed, there is a gap between the "is" and the "ought" that cannot be logically crossed. We might find that we are genetically wired to distrust, fear, and aggress against others who do not look like us, but this does not mean that we should. We might find that males are wired to be sexually promiscuous; but this does not mean that it is right to be promiscuous. Just because something, by nature, makes us feel good does not mean it is good.

If economics and science can offer no compelling reasons for why it is good for individuals to be good, can modern philosophy? Modern philosophy has spawned two great ethical systems that are necessary in order for the essential structures of democracy and a capitalist market economy to flourish: the deontological ethics of Kant and utilitarianism.[3] Kant held that persons could pursue their own happiness in any way they want so long as they do not violate basic moral laws—they can seek their own advantage in any way except by lying, cheating, murdering, making false promises, etc. The utilitarians realized that a society based on a market economics by necessity had to produce a group of people who lose in the competitive struggle. Hence, they proposed that moral persons must concern themselves with the general welfare. For the most part this obligation can be satisfied by rationally engaging in market interactions, as such activity has the consequence of pushing the cost of goods to the lowest level—thereby benefiting everyone, paying taxes to a government that has programs to aid those who have lost out in the competition, and generally having a compassionate attitude toward those who suffer.

In short, modernity has generated the two kinds of ethics it most needs: one that justifies a set of restrictions on how far individual pursuits can be taken and a compassionate attitude toward those who suffer because of the competitive nature of the modern world. Ethicists have fought over the past century and a half over which of these is the superior ethic, but, clearly, both are needed in order for a society of economic, social, and political individualism to flourish. That is, modernity has produced a fairly adequate concept of what it means to be a good person for this kind of world: play fair, don't violate basic moral laws that everyone needs to follow in order to have a trustworthy enough economic society, and develop compassion for those less fortunate. For the most part modernity seems to have a "good enough" sense of what it means to be moral, and we are, in general, held accountable to that concept.

However, the question remains: do we have good reasons to be good—do we have good reasons to limit our personal quests, especially if we can appear to be good while unethically pursuing our own advantage. This is the crucial ethical question for a society that values individualism: why should we do what is moral when it conflicts with our perceived individual interests?

The utilitarians, especially John Stuart Mill, claimed that we should want to be good because we are fundamentally social by nature (1863). Morality is grounded in our natural inclination to help our fellow human beings. However, the utilitarians also admitted that we have selfish, self-serving sentiments. There is no apparent reason why one kind of sentiment should be privileged over the other when they conflict.

The primary tendency of philosophy since Kant has been to answer the question of why it is good to be good by showing that rationality itself demands that we follow moral laws or the principles of justice—that they are built into the very concept of a rational life.[4] Kant thought that it was the power and use of reason that enabled us to individuate and become autonomous agents capable of willing our own lives (1797). Hence, to value individuality means necessarily to value rationality, and if there is any one crucial principle of rationality, it is consistency. To be consistent means that we cannot expect others to act on principles that we do not hold for ourselves. Ergo, all rational agents must find themselves constrained by moral laws that hold for all persons. This appears to be a compelling argument.

However, Kant recognized that there were two forms of rational self-direction, one that seeks personal happiness and acts on hypothetical imperatives—maxims which state what we should do in order to optimize our happiness—and another which states what is categorically required of us to be moral. Our question is why should a person favor one form of rationality over the other when the two conflict. One cannot argue that one kind of rationality is more rational than another without circularity, for one must arbitrarily presuppose a concept of rationality in order to give reasons for why one form of rationality is more rational than another. If someone reasons that he can get ahead by cheating while proclaiming the glories of honesty, why should he prefer to be rationally consistent? In some situations consistency might not be a virtue but, as Emerson said, "the hobgoblin of little minds" (1841, p. 183). There is no way of showing why a universal kind of reasoning is superior to individualistic scheming without presupposing that one kind of rationality is more rational than another.[5]

Since deontology and utilitarianism more or less exhaust the possibilities for ethical thinking in the modern world, it appears that neither modern society nor philosophy can say why it is good to be good. The only reason for being moral is the Hobbesian one of fear of what will happen if one gets caught. This is, obviously, not a convincing reason for those who think themselves sly enough to avoid detection. While the consequences of modern society's failure to offer compelling reasons for why it is good to be good are many and reach into every sector of modern life, I want to concentrate on three: the catastrophic increase in cheating with a concomitant rise in the instruments of public surveillance and punishment, the dangerous rise of fundamentalism, and the moral enervation of liberal modern persons who are good but who cannot explain to themselves why.

According to David Callahan (2004), America has seen an extraordinary rise in cheating that is affecting every arena of contemporary life. Ordinary persons in droves are cheating on their taxes; executives of some of the largest firms in the world are cooking their books; a large percentage of spouses cheat on their mates; and more than half of all college students cheat at least once. Callahan reveals how it is common practice for lawyers to pad their hours and for doctors to be in collusion with drug companies. Cheating even extends to the highest levels of government in matters involving issues of gravest significance, for example many felt that the Bush administration cheated when it claimed to have compelling evidence that Iraq had weapons of mass destruction. Cheating is not a terrifying moral crime like the genocides of Hitler or Stalin. It typically involves no violence and often does not target specific victims. And, yet, when we look at the effects of all the cheating in the socioeconomic sphere, politics, academics, marriage, and personal life, we can see that the coherence of social life is being fully undermined. Cheating is a small, almost invisible, moral failure, but like a hidden cancer it is destroying the integrity of both persons and modern society.

Cheaters are not confused about what is good nor are they moral rebels; they just do not want to do what is right when it stands in the way of perceived personal gains. It seems that they can find no compelling reason not to cheat except the fear of being caught. They do not believe it is good to be good. The epidemic of cheating (in which I include non-violent crimes that appropriate the property of others) has caused a corresponding escalation in the mechanisms of surveillance and punishment. Since 1970 the legal profession has grown three times faster than the economy. America is distinguished as the nation having the highest percentage of its population behind bars and the highest percentage of its resources devoted to the criminal justice system (Berman, 2006). Because modernity cannot offer substantial reasons for being ethical, it is becoming a society that is increasingly brutish, unsafe, and overly policed.

The second consequence of modernity's failure to provide a substantial reason for being moral is the rise of fundamentalism. While the causes of fundamentalism are complex, I believe that a major factor in the emergence of this powerful political and social force is modernity's inability to provide an understandable ground for ethical life. Fundamentalism's response to modernity's problem is to re-instate an absolute moral authority in the form of God, whose will and law is known with certainty by a sanctioned religious institution. The tightness, vindictiveness, self-certainty, willingness to impose values on others, and lack of epistemological humility that characterize this movement make it a counterforce to modernity, one that threatens the great gains modernity has made in the realms of individual and political freedom.

The third consequence of modernity's failure to establish a ground for being ethical might be the most disastrous of all—the enervating effect it has had on persons who are good but who cannot explain why. Insofar as good persons cannot give a coherent account for why they are good, their lives have a core senselessness in them. They can only say "I am good because that is what I choose to be" or "It's just the way I was brought up" with the first answer admitting the groundlessness of the choice and the second succumbing to a morbid developmental determinism. It is difficult to be energized by one's own goodness if one has no explanation for why one chooses to be good. One of the consequences of this moral incertitude is a tendency to engage in tepid childrearing, one that overemphasizes freedom and personal choice and fails to provide a strong sense of what constitutes living as a good person. This lack of moral energy in liberal modern people explains in large part why the fundamentalists have claimed the high moral ground in contemporary society and with it have become such a significant political force.

In sum, modernity has invented a culture of individualism that encourages and even requires persons to pursue their own advantage but needs these pursuits limited by individuals' adopting a moral point of view. However, it can provide no compelling reason why people should be moral except for fear of what will happen if they are caught doing what is wrong. Hence, modernity's entire project of establishing individuality, freedom, and openness is in grave danger of turning into a world that is being made untrustworthy and brutish by the cheaters, overly surveyed by disciplinary mechanisms, threatened politically by religious authoritarianism, and occupied by people who can not exuberantly proclaim the goodness of their lives for they do not know why it is good to be good.

Is there a way of establishing a ground for ethical life that is non-religious, non-authoritarian, and which does not diminish modernity's life-enhancing values of individualism, freedom, and openness? The search for such a ground must take place within a naturalistic framework in order to fall within modernity's framework of understanding human life as arising from natural processes and its need for values to pertain to living well as embodied creatures in this world. I believe that such a naturalistic ground is available, but accepting it involves challenging the reigning naturalistic conception of human nature that has been foundational for economics, the social sciences, Darwinian biology, and modern ethics. This naturalistic understanding of human beings has four fundamental tenets: (1) humans are independent organisms, each basically wired to be concerned about their own interests; (2) their interests are conceived of a maximizing satisfactions and minimizing pain; (3) there can be no universal concept of good, as what gives pleasure and pain differs for individuals; and (4) individuals occupy a world of scarce resources and must compete for its goods—compete for everything from winning the most desirable mate to acquiring the basic necessities of life.

In short, humans in this naturalistic framework are conceived of as pleasure-optimizing organisms engaged in an intense competition with one another for satisfactions. If this competition were entirely unregulated, it would probably doom us, in Hobbes' famous words, to a life that is "solitary, poor, nasty, brutish, and short." This naturalistic view of human nature gives us a very good reason why, in general, human beings need morality and respect for law: without it, few of us would fare very well. And it is easy to see why it is good to appear to be good. Since society is in such dire need of moral, lawful persons, it has created a massive arsenal of disciplinary punishments for wrongdoers—everything from doses of shame, humiliation, shunning, and guilt to confinement, torture, and death. However, it can offer no reason as to why an individual should be good if he can get more satisfactions by not being moral and is confident of not getting caught.

If the reigning paradigm were the only available naturalistic concept of what it means to be human, then I would have to conclude that modernity is doomed to be destroyed by its inner contradiction of needing persons to be moral and being unable to offer them any intrinsically compelling reasons for being moral. However, there is another naturalistic way of understanding human nature that contains the possibility for offering compelling reasons for becoming a moral person: the concept of human nature developed within the self-psychological school of psychoanalytic thought. While Freud's theory of psychological life adopts the reigning naturalistic paradigm that sees us as separated units each intent on optimizing personal pleasure and is therefore unable to provide a ground for moral life, Heinz Kohut's theory that psychological life revolves around the development of a largely unconscious self that is inherently dependent on others to sustain its vitality and functionality can give us compelling reasons for being a good person.

While it is not crucial that we buy Kohut's theory of the self lock, stock, and barrel, the argument requires that we accept the following four major tenets of his work: (1) that the development and organization of self structure is the key to psychological functioning and a sense of robust well-being; (2) that motivation which stems from the self is different from motivation that stems from other parts of the psyche—for instance, from drives, the ego, or social pressures; (3) that ideals form an essential part of self structure and that to have a coherent self one must have a set of cherished ideals; and (4) that the self is highly vulnerable to de-stabilization and fragmentation and has a lifelong need for others to provide selfobject supplies in order to maintain an optimal level of functionality. I believe that most of the theories of self that derive from or relate to Kohut's theory adopt these four premises.

SELF PSYCHOLOGY AND ETHICAL LIFE

My argument that self psychology can ground moral life constitutes, I believe, a conceptual revolution, for it makes narcissism—at least mature narcissism—the basis of being an ethically good person. If by narcissism we mean making one's particular, embodied self the central concern of life, then what I am positing goes against almost all previous ethical theories, which have claimed that ethical life comes into existence only when we are able to transcend the particular narcissistic self by identifying ourselves with universal values (ancient and medieval philosophy), limiting our narcissistic pursuits by obeying general moral laws (Kant), being selflessly altruistic (religion), or having a concern for the general welfare (utilitarianism). All of these ways of being ethical assert that the narcissistic individual person must overcome their particularity. In contrast, I hope to show that not only is there no intrinsic conflict between self-interest and ethical life but that the two require one another. The problem with pre-psychoanalytic morality is that it misconceived the self either in terms of making it an independent substance—a soul—requiring nothing other than itself to be itself or as a set of organized desires seeking satisfaction. Selves as independent substances do not need others, hence, do not need ethical life to be whole or self-realized. Selves as organized sets of desires are in competition with others for satisfactions and there is no inherent reason why, if our primary motivational intent is to gain satisfaction, we should respect others' desires for their satisfactions. It is only when the self is conceived of as the precipitate of a developmental process and as a psychological structure that continues to be vulnerable and in need of selfobject relations and which represents a different motivational source from desires that we can fully align ethical life with self-interest.

My argument will be in three parts: I will show (1) why a person's need for selfobjects demands they be able to engage in reciprocal relationships with others—that is, relationships in which one is willing to perform for others what one needs others to perform for them; (2) why persons who want to have flourishing selfobject relations must develop the traditional moral virtues, integrity, and a sense of responsibility; and (3) why persons who want the self to be the center of their psychological life must be willing to extend their ethical concerns to all human beings rather than just to those who can help sustain their selves.

THE NEED FOR RECIPROCITY

Since we need others who can perform selfobject functions for us throughout our lives, it is crucial for the development and maintenance of the self that we surround ourselves with such people. Persons who don't have such friends and decide they are strong enough to go it alone typically pay the price of having to live through the ego or other non-self structures, for the self, according to Kohut, has only two choices—allow itself to be helped by others or live with other centers of initiative motivating life. The cost of the latter is high, for it reduces our sense of aliveness, limits our developmental growth, and isolates us from the joy of shared existence with others.

Given the inescapable vulnerability of the self, it becomes essential for a person to be able to make and sustain friendships and/or intimacies. It is important to emphasize that while everyone has situational selfobject needs, they can typically only be met by someone with whom one has established a long-term relationship and whom one can trust. That is, we cannot sustain the self through the ups and downs of life without belonging to committed self-object relationships. While one of these relationships might be with a therapist, for the most part they are with friends and family.

If we ask what kind of person is able to make and sustain friendships, the answer is, obviously, someone able to engage in selfobject reciprocity—someone who is willing to empathically care for others as they expect others to empathically care for them. Persons best able to offer reciprocal friendship to others are those who have developed the character traits of being empathic, caring, and genuinely concerned about the well-being of another. Since we usually associate the traits of empathy, care, and concern for others with people who are ethical, I think Kohut's claim that all persons need to be in selfobject relationships to sustain their selves entails that it is personally good to become an ethically good person.

The key difference between an infantile or immature use of selfobjects and a mature one is the presence of reciprocity. The baby expects the mother to empathically mirror and sustain it with her greatness; it does not feel the need to do the same for her. As we grow older, infantile narcissism ought to transform into mature narcissism. We still want and need selfobject support, but we are willing to engage in reciprocity in order to get it. If we remain infantile and expect to get selfobject support without reciprocating, then we will have to pay for it in some way, or else we will not get it. But, with the exception of psychotherapy, all non-reciprocal payments for selfobject support (such as flattery, monetary payment, sexual favors, etc.) will involve the internal knowledge that one is manipulating love and care, and care achieved through manipulation typically turns out to be deficient care. That is, what the self needs to sustain itself is to feel loved and affirmed. If people buy love or affirmation, then the self is not getting love or affirmation. Rather, one's ability to pay is being affirmed.

Reciprocity of care is the essence of what many people think of as the quintessential moral maxim: "Do unto others as you would have them do unto you." Underlying this principle is another one, without which it makes little sense: "Love thyself fully and desire loving things to be done to one." Unless one narcissistically loves oneself, the command to love others as one loves oneself makes no sense. The combination of self-love and care for others is even clearer in the Biblical command to "Love your neighbor as yourself." If one does not love oneself, one cannot love the neighbor, and, from a self-psychological viewpoint, if one does really love oneself, one will have to love the neighbor—at least the neighbor with whom one has a self-object bond. What is not quite right about the commandment to love one's neighbor as oneself is that it seems to imply that self-love is easy and neighbor-love is difficult. However, achieving a mature self-love is no easy matter, for it involves coming out of narcissistic fantasies of who one is and accepting/affirming the flawed and limited particularity of who one is.

To engage in reciprocity we must treat others as independent centers of initiative, as persons who can suffer or flourish, and as beings who have intrinsic value. If we do not do this, we cannot reap full selfobject support from them when we need it, for that support cannot be experienced as worthy if it comes from someone whom we do not value or do not think is acting as an independent agent. Engaging in selfobject reciprocity demands that one treat others with moral respect, treat them as ends in themselves. This is what it means to engage in what Buber calls an "I-Thou" relationship (1970) and what Jessica Benjamin calls "recognition of the other" (1988).[6]

I think that reciprocity also entails that one develop a keen sense of "fairness." Indeed, one can hardly imagine what reciprocity would look like without fairness. Fairness is, however, what John Rawls found to be the essence of the notion of justice (1971). Thus, we can now say that in order for persons to sustain their selves they need not simply to be caring, empathic, and concerned with others, but also they must be just—at least in their friendships. Since Rawls and many other modern theorists have found justice to be the essential notion of morality, we have a further reason from self psychology as to why it is good to be good.

In short, if we ask what kind of person can most adequately engage in the selfobject matrixes needed to sustain optimal self-functioning, we find it is someone who is caring, empathic, able to acknowledge and respect the worth of others, and who is capable of fairness—at least in the context of friendship. As these are the traits most associated with being an ethical person, we can conclude that the psychology of the self developed within the psychoanalytic framework provides us with compelling reasons for becoming moral persons.

Note that this theory locates ethical activity not in a realm of pure reason or abstract generalized love but in the robust matrix of friendships in which there is lived mutuality of respect and care. I think that this kind of reciprocity is the natural breeding ground for people to become fully ethical. Without it a person falls into the dangers of becoming a harsh moral legalist requiring strict obedience to the law or becoming a moral spiritualist who hopes and prays for the good but does not know how to help restore the self-functioning of those closest to them. It is the hearty world of self-selfobject friendships and love relationships that gives birth to an embodied, sensitive, caring person—the essence of what it means to be ethical.

THE NEED FOR MORAL VIRTUES

My claim that only people capable of empathic, caring reciprocity can engage fully in mature selfobject relationships is consonant with Aristotle's contention that only good people can participate fully in the practice of friendship (1962). By "good person" Aristotle means someone who has developed the moral virtues such as courage, justice, moderation, and generosity. It is fairly easy to understand why a person who lacked such virtues could not sustain a friendship. Very few psychologically healthy people will put up with unbalanced reciprocities, excessive consumption of shared resources, cowardice in the face of challenges (especially the challenges of sustaining love and friendship), and a tightness of giving. The only kind of person who would remain friends with such an un-virtuous person is one who is either a saint or suffers from such significant psychopathology that they will take any kind of friend they can get, or worse, be driven by repetitive structures to seek out friends who would injure them. I do not believe that such injured people can provide free, genuinely caring selfobject functions, for their nourishment will always have a toxic residue—a need to control, to take revenge, to keep the other in a state of dependency so they won't be abandoned, and so on. That is, such "friends" do not seek to promote the development of a genuine self but wish to keep it in a state of pathological neediness.

The Aristotelian virtues are necessary not only for friendship, but also for the development of a nuclear self capable of living in reality. Kohut says that for infantile grandiosity to transform into mature ambitions, the child must undergo events of optimal frustration. I contend that the process of optimal frustration is very close to what Aristotle describes as the development of the moral and intellectual virtues. For Aristotle the moral virtues are character traits that represent the mean between the extremes in relation to situations that arouse basic human emotions and desires. The mean allows the emotions or desires to be experienced without either overwhelming or underwhelming us. In allowing an emotion or desire to appear the virtues provide motivation for action, while in not allowing an agent to be overwhelmed, they provide the calm necessary for thinking about what to do (1962).

Optimal frustration generates a similar kind of character structure. It occurs in situations in which we cannot simply opt for immediate gratification or feel nothing at all—rather, we are presented with a problem that demands we hold our responses in abeyance until we can figure out how best to solve the problem. We will not be able to tolerate the delay in satisfaction unless we have begun to develop the virtues, for the virtues constitute the kind of character we must have in order to tolerate frustration in any particular kind of situation. For instance, courage is what allows us to tolerate the presence of fear rather than denying it (rashness) or running away (cowardice). Not only are the moral virtues needed to block the demand for immediate gratification, but the intellectual virtues are also required to solve the problems. A solution based on immediate desire or emotional discharge fails to constitute an experience of optimal frustration.

The difference between Kohut and Aristotle is that Kohut uses optimal frustration in a general application to all developmental problems while Aristotle is careful in specifying the crucial kinds of situations that require virtuous responses. Thus, he can name the virtues while Kohut has no similar characterlogical inventory. I believe that Kohut's general theory of development through optimal frustration entails Aristotle's specific virtues. In essence, optimal frustration creates the same character structure as the Aristotelian virtues.

Another way of saying this is that if a person has insufficient optimal frustrations, they will tend to remain infantile (spoiled) in their demand for instant gratification, while if they have been overwhelmed rather than optimally frustrated, they will be traumatized, become defensive, and have a lessened ability to feel their emotions and desires. The Kohutian self and Aristotle's ethical person appear to be very close—I would even say, one and the same.

The virtues for Aristotle are not an end in themselves, but a means by which we are able to best accomplish our human function of self-directing our lives in a rational, thoughtful way.[7] What Aristotelian virtues give a human being is the possibility of choosing a life. What a successful developmental pattern of optimal frustration gives a person is ambitious vitality for achievement in life. Aristotle knew that to have a life, a person needs to moderate the power of the passions (the id); Kohut knew that in order to have a life, one's grandiose narcissistic energy had to be transformed and organized. Infantile grandiosity has no impetus to action, for it is already perfect; injured grandiosity has no impetus for action as the spirit of the person has been crushed. Only grandiosity that has been optimally frustrated can ground the possibility of someone becoming a mature agent.

Thus, the goal of both the virtues and optimal frustration is the same: the possibility of agency. Action requires the presence of the moral and intellectual virtues because in order for someone's ego to choose between alternative possibilities, the power of immediate responses must be moderated and the ability to think about the consequences and meanings of different courses of action developed. The more one is capable of being an agent, the less one is a vehicle for forces acting through one. It is the possibility of agency that grounds what many consider to be the most important trait of a moral person: responsibility. Because we can, through the moral and intellectual virtues, control forces working on us and act according to a deliberated choice, we are responsible for what we do.

However, Aristotle missed a crucial condition for the possibility of agency—one which self psychology understands—namely, the presence of psychological integrity. A lack of psychological integrity means that parts of the psyche can motivate actions without either the knowledge or consent of the other parts or of the person as a whole. I believe that most acts of cheating are accomplished when the psyche engages in vertical splitting—the same kind of splitting that Arnold Goldberg has analyzed in the perversions (1999). It is hard to explain the possibility of integrity without a self to center and organize the other parts of the psyche, and with a self, it is easy to see why integrity is such an important value. Most previous theories of integrity have tried to locate it in the conscious rational ego acting according to consistent principles. These theories are deficient in two ways. First, parts of the unconscious can be and often are out of the realm of control and knowledge of the ego. They can act independently of it without its awareness. Second, the ego is marvelously prone to self-deception and rationalization. The self, on the other hand, is an unconscious structure that relates to all other parts of the psyche, and, when its ambitions and ideals are stabilized, is not prone to deception or fabrication. Vertical splitting is a pathology of the self, not one of its functions.

In conclusion, if we accept self psychology's primary tenet that the most important psychological task is developing a nuclear self, then we have good reasons for wanting to be a person with integrity, empathy, care and respect for others, a sense of fairness, the moral and intellectual virtues, and a sense of responsibility. But these are exactly the terms we associate with being an ethical person. If we want to have a self, then we need to develop the traits of an ethical person. If asked why developing a self is so important, self psychology can show that a psyche grounded in a coherent self is capable of more liveliness, joy, and agency than any other kind of psychic arrangement. Without an intact self, a certain emptiness and ungroundedness pervades experience, even experiences of immense pleasure and success. To feel fully alive with a strong sense of meaningfulness and agency, one needs a self. And to sustain the self, we need to become ethical persons. [8]

Thus, self psychology offers to our culture an immeasurable gift, for it provides an answer as to why we should be moral that does not involve improvable metaphysical claims about God or a demand that we transcend our particularity. For those who try to be good and act with integrity, it offers the great solace that they are not being dupes but are living the only kind of lives that offer genuine happiness. For those who are tempted to be cheaters, it offers a great caution. What cheaters think their cheating will get them only appears to be in their best interest, for by cheating a person is making himself into the kind of person who is lessening his chances of developing and sustaining a self.

However, a problem remains. Just because someone has the moral virtues and empathy does not mean that he will apply them to all people at all times. That is, we can be ethically caring with those close to us or seen as belonging to the same group as us, and vicious with those who are not in the chosen group. Nazis, racists, and Mafiosi have been known to be loving humans with those they considered to be the same as themselves. That is, the exercise of virtues and reciprocity tends to be group- or context-dependent. To be fully ethical is to be predisposed to treat all people respectfully and with compassion. Why would someone who believes that the fundamental psychological task in life is the development and realization of a self want to be a universalistic in the scope of his values rather than someone who re-serves them just for friends?

THE UNIVERSAL EXTENSION OF ETHICAL CONCERN

In order to explore this question of why a healthy narcissist should want to extend ethical concern to all persons and maybe all sentient beings, we need first to turn to the nature of ideals and how they function in life. For Kohut, the idealized pole is that part of the self that carries teleological values. It is extraordinarily important that self psychology finds that teleological motiva-tion—being moved by ideals—is essential to having a healthy self, for many of the most important thinkers of the past one hundred years, including Nietzsche and Heidegger, have found ideals to be problematic in that they destroy individuality by forcing people to conform to generalized values. Scientists, in general, have also been skeptical about whether ideals can be motivators. They, like Freud, tend to believe that only forces, such as the drives, can cause actions.[9]

For self psychology ideals are not cages that repress the drives, self-expression, or the erotic body, but vehicles for giving life meaning and making the future a source of dynamic interest. Ideals open up time and extend the self into time. Yet, Freud and Nietzsche are not wrong in being wary of ideals, for they can be imposed punitively on the self by a harsh superego and/or a rigid society. Whether ideals generate liveliness and meaningful systems for the organization of life or function as sources of repression depends upon whether the ideals represent the internal strivings of the self, derive from the impositions of social forces, or represent a defensive and over-controlling superego. Ideals imposed by society and/or a repressive superego can be cages; those structuring the self are beacons pointing toward new possibilities of enhanced life. Note that it is not the content of the ideals by which we can say whether they are self ideals or social ideals; it is how they function in the psyche. Someone might have as a part of a self ideal to become a lawyer, while another person might be using the same ideal to hold himself together defensively or adopt it to please their parents. Ideals, if they are part of self structure, are crucial for the maintenance of a sense of meaningfulness.

However, as strong a proponent of ideals as Kohut is, he does not address the question of whether persons with coherent selves need to hold ethical values and extend them universally. He does say that the mature narcissist needs to identify with wider, more enduring values to overcome the narcissistic injury of mortality (1966), but does not specify what these ideals should be. However, we have seen that part of any self's set of ideals ought to be the ideal of being an empathic, caring, virtuous human being, for only when this ideal infuses our lives do we become optimally able to engage in what strengthens the self more than anything else—selfobject relationships. Other parts of a self's ideals are optional, but not these ethical traits for they are the traits necessary for any self to sustain itself. Hence, if we are to be persons who value having a vital self, we must also value being ethical persons.

However, a further problem arises, namely, that character traits and values tend to be highly context-specific. Aristotle says, we exercise our virtues differently in relation to different situations. For instance, we exercise the trait of generosity more fully in our families than we do with friends, and more fully with friends than acquaintances. But how about in situations with those we do not know or those trying to harm us? If we do not extend some empathic generosity and care to such people, can we say that we are really caring, empathic, and generous people? Are we injuring our abilities to be the kind of people able to get selfobject supplies if we do not exhibit at least some range of the virtues in these difficult situations? Are the ethical traits of self and character so context-dependent that they can entirely disappear if certain contextual variables are absent?

The full ethical position demands that we extend our empathic concern to others with whom we are not in a reciprocal relationship, that we give respect to all human beings and maybe even all sentient creatures. What would lead a mature narcissist to this position? The answer is compelling: not to do so involves a fragmentation of ourselves, a loss of agency, and a replacement of the self as the center of experience by the ego.

To say that we will exhibit our virtues and empathic sympathies in some situations and not in others entails that a decision must be made as to what distinguishes the situations. This kind of distinction is the kind of thing that the ego does, and, as such, it puts the ego in charge of the life of the soul. The ego has the extraordinary power to abstract itself from everything, including a person's character. However, while a psyche organized around a rational ego might give one the most control over life, it is not the most alive way to live, for it lacks the vitality of the self which is immersed in connectedness with others, tied to cherished ideals (including the ideal of being an ethical person), and devoted to accomplishment in chosen arenas of endeavor. It cannot so easily distance itself from the character traits or ideals with which it engages life. The self cannot, like the ego, just turn these traits on and off depending on the context. In short, the ego can live a kind of disembodied, un-situated kind of existence; the self is inherently embodied and situated.

Another way to make this psychological argument is from the value of psychological integrity. We have seen that integrity must be a value to a psyche centered on a self, for it is the value that essentially supports the self's being the fulcrum of the psyche. This does not mean that we must have one highest value or that our lives cannot have multiple dimensions. It means that when a person with an integrated psyche engages in the manifold dimensions of life, she is fully present, active, and alive in them. The parts do not war against one another in an integrated psyche, but work together to produce a focused meaningful life.

Integrity means being who you are, regardless of situation. If one is an empathic caring person, then one remains empathic and caring, even in difficult situations. This does not mean that we cannot be aggressive. If I need aggression to protect myself or what is precious to me, or if I need aggression where it is legitimately called for—on playing fields or combat, then it is right (and natural) to be aggressive. But one can be aggressive in a just, caring, and empathic way. Indeed, on the sporting fields this is precisely what is called for—aggression without loss of virtue or humanity. Empathically caring for one's enemies makes life much more difficult than being able to aggress against them without counter-feelings, but this might be the price for being an integrated human being living from a core self.

Finally, I believe that keeping one's character and empathic predisposition in all situations leads to more aliveness of the soul, for it makes one active and assertive rather than dependent upon circumstances to determine who one is. If I have to change my character depending on whom I am with or what circumstances I am facing, then who I am is contextually determined, and this is a passive way of being human rather than active. When I retain the essence of myself regardless of circumstance, then I actively assert my being in the world. This, I believe, is the power of Socrates' death and the deaths of many heroes who retained their integrity at the cost of death rather than selling out. [10]

Why is it good to be good? Because it is only by being good people that we can fully develop or sustain our selves and without a developed and sustained self we cannot be as intensely alive as possible. Here is a return to one of the most profound insights of Greek philosophy but without the transcendence of particularity that Greek thought entailed: the person who is able to reap the most personal happiness is the good person. Bad people cannot be fully happy for they have unjust souls that are anarchically controlled by whims, can't be fully empathic with themselves or others, and can't engage in the kind of friendships that supply necessary selfobject support. Note that there is no reason why bad persons cannot have highly functioning egos capable of crafty, even brilliant reasoning and action. There is no reason why bad persons can't have lots of pleasures. What bad persons can't fully have are selves and the profound joy that accompanies this psychological state, for it is the self—not the ego—that needs to dwell in human connectedness.

I have tried to show why it is personally good to be morally good; but it can also be shown that it is morally good to have a narcissistically healthy self. When we inquire into what kind of human being creates the most human misery and suffering, I think we will find that it is those humans who have suffered severe trauma to the self and harbor an unremitting narcissistic rage. Narcissistic rage differs radically from ordinary anger and aggression. Ordinary anger is typically caused by a specific injury or obstacle, has a specific target, and once discharged it disappears. Narcissistic rage, on the other hand, can fester forever and seek revenge on any and all persons who might get unconsciously associated with the cause of the trauma. It is never satisfied, regardless of how many victories of revenge and acts of destruction it commits, until the self is repaired (Kohut, 1985b). I believe the harboring of unconscious rage due to injuries to the self forms the core motivational structure of evil persons—persons who seek to harm others for seemingly no reason other than seeing them suffer. The great antidote to evil is the development of persons with healthy nuclear selves.

Finally, as Kant has shown (1797), morality inherently involves the adoption of a universal point of view. We must be willing to universalize what we believe to be right and affirm a world in which we find all persons acting on the principle that we are acting on. I think that Kant is right about universalization, but wrong that it is principles that need to have universal validity, for there are no principles that do not have exceptions or conditions that invalidate them. What we need to do is to combine virtue ethics with Kant's deontological ethics and ask "Can we universalize trying to foster the kind of person being posited here as an ideal way to be human?" That is, would I be willing to live in a world in which persons had firmly developed, coherent nuclear selves that they were actively attempting to realize and who had developed the moral virtues, a fine sense of fairness, and who extended empathy to all other humans (and maybe all sentient creatures). My answer, of course, is "Yes, absolutely, for this is a world without narcissistic rage, a world of genuine happiness rather than meaningless pleasures, a world of strong vital individuals (Nietzsche would like this) pursuing their deepest values but who recognize the inherent worth of others and have a keen sense of the selfobject needs of others." For sure, there will be competitive conflicts; it is a world based on individuality, not communist harmony. But empathy, care, and concern for the other will provide the means by which the difficulties of competition and suffering will be assuaged. We do not need to be split between our moral selves and our narcissistic selves, as Kant thought. We can have an integrity in which we are most our selves when we are being ethical. This is the kind of world that I can heartily affirm and the kind of human being I can will to universalize.

CONCLUSION

If I am right that the understanding of self developed in psychoanalysis and the ability to live as an ethical human being are deeply intertwined, then a number of stunning conclusions follow. First, psychoanalysis needs to become as central to modern culture as philosophy was to ancient Greek and Roman cultures. In those cultures, philosophy was not an academic discipline, but the practice of a way of life that many in those cultures thought as the highest and best form of human existence. Engagement with philosophy was meant to give not just wider perspectives and a deeper sense of meaningfulness to life, but also to transform the soul from a confusion of desires and passive responses to external pressures into a calm seat of activity that had integrity and self-control. Practicing philosophy was the best-known way to care for the self.

Philosophy held reign in the West for close to a millennium before it was superseded by an enticing new monotheistic religion promising personal eternal salvation. Religion had its reign, but, as Nietzsche so succinctly put it, God is now dead. Religion could not stand up to the new empirical methodologies that have made science so successful and its price of diminishing this life in the here/now for an improvable afterlife was too high both in terms of the relinquishment of personal enjoyments and in terms of simply making sense. The void left by the demise of religion has not been filled (see chapter 10). Neither the shallowness of a life devoted to personal enjoyments nor the materialistic worldview of science can offer humans enough meaning to sustain the deepest longings of their psyches. Modernity teeters on the brink on nihilism.

Freud had hoped that psychoanalysis could become the new way of thinking about human life that could offer meaning and guidance to humans in their post-religious worlds. Despite his brilliant opening up of an entirely new realm of human subjectivity—the unconscious—his theory, after making enormous cultural headway in the first half of the twentieth century, has failed to become the cultural centerpiece he had hoped for. His theory was simply too biological, too deficient in teleological meanings, and too deeply connected to the old naturalism to provide an adequate ground either for ethical life or for a personal life of meaning.

Kohut's re-visioning of psychoanalysis in terms of self psychology, as I hope to have shown, offers the genuine possibility that psychoanalysis will claim what Freud thought was its heritage. If what I have said is true, and I believe it is, then self-psychological psychoanalysis is the only foundation within secular modernity that can offer a genuine ground for ethical life. I believe it does this not only in its theoretical understanding of human nature but also in its practice. The practice of psychoanalysis is the most profound way ever conceived to enhance both the particular narcissistic vitality of persons and their ability to be good persons. It does not do this in the old way by offering moral advice or social pressure—what Arnold Goldberg calls "moral stealth" (2007), for this can destroy the openness and trust of the psychoanalytic dyad. Rather, it is by helping heal wounds in the psyche that harbor narcissistic rage, building selves through the presence of empathic responsiveness, integrating unconscious aspects of the psyche, and providing forms of self understanding that include both conscious and unconscious aspects of who we are that psychoanalytic practice can help its clients become more ethical human beings. In providing both a theory for why it is good to be good and a practice of interaction that helps human beings become good, psychoanalysis has the most profound gift that any discipline can offer a culture.

NOTES

1. This chapter is an attempt to encapsulate the general argument I make in *Why It Is Good to Be Good: Ethics, Kohut's Self Psychology, and Modern Society* (2010).

2. Although I have distinguished them in previous books, I will be use "morality" and "ethics" interchangeably in this book. "Morality" tends to have the sense of a set of social values that governs our relations to others and which is justified independently of established custom. "Ethics" tends to be more personal and attempts to find a set of values by which an individual can live a good human life. Since I will be arguing for a theory in which the best way for an individual to live is in empathic respectful relations with others, the ethical and moral come together fully.

3. See Ross Poole's *Morality and Modernity* (1991) for a further elaboration of modern moralities and their failures.

4. For instance, see the works of Rawls (1971), Hare (1963), and Gewirth (1978), all of whom adopt variations of Kant's stance that we are required to be consistent with ourselves as the key reason why we need to universalize our values. I will later try to show why rational consistency is not a compelling value but that psychological consistency—integrity—is.

5. Bernard Williams makes this point in one of the most important books in moral philosophy over the past half century, *Ethics and the Limits of Philosophy* (1982).

6. Frank Summers in his *The Psychoanalytic Vision* (2013), while praising my *Why It Is Good to Be Good* (2010) as "the most significant breakthrough in using analytic thought as a foundation for ethical behavior since Erich Fromm" (p. 33), also criticizes my position as one which affirms only the selfobject use of other persons or at best, a reciprocal selfobject use. He finds this position to be sub-ethical and agrees with Jessica Benjamin (1988) that humans must come to *recognize* others as having independent self worth, not just see them as possible selfobject reciprocators. Summers is, of course, right; but I fully intended for my concept of selfobject reciprocity to include the recognition of others as independent separate agents with intrinsic worth. Without such recognition, one could not enter into the kind of relation in which maturity of human functioning could be reached. Summers might have thought that I did not include this understanding of recognition and respect in my notion of reciprocity, because I was coming at the question of why, from the viewpoint of self-interest, one would want to engage in reciprocity.

7. The Greek *arête* is closer to the virtue in the phrase "by virtue of" rather than some abstract concept of what good character is. A Greek would say "Achilles was able to defeat Hector by virtue of his strength, speed, and closeness to the gods." Hence, strength, speed, and piety are his virtues.

8. This position is mirrored in Frank Summers' *The Psychoanalytic Vision* (2013, ch. 3).

9. It is important that Freud shifted his theory from seeing humans as motivated by an ego ideal in "On Narcissism" and *Mourning and Melancholia* to be compelled by a superego in *The Ego and the Id* and other later works. Like Kohut's idealized pole of the self, the ego ideal is a transformation of narcissism, a place where we can locate our previous perfection. However, Freud sees it more as a pressuring force making demands on the ego rather than a teleological lure for development. This is fully the case when the superego replaces the ego ideal in Freud's later work.

10. See Kohut's "On Courage" (1985a, p. 5–50) for a stunning account of how several "heroes" retained their integrity at the cost of their lives during the Nazi era.

Chapter Eight

Self Psychology and the Problem of the Other

One of the most important ethical problems of the contemporary world with its unceasing flow and mixtures of peoples is the problem of relating to difference or alterity. We are presently faced with the problem of how to negotiate otherness as in no other time in the past—not just diversity of race and culture, but differences in sexual orientations, religion, politics, aesthetic preferences, metaphysical commitments, and epistemological convictions, to name just a few. It is a problem that has caused massive suffering throughout history and still causes aggression and inhumanity all over the globe.

What is the problem of difference? It can be schematized in the following way. First, an essential difference is noticed: men are different from women, the strong are different from the weak, fair-skinned people are different from dark-skinned. Then, the crucial move comes, for rather than simply accepting that the world has differences, a normative judgment is made as to which side of the difference is superior to the other side. If the evaluative judgment is made by a person or group in power, then their side of the difference becomes privileged and the other side is unfairly discriminated against. Men are not just different from women, they are the superior gender. Rich people are not just different from the poor, they are better. White folk are not just different from other races, they are more advanced. Wherever significant differences are noted that are important in the construction of identity, value judgments seem to follow instantaneously, followed by structures of privilege and discrimination. Once these configurations of injustice have been constructed, then social and political tensions ensue, with the result being the turmoil, suffering, and tragedy that we have witnessed throughout the world for most of human history. Negotiating the problem of difference is not just any social problem, it seems to be *the essential and unavoidable problem* that must be solved in order for the world to stabilize and progress into an international harmonic order.

Can psychoanalysis in general and self psychology in particular help with this problem of how to deal with difference? My answer must be nuanced, for psychoanalysis and self psychology both have the appearance of being Enlightenment-type theories, theories that hold that all differences between humans are superficial and that at core we all have the same nature. This Enlightenment outlook was the key conceptual framework that came into being in order to overcome the religious violence that was decimating Europe in the seventeenth century. It held, first, that humans should practice tolerance toward differences, at least differences of religious beliefs. Second, it held that political differences could be negotiated through democratic institutions in which the majority ruled but minorities had rights that could not be abrogated by a hostile or fanatical majority. Its third value was to instantiate inquiry into alterity, inquiry that could break through the superficialities of difference and locate a common human core in all individuals, regardless of culture or religion.

This has been a remarkable strategy, the strategy upon which the modern liberal world has come into existence. It is probably what you and I believe as the proper way to deal with difference: tolerance, inquiry that dispels surface differences, and democratic institutions for the resolution of disputes. And, yet, this liberal strategy of toleration and "getting-to-know-you, getting-to-know-all-about-you" has been rejected by a number of important feminist and ethnic theorists. They say that the Enlightenment's attempt to erase all difference as superficial is a falsification of reality. African-American philosopher Charles Mills sees "mainstream liberal color-blindness and gender-blindness as simple blindness" (2007, p. 175). It makes an essential difference in this culture if one is born a woman or an ethnic minority. Those who are privileged experience the world very differently from those who suffer from systemic discrimination, prejudice, and the lack of equal opportunities. The new politics of identity proclaims that differences in sexual orientation, gender, race, and religion not only cannot be erased to find a core humanity, but these differences are essential ingredients in how we construct our identities.

Further, liberal tolerance too often turns out to be indifference, and exploring difference too often turns out to be eating tacos, doing yoga, or engaging in exotic world travel. Difference is never really encountered or validated. Hence, it turns out that the Enlightenment strategy for dealing with difference, while certainly containing the essential values of common human rights, toleration of tolerable differences, and inquiry into the Other, has failed to really engage otherness and difference. Insofar as psychoanalysis in general and self psychology in particular pose "universal" understandings of human nature that are supposedly true for everyone regardless of culture or gender, they appear to fall victim to postmodernist and post-colonial criticisms that they fail to validate the genuine difference that difference makes.

However, I believe that the rejection of psychoanalysis and self psychology as universalist psychologies that fail to validate difference and offer strategies for dealing with difference is misconceived. For one, psychoanalysis can help us understand why humans tend to leap to judgmentalism and negation when difference appears. Since the "other" is unknown, they are inherently unpredictable, and, hence, pose a threat, but what is threatened is unclear. Unclear threats cause anxiety to arise, and no other discipline has explored anxiety more profoundly than psychoanalysis.

What psychoanalysis teaches us about anxiety is that it is such a debilitating emotion that the conscious ego will do almost anything to rid itself of it, including bringing into play the psychological defenses in which repression, dissociation, etc. cast anxiety and its traumatic causes out of conscious awareness. It is the presence of anxiety that explains why we so quickly want to resolve moments in which difference is experienced, by forming value judgments in which the different other is found to be wanting, inferior, or impotent. Remaining in the experience of difference seems to subject us to more anxiety than we can easily tolerate and hence rather than tentatively exploring the otherness before us, we leap to the discriminating evaluative judgment to control the situation.

Psychoanalysis can point to even more profound reasons as to why the experience of the Other can cause anxiety to arise, for it reveals that the dangerous other is not only outside of us but inside of us. In positing a theory of unconscious mentality, psychoanalysis understands that we all carry around repressed material that has been thrust from consciousness and which, as unconscious, constitutes an ever-present threat to our psychological coherence and ego-identities. When we unconsciously associate the threat from the other that resides within us with the other who appears outside of us, an over-determined anxiety arises. We feel threatened from both the inside and outside, but can manage only the threat from the outside. The vehemence by which we denigrate those different from us, and the ferocity with which we attack them reveals this over-determination at work. We are attempting to control and dominate the other outside of us because we can't accomplish a negotiated integration inside of us.

For Freud, of course, the root of all anxiety is the fear of castration. While the notion of castration anxiety, if castration is understood as any event in which our agency is threatened, might help us understand why anxiety arises when we are faced with difference, it seems too contrived and gender-specific to be of genuine use. It is self psychology's understanding of anxiety being at root about the disintegration of the self which, I believe, sheds light brilliantly upon the problem of difference and will offer original ways to overcome the devastations that surround the problem of relating to alterity.

For Kohut the development and sustenance of the nuclear self are the most crucial of all psychological tasks, and essential to the generation and preservation of the self's grandiose pole is empathic mirroring. Mirroring is a process in which the self finds itself in some important way duplicated in another person. This doubling seems to happen best where the mirroring person has some essential sameness with the person being mirrored. In junior high school when young persons are separating from their families and in desperate need of peer mirroring to sustain themselves, they tend to form groups that look alike, talk the same talk, dress the same dress, listen to the same music, and denigrate everyone who is different. The mirroring process that is crucial for sustaining the grandiose self seems to need a background of essential sameness.

Also, when we locate ourselves with others who are essentially the same as we are, we participate in a group-identification that enhances the feelings of omnipotence, specialness, and greatness in the grandiose self. The individual self might be insignificant but the group it is identified with is great. Hence, when we are with others who are the same as us, we get grandiose enhancement both in terms of mirroring and identification with a greater, more powerful entity.

Thus, we can see that the appearance of someone who differs in some important way from oneself or one's group threatens the esteem of the grandiose self and causes anxiety about disintegration to inundate the psyche. If one is organizing one's personal identity around such crucial components as gender, sexual orientation, class, ethnicity, and nationality, then those who differ from us in these categories will constitute a danger. The appearance of the other calls into question not only the background conditions necessary for empathic mirroring but the components of grandiose identity that allow one to feel so confident in situations of sameness. The disruption of sameness threatens self-dissolution, thereby provoking anxiety and all of the defensiveness and rage that occur when the self is threatened.

Given Kohut's understanding of grandiosity as an essential component of the self, the need for mirroring to sustain that component, and the need for sameness as a backdrop for effective mirroring, we can understand why difference is so difficult for human beings. It threatens the coherence and esteem of the grandiose self! With self psychology we now have a deep psychological explanation for why there has been such a devastating human history of violence toward those experienced as other.

However, self psychology can also offer us a profound understanding for why we need to engage with otherness. There is no essential reason why Freudian drives need to seek objects that are different, aside from heterosexual libido, and here the drive does not essentially seek to relate to the other so much as to discharge on the other—to use the other to gain satisfaction. When Kohut replaces drive satisfaction with self construction as the fundamental psychological task, our understanding of what it means to relate to the other changes dramatically. Unlike the Freudian drives, the Kohutian self is a dynamic structure. By this, I mean that the self must always be striving, adventuring, exploring, or developing in order for it to remain vital. However, as we have also seen, the self also wants repetition and sameness in order to feel secure and non-anxious.

In short, there is a strong dialectical tension at the core of the self between staying within a repetitive identity and seeking new life through development. It makes a great deal of difference which side of this tension gets the upper hand. In general nothing stimulates development and adventure more than the encounter with otherness. When we are in familiar situations with familiar persons doing familiar things, there is typically a lot of soothing comfort and little growth. To grow we need to encounter that which is other than who we are now and relate to it in such a way as to be able to ingest it or respond to it with more maturity than previously. In terms of psychotherapy, encounter with the other involves an opening up to and owning of unconscious material—material that has been declared to be other than who I am. In terms of selfobjects, we need to have more realistic, less merged, less dependent relations with our selfobjects as we mature, and this involves allowing the otherness in them to appear, as when, for instance, one experiences the mother not merely as a source of psychological and physical nourishment but as having an existence independent of oneself. In terms of sociality the encounter with otherness means being open to what is strange and foreign. It is the ability to live in a democracy.

This view of self-formation through negotiated experiences with alterity is not only a corrective to the universalist views which find us all to be, at bottom, the same, but also those views which understand identity-formation to involve a necessary abjection of different others. These abjection theories, such as those of anthropologist Mary Douglas and philosopher Julia Kristeva, hold that humans form identities only by establishing who they are not (Oliver, 1998). Men are not women; Christians are not Jews or Muslims. It is only by defining ourselves as different from select others that we come to be who we are. These abjective theories, however, are as highly problematic as the universalist ones. While their understanding of aversive identity-formation can explain why there has been so much violence in the world arising from situations of difference, they offer us no hope that we might overcome such aggressions.

In contrast, self psychology's theory of self development does offer us hope that human beings might eventually overcome their rejecting styles of identity-formation. In its understanding of the self as needing to engage otherness in order to develop, it can show why there is a need to engage the other positively. While the achievement of definiteness is crucial in identity-formation ("I am a this, not a that"), the definiteness ought not to be totally exclusionary of otherness or aggressive against it. I might not be a Muslim, but by learning about this faith and interacting with others in it, I might deepen and expand my own faith.

Self psychology also has the most profound theory available for grasping what it means to genuinely engage the alterity of the other. Being open to otherness means being willing to empathically immerse oneself in the experience of the other. All other forms of attempting to know or encounter the other will involve epistemological processes that objectify the other—that turn the other into an object. When we learn "about" someone, we attempt to determine their defining traits. That is, when we try to know the other through knowing truths about them we do the same thing as we do when we are trying to know truths about any object. When we interview for a position in philosophy, we seek to know whether the candidate has been adequately trained, whether they exhibit a scintillating intelligence, and whether they are prepared to produce the courses we need taught. We don't empathically engage them; we examine, interrogate, and assess them to see their level of excellence in the field. This is not unlike finding out that the molecule before me is water because I can detect two atoms of hydrogen and one of oxygen.

Knowing through objectifying epistemological methods produces a conceptual frame of what the object or person is. For Heidegger, conceptual enframing is, in essence, an act of power, an act in which we engage in knowing in order to achieve control over the object (1949). As such, it is a way of attempting to dominate the other. Emmanuel Levinas says that in objective knowing there is a "seizing of something and making it one's own, of reducing to presence and representing the difference of being, an activity which *appropriates* and *grasps* the otherness of the known . . . The immanence of the known to the act of knowing is already the embodiment of seizure" (1989, p. 76).

Empathic immersion is different. It is the vulnerable attempt to learn what someone is experiencing from the inside of that person. With empathic immersion, our paradigm shifts: the other appears, causes anxiety, but rather than binding the anxiety with normative judgment, we gather ourselves and empathically inquire into who this person is or who these people are. What does it feel like to be them? What does it feel like to be in their worlds rather than mine?

Replacing normative discriminatory judgments with empathy is, to me, the only plausible way to overcome the tensions and violence that are associated with the experience of difference. When we ask who is most able to tolerate the anxiety associated with difference, self psychology has a surprising—stunning—answer. It is not the humble or poor in spirit; it is persons with coherent, vitalized selves who are most likely to be empathic with others.

I believe self psychology's advocacy of empathy as the way of knowing another that does not objectify the other fleshes out what Buber means by proposing that we have "I-Thou" relations rather than "I-It" ones (1923), and what Kant meant when he said that we must treat others as ends in themselves (1797). To treat others as a "thou" or as "ends in themselves" means seeing other human beings as subjects—as having subjective experiences that are the basis for their being independent centers of life and initiative. But to see other human beings as subjects means to validate their subjective experiences rather than reducing them to objects, and this is exactly what empathic responsiveness does.

Empathy also seems to be the core of what Emmanuel Levinas means by ethical responsibility. Levinas, one of the most important ethical philosophers of the twentieth century, realized that the old moral way of being—one in which an agent mediated his experience with others through moral laws or by tending to the general welfare—tended to objectify human beings and not encounter them in their singularity—in their particular beings. He then articulated an ethic in which the appearance of the face of the other immediately (that is, without mediation of any concepts or moral rules) places one under a full responsibility to that other (1989). But what could this mean? What kind of responsibility do I have for the other who appears opposite me on the subway or next to me on the plane? It can't be to improve their welfare or else I would soon find myself destitute of all resources. It can't be to not cheat them, maim them, etc. for these acts are forbidden by moral law not by immediate responsiveness. I propose that the only concrete way to actualize an immediate responsibility to the other whose face appears before me is to empathize with the subjectivity present in the face. The face is crucial to Levinas, I suggest, because it expresses that the being before me has an inner life. To respond to the being of that inner life is to empathically resonate with it. In this way I can be responsive to the black woman sitting across from me on the subway or the busy businessman next to me on the plane. I don't have to do anything more than empathically acknowledge that they are beings who have an inner reality that I can sense and respond to. That is, what I am doing is the most significant act of all—I am confirming that they are subjects and not just objects.

Self psychology also resonates with the ethical work of Hannah Arendt, whose book *Eichmann in Jerusalem* (1968) has been hailed as one of the most important works on the nature of evil and the causes of the Holocaust. What she famously found in the man who sent millions of Jews to their deaths was "the banality of evil." Eichmann was not filled with black hatred nor had he been taken over by some dark force residing in the universe. Rather, he was a little man efficiently and effectively doing his job without inquiring into what he was in fact doing—committing one of the most hideous crimes in the history of humanity. His consciousness was constructed in such a way as to be obedient—to do what he was asked to do, to follow the values that were espoused by a reigning authority. Eichmann and other Nazis had the kind of structured consciousness that traditional ethics championed— a consciousness obedient to higher norms. When the norms shifted from those of a general respect for all citizens to norms that condemned certain populations and authorized them to be subjected to horrific violence, Eichmann and others simply adopted the new norms and kept their familiar structure of consciousness. What the Nazis did not seem to have was either an ability to be self-critical of the norms they were following or the ability to empathically encounter the other as a subject having intrinsic worth. Once someone was seen as having a crucial objective characteristic—being a Jew—then they could be treated as an object and not as a subjective other.

Arendt said that ethical consciousness was not one of obedience to rules or customs but an ability to live with ourselves, where "living with ourselves" involves engaging in an internal dialogue with ourselves. In this internal dialogue, which is usually silent, we cease being a single entity and become beings able to question ourselves, look at ourselves, and hear different sides of ourselves speaking. That is, being a genuine self is being able to be a friend to oneself within oneself. If one is evil then one cannot be a friend to oneself. That is, we must both be the same as ourselves and also other to ourselves in order to be both genuine selves and ethical beings (Arendt, 2003).

What self psychology can add to Arendt are two crucial ideas. The first is that we cannot genuinely listen to a voice either within us or without us if we are not first capable of empathically attuning to the other and what the voice of the other is trying to say. That is, I believe that the capacity for empathy is the necessary precondition for any dialogical interaction to take place, be it inner or outer. The voices within us that are unconscious are always difficult to hear for they are not formulated in the clear language of ego consciousness. We must practice empathy in order to be responsive and to understand the inarticulate articulations within ourselves and those coming from others. Second, the dominating unity of consciousness which Arendt finds to be dangerous because it casts out any voices that disagree with its primary outlook is, from the viewpoint of self psychology, the ego. The voice of the other which the ego needs to hear is not just any voice of any part that might be residing in the psyche, but the voice of the self. It is the self that has been nourished by selfobject relations, that has come into being through empathic mirroring and the care of others, and which needs to love and be loved to sustain itself. The ego is happy with distance from others, critical acumen, and obedience to rules. It is the self that needs and experiences connectedness, can flourish only in a warm sea of empathy, and which, when mature, needs to practice selfobject reciprocity in order to sustain itself. It is the self that grounds moral life.

In sum, we have reached the surprising conclusion that the key to resolving difficult problems with otherness is the formation of a strong nuclear self that is secure and vibrant in its singularly. Persons with coherent vitalized selves are, first, less likely to feel anxiety when the other appears, less likely to feel threatened than those who have fragile, vulnerable, or fragmented selves. Persons with healthy selves also will not contain traumatized sectors of themselves that the appearance of the other threatens to expose. Second, persons with healthy selves do not harbor vast reservoirs of narcissistic rage, rage that often is mobilized indiscriminately against others. Third, persons with healthy selves are more likely to be empathic toward both themselves and others, for the self is the psychological home where empathic responsiveness dwells.

Example:

In the spring of 1999 I was asked by the president of my college to create a bridge group for first-year minority students. At the time the college had a dropout rate of over 50 percent for students of color and she thought that a bridge program might help with this terrible rate of attrition. When I responded that I didn't seem to be the right person for this task, given that I was the most privileged member of the society—white, male, and from a middle-class background—she countered by pointing to my reputation for being very student-oriented. I requested some time before making the decision and asked a number of friends and students about whether I should take on this task. About half said "No, minority students will feel comfortable only with someone who has suffered the kind of discrimination they have," while the other half thought I would be terrific. What was at stake was whether "sameness" would create a higher level of comfort at the college or the presence of "otherness capable of empathy." Reluctantly, I decided to take on the task but not without a great deal of apprehensiveness and, yes, anxiety.

The students were invited to come to college two weeks early to take a course that would give them a half unit of credit (for free) and told they would also get a free computer. They were not told that they had been selected because they were students of color. Eleven accepted. When they came and looked around, they quickly noticed that I was the only white guy in the room. One very articulate black woman, Carolyn, then asked, "Are we in this program because we are minorities?" After I answered, "Yes," she continued by saying that she was not sure she liked that, that it smelled a bit like a remedial program which assumed that students of color were underskilled and needed extra support and preparation. It was a moment of crisis—right in the first few minutes of being together. It was not hard to be empathic with Carolyn's growing outrage and the sudden concern of all the other members at the possibility of being typecast as "deficient." I responded truthfully: "You are being invited to join this class and being given the computer because the college has proven itself to be deficient in its ability to attract and retain qualified students of color. You don't have a problem; we have a problem. This program has been set up to make your college experience more satisfying to you such that you might stay."

I knew enough self psychology at this point and seemed to have had enough empathy and understanding of victimization and trauma from my own difficult past to make an alliance with them. My interpretation of the above moment is that self-esteem was at stake and my students were questioning whether the price they had to pay for getting the benefits of the program was a loss of self-esteem. My response let them know that it was not their esteem but the college's that was at stake.

We met not only before school but for lunch once a week every week during the school year. During these sessions I would open up the discussion to what they had experienced during the week, how their classes were going, etc. They reported suffering many blows, from being in classes that were much harder than anything they had anticipated, to feeling isolated by the social life of the college that was dominated by wealthy white students, to being un-empathically asked in classes to provide "the African-American perspective" or the "Hispanic perspective." They felt like freaks not being like the 90 percent majority of white students. At one point just before winter holiday break Carolyn said, "I have to transfer. It is just too hard to be a black student here." Two other African-American students announced that they had the same intention. The others were nodding their heads in agreement. Their feelings of alienation and despair, sense of isolation, and living in a hostile environment were different to me, for I had always felt a high degree of comfort at the college. Why not—almost everyone here was just like me!

When they presented their feelings of anguish, I was tempted to convince them of the glories of the college that they were overlooking, offer alternative ways of interpreting their experiences, or provide pragmatic solutions to the problems they had encountered. But I didn't; I just empathized with their despair and pain, and kept empathizing week after week. It was not easy as their pain seeped into me and their finding failure with the college that I so identified with and their intentions to transfer made me feel like a failure. However, in the midst of our shared pain, we connected more deeply—that is, formed more profound selfobject bonds. The students started to visit me individually in my office and started to feel more at home as students at the college. They also started to form deeper bonds with one another.

A corner turned. The reciprocal empathic group support along with the feeling of specialness that came with belonging to the group (which they named "the CC 11") began to transform their experience of the college into a positive one. They decided they did not want to transfer at least during their first year because they would miss our group meetings too much. The trust and connectedness grew, and by the end of their first year, there was a shift from "we need to get out of here" to "we need to make this a better place for students of color."

And they did. They, and subsequent students in the program, took on positions of leadership at the college. They soon became heads of the Black Student Union, the Hispanic Student Union, and even the general Student Council. They got themselves placed on important committees. When several challenging instances of racial prejudice occurred on campus, they gave nuanced and balanced responses, responses that made justifiable demands on the college and decreased rather than increased the sense of alienation.

All eleven of those students graduated in four years—their dropout rate was zero. Several have gone on to earn advanced degrees, some have become therapists, and at least one has become a rather wealthy business entrepreneur. The self-psychologically-based group experience proved so successful that several more groups were added. The dropout rate for minority students plummeted to 7 percent—a rate lower than the general dropout rate for the college. With the success in retaining students of color we have been able to triple the percentage of minority students and helped transform the college from something that looked a bit too much like a prep school for wealthy whites to a vibrant cosmopolitan institution of higher learning. The alienation and sense of being strange, while still present in students of color, is so much less intense that it is not uncommon for me to hear some say that they feel no sense of estrangement at all at the college. In a mere decade the entire atmosphere surrounding difference and otherness has changed.

I do not mean to make myself out to be a hero, but to present the above as what a layperson with an understanding of the theory and methods of self psychology can do to transform situations of difference from ones of alienating tensions to energizing, growth-enhancing engagements. With the aid of the self-psychological perspective, I was able to understand that the development of trusting self-object bonds was more crucial for the transformation of the problem rather than, for instance, enhancing academic skills or constructing sociopolitical agendas. The agendas for equity are, of course, crucial. Entrenched structures of privilege and discrimination need to be dealt with at the levels of power and policy. But at the micro level of existence—the lived experiential level of experience—it is empathy that has the power to transform individuals and communities.

In conclusion, I think that self psychology has a tremendous amount to say concerning the problem of difference. It gives us profound insights as to why the encounter with alterity is so threatening, why we need to engage with difference to grow, and how through empathy genuine engagement with the other is possible. With self psychology's profoundly novel understanding of human nature, the possibility opens up for a human future that does not resemble the past, a future in which alterity is welcomed, and where engagement with genuine difference generates both new arenas of personal self growth and the hope of a harmonious world order.

Chapter Nine

What do Humans Need to be Human?

Economic Society, Self Psychology,
and the Problem of Social Justice

MODERN ECONOMIC SOCIETY AND THE ACCEPTABLE COST OF DEVASTATED HUMANS

The essential feature of market capitalism is competition, for it is competition that drives prices to their lowest level, increases the value of goods and services, and stimulates the invention of ever new products. This economic system has been world transforming. According to economist Deirdre McCloskey, the per capita expenditure for humans had not increased from the beginning of recorded history until the modern era. However, it has increased for all humans a miraculous ten times in the past two hundred years, led by the West and its economic transformation of the globe (2010). That is, the standard of living for all classes has increased so markedly as to constitute a genuine miracle, something much more astonishing than the healing of a blind person now and then or making someone's leprosy suddenly disappear. So, we should all be jumping for joy and singing alleluias to our true savior, capitalist market economics.

But the shouts of joy do not come so easily, for our economic world has built into it the necessity of an indefinite subset of people who must fail and thereby suffer not only poverty but, in many ways, the loss of their humanity. In short, any competitive system must have losers—persons, classes, or countries that are beaten out in the Darwinian competition to determine the economically fittest. Unfortunately, not all begin from the same starting line, as some are given such unbelievably powerful headstarts through the luck of birth, inheritance, educational opportunities, etc., that in general they can not be caught by those who start later—by those who begin with less advantages. That is, the competition is never fair and so injustice is built into the very heart of the system. In short, the losers tend to be those already disadvantaged because they were born poor, female, non-Caucasian, or non-first world.

Hegel saw this problem at the beginning of the nineteenth century and proclaimed that economic civil society, due to the inequality of talents and other advantages, would always produce a "rabble" that could destabilize modern society unless the state addressed its primary needs for survival and some degree of affirmative recognition (1821). Karl Marx, of course, found the brutal competitiveness of the capitalist market economy to be so dehumanizing and destructive that he called for an alternative economics, one that was fully co-operative rather than competitive and that valued social relations and the dignity of each human being. As we now know in hindsight, such an economic system fails to be as productive as a competitive one and is one that unfortunately gives rise to political tyrannies. With the fall of the Berlin Wall and breakup of the Soviet Union, the triumph of capitalist economics seemed complete and globalization went into full swing. While a number of Islamists committed to the primacy of a religious life fought back with terrorist attacks, and the Chinese are trying to balance communist values with competitive capitalist ones, it seems that the tide has turned and the inevitability of a global capitalist market as the primary way in which human beings relate to one another and construct their values seems like a foregone conclusion.

But what about those systematic injustices? Why are they not causing grave hesitation or profound thinking as to how best to alleviate them? They are either denied or covered over by welfare systems which, at least in the United States, are accompanied with structures of shame and humiliation rather than a sorrow that such suffering is the necessary cost for a subset of people becoming well-off.

Discourses that deny the systematic injustices are famous and have become part of the system itself. One of the denials is to proclaim the possibility of social mobility for all by pointing to a few heroic cases in which someone who was underprivileged, like Obama, rose to greatness, fame, or wealth—ignoring the statistic that only a slim percentage of those born into poverty ever leave it. Another denial is the conservative one which claims every person has a fair chance in a free society, and, therefore, those who succeed deserve their wealth and those who fail do so out of their own shortcomings—usually portrayed as sloth, indolence, ignorance, and/or weakness of will—and thus deserve their suffering. Of course, there are liberal constituents in modern societies who understand the injustices of modern economic life and support the welfare efforts of governments, but often do so abstractly, without being empathically present to the suffering of those whose humanity has been decimated by the economics of competition. They often think that if the economic necessities of life are provided for the underprivileged, along with minor increases in structures that enhance mobility, that that is enough. Of course, the great institution for mobility is public education, and for almost every major city in the United States this institution is in shambles—underfunded, under-resourced, and unsuccessful in being a vehicle for transformation.

What can self psychology do to help with this problem, if anything? I think it has the conceptual tools to make several remarkable challenges to modern economic society. First, it can diagnose modern society as participating in a vertical split and therefore existing in contradiction to itself. Second, it can challenge the economic conceptualization of human beings to such an extent as to open up the possibility for a new paradigm of what it means to be human and a different grasp of what persons really need to feel human.

VERTICAL SPLITTING

Kohut speculated that societies, like persons, can be analyzed in self-psychological terms, because societies, like persons, have ideals, ambitions, and idiosyncratic strengths, and, like persons, they can suffer from fragmentations and inner contradictions (1985c). Insofar as modern liberal democracies proclaim as their highest values liberty and justice for all but in fact produce, not by chance but necessity, unfair economic advantages and disadvantages that doom an indefinite portion of their populations to unjust suffering, they are fragmented and in contradiction with themselves. Since participating in the willful and unfair destruction of human beings is shameful, we must find some way to deny what we are doing and hide from the shame. The primary way of dealing with this contradiction is to engage in vertical splitting—a kind of repressing of what our world is doing while remaining aware of it. Modern society's major conscious structure of subjectivity affirms the economic world as the great uplifter of human life—the splendid vehicle that has transformed human existence for the better, while the split-off part knows that in adopting a market economics, modern liberal democracies doom a subset of people to unjust suffering—usually those who have previously suffered forms of social/political discrimination. The various forms of denial previously mentioned are the fundamental defenses against this vertical split.

In psychological life, vertical splitting saves the psyche from being in a state of debilitating trauma, but always at a cost, including the dissipation of what Emerson calls "spirit" or what I am terming "the life of the soul." Integrated souls and societies—that is, souls and societies that have integrity— have a fullness of spirit for being present to experience and engaging life at its liveliest. Insofar as a society must engage in vertical splitting in order to conduct its patterns of life, its members lose the fullness of spirit and instead have a tendency to become mechanical, defensive, isolated, and/or driven. Hegel wrote that a person could not be fully spirited—fully whole—without being able to wholly affirm the wider social context of which he is a member (1821). Whenever a society participates in the unjust repression or negation of a subset of persons—be they identified as Jewish, Palestinian, poor, black, or female, its members will suffer an impoverishment of spirit. *When our society is inhuman to some, all lose some of their humanity.* That is, human beings have yet to realize the fullness of what it means to be human.

The major symbol of this vertical split in economic society is the fragmentation of the social and geographical landscape into pockets of wealth and ghettoes of poverty, making our lands as incoherent as a severely dissociated psyche. Because the dispossessed have no legitimate way of making a living and achieving dignity, they often turn to violence and participation in illegal activities, especially the drug trade, within the ghetto and beyond, causing the majority culture grave anxiety and endangering its sense of security and well-being. In response to the presence of illegality and violence, the majority society often performs massive defensive maneuvers by increasing its police forces and expanding its penal system at outrageous expense, thus squandering its valuable resources—resources that might be used instead to create a more just solution to the problems of injustice.

Thus, even the winners in the economic world must suffer from this splitting. For those in denial, there is always the anxiety of some dark irrational uprising happening to endanger their worlds and often bringing about a hideous obsession with guns and violence to keep themselves safe. For those who are clear-sighted and empathic enough to see the dire and unjust suffering which the modern economic world has created, it is difficult to sustain a robust sense of well-being regardless of the felicity of one's personal circumstances. We dislike seeing the homeless and the beggars, for they remind us that our well-being has been partially purchased at the cost of their well-being. Of course, one can be less sensitive, empathic, and understanding, but the loss of these virtues is akin to the loss of one's self.

In short, the concepts of self psychology are extremely helpful in diagnosing the vertical split in economic society and revealing the psychological and social costs of that split. But can it help with this problem?

ECONOMIC SUBJECTS VS. PERSONS WITH SELVES

The economic world is not just a set of methods for optimizing the production of goods and services, but a whole way of being in the world, a way of being that tells us what is real, what it means to be human, and what is most valuable in human life. Indeed, the economic world could not have come into existence if the metaphysical, ethical, and social concepts of what it means to be human from previous eras had continued to prevail. In the earlier religious age human life was conceived of as a great cosmic struggle between the forces of darkness/sin and light/salvation, and the battleground was each individual soul with God being the omnipresent audience and judge as to which side won. The well-lived life was one that overcame material/sexual desire and achieved a spiritual goodness that would be rewarded by bliss in an eternal afterlife. Given this conceptualization, persons in general did not concern themselves with economic betterment, for to do so would have been to tilt themselves toward the realm of the material/sinful.

What an enormous, perhaps traumatic, shift it must have been for human beings to declare that experiencing material pleasures in this mortal world is what is most important, and the achievement of socioeconomic success through engaging in market activity is the rightful goal of a well-lived life. Why and how this radical change in philosophical anthropology came about is a fascinating question, but one which we cannot treat here. What is most important is that a new kind of human being comes into being, namely, the economic subject. The rise and flourishing of the economic world is based on the conceptualization of the economic subject—for it is these subjects that are producers and consumers of economic goods—in a way that religious persons could not be, nor the political aristocrats of ancient Greece and Rome, nor the family members of a Confucian society intent on the ritual reproduction of social structures.

The essential categories through which economic subjects understand life and construct themselves are as follows. (1) Each person is an individual subject fundamentally concerned for his own self-interest. (2) Self-interest is primarily thought of in terms of what maximizes personal pleasure (hence, leaving the individual free to determine what gives pleasure). (3) The pursuit of pleasure takes place in a highly competitive world in which one can achieve varying degrees of success. (4) The key to competing successfully in the economic world is the development not only of talents and assets that one can trade but also the development of a rational economic point of view in which one can engage in accurate cost-benefit analyses and choose that course of action which will be most beneficial to the self-interests of the subject. (5) The rational individual who is best able to succeed in this competition is one who is willing to become abstract—willing to abstract himself from all other values and contexts and allow his decision to be based solely on an economic calculus. (6) In general, the ability to achieve pleasure is based upon having the means to acquire goods and services in the marketplace and, hence, as Jeremy Bentham stated, money is typically equated with happiness (1789, p. 7). For the economic subject, morality is understood as a set of limitations on his pursuit of happiness, or, as Kant said, a set of constraints. That is, ethics is not conceived of as a way to self-realization, as the Greek philosophers thought, but as a socially necessary obstacle limiting how one can pursue pleasure. In short, one ought not to achieve success through lying, cheating, murder, etc. (Riker, 2010).

This conceptualization arose from a number of strange bedfellows during the eighteenth and nineteenth centuries, not all of which can be mentioned here. First, the rise of democracies put an emphasis on the individual subject who has the freedom to engage in "life, liberty, and pursuit of happiness." Second, there were the great economic theorists, such as Adam Smith, who declared that individuals seeking their advantage would produce the greatest wealth for the whole of a nation. Third, and closely connected to economists, were the utilitarians—Hume, Bentham, and Mill—who proclaimed pleasure to be the fitting and final goal of human life and also asserted that each individual ought to have the most amount of freedom compatible with the freedom of all to seek what gives them pleasure. This notion was profoundly substantiated by Darwin's concept of natural selection in which each organism is wired to seek its own advantage in an intensely competitive world. Even the radical individualism of the existentialist thinkers, such as Nietzsche, could be incorporated into this picture. Although the existentialists eschewed pleasure as the end of existence, they did assert the radical primacy of the individual over the collective. And, finally, Freud's psychoanalysis fits perfectly with this conceptualization, as he sees each person as an individual organism that works according to a fundamental pleasure principle.

While there may be many modern persons who still define themselves in a partially religious way or who proclaim the primacy of family, the above conception of what it means to be an economic subject has become predominant and for the most part governs the patterns of lives of modern persons and institutions. It is in reference to this concept of human nature that we must further examine the misery of the dispossessed, for not only do they bear economic deprivation, but, worse, they suffer the loss of personal identity and dignity, for without an economic status, they become "nobodies," not only to the world but often also to themselves. In the previous religious age, everyone had an identity and dignity before God and everyone, regardless of wealth, had status within the realm of good and evil. But in the economic era where money and productivity in the marketplace reign, it is very difficult for the unemployed or underemployed to sustain a sense of human worth and dignity.

With poverty and non-recognition comes incredible psychological stress, so powerful that the rates of physical and psychological disease for the poor are astronomically higher than those of the well-off, as indicated by recent data showing that the wealthy in general live twelve years longer than the poor. In short, contemporary economic society produces, by necessity, a set of people who suffer not only economic deprivation but social non-recognition and psychological/physical vulnerabilities that are devastating. Economic society seems quite willing to produce such a sub-set of deprived persons as acceptable collateral damage—they are just part of the cost of having a robust economy.

The most important gift self psychology has for the modern world is to confront the conceptualization of human beings as economic subjects and reveal its profound inadequacies both for the losers and the winners by offering contemporary society a different way of conceptualizing what it means to be human, one that can compete with the economic/Darwinian/Freudian model because it is a naturalistic theory grounded in clinical observations and which, for many, illuminates personal experience better than any other theory. For self psychology, human beings are not atomized pleasure-optimizing organisms who ought to abstract themselves from sustaining matrixes of friends and family if better market opportunities arise; rather, they are beings who harbor within themselves a self, that psychological configuration of subjectivity which, when a person is actively realizing its cherished ideals and ambitions, they become zestfully alive and feel intensely real. Self psychology has also discerned that the self is the most vulnerable of all psychological configurations and needs immersion in matrixes of others willing to play self functions when such are needed. This is a very different view of human nature than that offered by economics.

While it is, of course, true that human beings need basic economic necessities—food, shelter, warmth, etc. to survive, the provisioning of these material necessities does not in the least address the problem of psychological survival. For self psychology, this means recognizing that a person is not just a set of drives or desires for pleasure but a being who has a self that needs both empathic concern and opportunities for realization, a realization that need not take the form of socioeconomic productivity. In the old religious language, every person was worthy because they had a soul; for self psychology every person is worthy because each has the possibility of a flourishing self. This is an enormous difference from human beings being seen as economic subjects who do not become worthy until they are productive or wealthy.

In short, self psychology has a great gift to bestow on contemporary culture, a gift which, if it is accepted and the conceptual foundations of the culture begin to shift, we might be able to overcome the horrendous societal splitting which enervates the culture and openly address the suffering that our economic society systematically imposes on some. But do the gifts of self psychology have any possibility of being received? In an economic/scientific world that seems to value only the objective and quantifiable, self psychology is going to be a hard sell (Summers, 2013). The keys to the sea change from an economic to a self-psychological culture occurring are first the realization of how profoundly the economic world undermines self struc-

ture, and, second, the coming into being of an alternative way to be human—
that is the coming into being of a set of persons for whom self psychology is
not simply a theory of human nature and a guide to clinical practice, but a
way of being in the world.

Economic society is not going to wither and die or be violently over-
thrown as Marx predicted, for it produces incredible goods and services
which most of us enjoy and would not want to forego, and, more important,
offers, for those who are privileged, more variegated possibilities for adventurous, lifelong ways to realize the self in its multiple professions, extraordinary leisure activities, and open personal relations than any previous society.
Yet, it fails the self wretchedly in two crucial ways: first, by undermining the
ability of parents and caretakers to provide necessary selfobject supplies to
children and, second, by significantly decreasing the abilities of adults to
receive and give selfobject supplies in the one great remaining social space—
the workplace.

There are a number of elements that have contributed to economic society's generating negative conditions for children's developing robust nuclear
selves. First, the mobility demanded by economic society has significantly
diminished the possibility of having an extended family (grandparents, aunts,
uncles, etc.) participate in the difficult chores of childrearing. Second, and
most important, it is quite common for both parents to have to work, in part
because two incomes are necessary to sustain material adequacy for many
households, but mainly because having a position within the socioeconomic
world is necessary for one to have an identity—to be "someone." It used to
be that "being a mother" was a recognized and honored identity, but since
there was neither a salary nor economic status attached to it, "being a mother" ceased to provide the all-important source of recognition that persons
need to flourish. (To be fair, the pressure to be more than a "homemaker"
does not come simply from economic society, but from individuals who
often feel that the workplace is a more exciting and fulfilling site to actualize
the self than is the home.) Third, when caretakers do come home from work,
they are often exhausted and tense from the hassles of the day and unable to
be the source of self-object supplies either for one another or for their children. It is not unusual for caretakers to soothe themselves with an alcoholic
elixir, making them less able to be fully responsive to the self-object needs of
their children, who all too often disappear into their rooms to electronically
network with other desperate children in other homes. In short, if intensive
care, empathy, and the presence of calm, strong caretakers are needed in
order for selves to come into existence, the contemporary Western household
is incredibly impoverished.

There is another way in which contemporary economic society fails to
sustain whatever self structure there might be in adults. Before the last quar-
ter of the twentieth century, it was not uncommon for friendships to develop

within the workplace; indeed, for many the workplace came to provide the supportive social connections that the village used to. Two prongs of modern society intersected to significantly diminish the availability of selfobject supplies for adults in the workplace. First, the increasing demand that all decisions about personnel be made on the strict basis of objectively certified competence and objective economic factors rather than "old-boy networks" or friendships significantly increased the insecurity and competitiveness with one's fellow workers. Second, when women entered the professional workforce in large numbers, there was a tendency of men to sexualize the workplace in an egregious and unjust way. This sexualization had to be eliminated, but with its elimination a certain amount of normal human warmth, care, and concern also left the workplace. In short, the workplace is less a realm of friendship and camaraderie than it used to be, and as such has become an institution less able to give empathic selfobject supplies to adults.

To be clear, I think that operating under a code of objectively determined merit is a great improvement over the "old-boy networks" and that the workplace needs to be as free of sexual tensions as possible. However, genuine empathy and care for one's fellow workers need not be diminished in any way in order for these values to be achieved. Indeed, empathy counters sexualization by being genuinely concerned for an other rather than being concerned about one's desire for that other, and, while it is certainly harder to criticize or fire someone with whom one is empathic, it is certainly possible and much more humane. There is no deep opposition between productive efficiency and empathy. Indeed, the more the workplace is experienced as a place of empathic selfobject responses, the more workers will be committed to making it flourish.

Finally, for those persons who have been systematically excluded from the benefits of economic society and thus unable to take advantage of the avenues for self-exploration, the economic world offers very little, if any, support for self structure.

As devastating as the above critique is for the development and sustenance of the self in contemporary economic society, the absence of coherent self structure is hardly noticed because the paradigm for being a successful human being is to be an autonomous, ego-dominated, rationally calculating player in the socioeconomic world. The ideal is "to be an individual" not "to have a self." The self and its needs for love, responsiveness, ideals, and meaningfulness often get in the way of being an ideal economic individual competitively establishing his greatness in the world, and so its needs are often stifled.

However, as we know, an injured or neglected self does not just disappear, but produces symptoms in a person—including a sense of drivenness, of never being deeply nourished by successes, of forever needing excitement and ever greater narcissistic markers to supplement the depleted self, and a tendency to be so needy and demanding in relationships that they are very difficult to sustain. In sum, while the contemporary economic world provides more avenues for self-actualization than any previous culture—at least for the economic winners, it undermines the possibility of persons developing and sustaining selves due to its radical destabilization of family life, its cold objective standards ruling the workplace, and its suppression of a large sub-set of people from its benefits. In the end, what destroys societies more than any other factor is unhappiness, and it will be this unhappiness that will in time produce the grounds for a shift from a purely economic world to one that balances its values with those of self psychology.

However, another element besides unhappiness is needed for this great shift to take place and that is the presence of a set of humans who do not define themselves primarily as economic subjects nor do they regressively attempt to restore past forms of life such as patriarchal religiousness, but who attempt to construct a way of being in the world in which they foster their selves and the selves of others, one in which they can compassionately use the profound understanding of human nature that has been developed in self psychology to help lessen the impetuses for revenge and domination that afflict every society. Such a way of being has just begun being explored in Lod, Israel, where Ranaan Kulka is establishing the Human Spirit Institute that combines psychoanalysis, self psychology, Buddhism, and the human-ities into a program that not only produces self psychologists but gives to the impoverished of Lod free clinical assistance.[1] However, the deeper goal of the institute at Lod is an attempt to generate a new kind of human being, ones who not only are capable of practicing self psychology in the clinic, but who also invest themselves with both the humanizing themes of self psychology and the quiet compassion wrought by Buddhist meditation, a practice which moves the self beyond its singular involvements in the world into wider concerns for all humanity and even all sentient creatures. There are, of course, many persons who have selves and act from the fullness of these selves and many who are Buddhists and act from a profound compassion for the suffering that life brings, but there are very few persons who have quieted the demands of their egos through meditative practices, developed core selves that can act from a human fullness rather than deficit, and attained a theoretical understanding of what it means to have a self and how selves are brought into being, how they can become devastated, and how they can dissolve their singularities into wider cosmic visions. I think that it does make a difference that persons not only have selves but a self-conscious theoretical awareness of what it means to have a self and the compassion to care about the extent to which others have this greatest of all gifts. Some know the theory and apply it in the clinic; but they lose track of their empa-thy and insight when they walk out the clinic's doors. Those trained in Eastern practices of meditation might be compassionate, but without an knowledge of the self, they might not be able to give to others what their selves most need. The vision of what it means to be human that is guiding the birth of Lod's very special program in the Human Spirit I believe is a unique and small glimmer of light, especially in this sector of the world so devastated by darkness. I believe that it can offer the world a novel way, a more profound way, for us to inhabit our humanity. If such a small center and its new persons seems insignificant, we must remember that often ontological changes in ways of being human start with just one person or a small group—think of Zoroaster, Socrates, Confucius, Siddhartha, Mohammad, Jesus, and Abraham and their small bands of followers who, in the fullness of time, transformed the world.

However, when self psychology merges with Buddhism a different kind of help needs to emerge rather than the old blanket of extending a hand to all who need it. To repeat what Emerson said: "do not tell me, as a good man did today, of my obligation to put all poor men in good situations. Are they *my* poor? I tell thee, foolish philanthropist, that I grudge the dollar, the dime I give to such men as do not belong to me and to whom I do not belong" (1841, p. 53). This statement, like those of self psychology concerning the self, stands opposed to Enlightenment totalizing kinds of moral injunctions— that we are humans who always must help all other humans in need. Insofar as we take this stance, we act from a kind of Kantian rationality, from a categorical imperative that has nothing to do with the singularity of our selves. As such, the deed can be done, but it will have none of the life-affirming zest which gifts given from the singularity of one's self have. For a while, I attended a church with a philosophically adroit pastor, but one who in the end proclaimed the moral duty for everyone to volunteer in the trenches where the poor can be met face-to-face—serving at the soup kitchen, hammering nails for Habitat for Humanity, working at shelters for the homeless, and so on. However, such activities may diminish one's ability to give to the world one's genuine gifts. The world needs more than full stomachs; it also needs art and music, literature and philosophy, architectural masterpieces and well-kept nature preserves, and, of course, psyches that are vitalized and whole. What both Nietzsche and self psychology call for in the place of self-negating sacrifice is the joyful presencing of oneself in being oneself, for such actions grant permission to others to be themselves, and, in the end, no better gift can be bestowed.

When the impoverished I help *belong* to me and I to them, then I proclaim a solidarity of worth with them and avoid the profound problem of engaging in a kind of giving that simultaneously humiliates, for it is experienced by the receiver as coming from someone occupying a superior, enviable place. When my self and its gifts are engaged with others who can receive them, then their reception is as much a gift to me as my overflowing is a gift to them. I can affirm them not as empty, needy beings, but as fellow travelers in this strange wilderness that we as humans must traverse. People who belong to me are those who can benefit from my singular gifts. Put me in the classroom, not the soup kitchen; my gift is to help minds learn how to think more deeply.

But this cannot be the whole story from self psychology, for this profound theory also tells us that if I wish to retain a psyche centered on my self, then I do, in fact, need to be empathically responsive to all and all the time. Empathy cannot take a moral holiday, for to be sustained, the self needs to dwell in an empathic milieu and this can happen only if a person is actively empathic with others. When we turn off our empathy, we lose track of our selves, quaver in our integrity, endanger our empathic surround, and hand our psyches over to our economically constructed egos. Being empathic with the homeless man asking me for a handout does not require that I give him my last dollar or any dollar, but it does require me to empathically respond to his plight. What I do more than offering him recognition and affirmation will depend on many circumstances, and, in the end, a dollar grudgingly given might be less helpful than a smile and a warm greeting. In short, there is a universal ethic in self psychology: empathically respond to all human beings, even those who would attack you and annihilate you, for if you do not, you will lose your soul.

In conclusion, what I have been advocating in this chapter is nothing less than a radical shift from an economic culture to a psychoanalytic one in which the discoveries about what we humans need to have fully vibrant and coherent souls from psychoanalytic self psychology form the dominant conceptual structure for how we think about ourselves and our lives. I have already spoken about the beginnings of this change in first becoming aware of the systematic injustices and other forms of dehumanizing oppression of the economic world, and how to confront them with care and empathy for all. Further, individuals, either singly or in small groups like those at Lod, can point toward a new way of being human by living out of their selves rather than economic pressures.

Obviously, there must also be radical changes in social practices, such as once again re-invigorating family life, insuring that childcare centers are staffed with persons who are empathic and who understand what the nascent selves of children need, and promoting selfobject connectedness in the workplace. Further, the transformation of society probably cannot come about without a massive number of persons engaging in psychoanalytic psychotherapy—hopefully guided by a self-psychological understanding of the psyche. Impossible? At the turn of the twentieth century, it was impossible to think of a country in which everyone was driving a car for there were not adequate roads and gas stations did not exist. Then, a sudden miracle occurred: gas stations popped up everywhere, roads got paved, and the world transformed. Need creates supply. If humans could see how much they need to recover themselves, then a like transformation of society can occur.[2]

I am not a starry-eyed radical, for I know that we contemporary humans can no more escape the economic construction of human existence than a fish can escape the water that surrounds it. However, we can do much in our own personal lives and how we live them to help this new way of being human to come into existence. In the end, what it comes down to is caring. I believe that Heidegger is right when he says that what we care about is what constitutes our worlds. By caring about one's self and the selves of others, we help bring into existence a self-psychological world. In so doing we become beacons of light pointing toward a new world, one in which the needs of persons striving to have a coherent, vital psychological existence is the commanding value and all are respected as deserving the right to have a self.

NOTES

1. An earlier version of this chapter was given in a session dedicated to the founding of the Human Spirit Institute at the 2014 meeting of the International Association for Psychoanalytic Self Psychology in Jerusalem.

2. I have written about these small revolutions in the last chapter of *Why It Is Good to Be Good* (2010).

Chapter Ten

Self Psychology and Historical Explanation

The Death of God and the Birth of Impressionism —
Forms and Transformations of Narcissism in the
Nineteenth Century

Since history concerns human actions, it must espouse a psychology for understanding why humans do what they do. The usual psychologies that have dominated historical explanation are, first, a political psychology of power in which humans seek to gain as much control over their circumstances and others as possible or do what they do because they are caught up in power/knowledge systems, and, second, an economic psychology in which humans are fundamentally motivated to secure the basic economic necessities for survival and the enhancement of material life. Self psychology has a very different understanding of what basically motivates humans. While it, of course, does not deny that humans are motivated by economic and power needs, in addition it finds that all humans, both individually and collectively, are, at the very nucleus of psychological life pressured by narcissistic demands to achieve a satisfactory relation to perfection and grandiosity.

Kohut, himself, proposed that self psychology could be a powerful vehicle for understanding historical peoples and events, because nations, like individuals, need to realize ideals and think of themselves as participating in greatness. In "On Courage" and "On Leadership" he offers an insightful—indeed, compelling—self-psychological account of why the German people fell under the spell of Hitler and Nazism (1985). What I want to do in this chapter is to extend this kind of self-psychological analysis not to a particular

139

nation but to the whole of European culture during the nineteenth century. I want to claim that what the historians call "the long nineteenth century," which began with the French Revolution in 1789 and ended with WWI in 1914, commenced with a double narcissistic trauma: the beheading of the most powerful king in Europe and the slow loss of religious life, culminating in what Nietzsche called the death of God (1882). Hence, the culture's ideals and grandiosity that had for centuries been organized around a connection to monarch and God, collapsed, an event that both freed these narcissistic energies for new creative outlets, but also carried the narcissistic rage and fragmentation that ensues with trauma. I believe it is possible to see the extraordinary creativity of the nineteenth century as stemming from the shift in ideals from those in which persons were subservient to God and king to those which championed democratic individuals creating their own lives, but also to see the devastatingly destructive nationalism, anti-Semitism, and colonialism as a derivative in part from the trauma.

Surprisingly, this notion that the fundamental task for both persons and cultures is to manage narcissistic pressures can be found in the first two historians of the West, Herodotus and Thucydides. Herodotus' monumental *Histories* (1972) is an account of the how the wheel of fortune endlessly revolves around failures to manage narcissistic pressures, by showing that great men and great cities tend to become hubristic—that is, overly grandiose. Their grandiosity then blinds them to important limiting structures of the realities they inhabit, causing them to make devastating errors of judgment that in turn brings nemesis upon them. Thucydides claims that the fundamental driving forces of history are "fear, honor, and self-interest"—two of which clearly have to do with narcissism (1996)! Likewise, in the first piece of literature in the west, *The Iliad,* we find heroes desperately competing to establish their singular greatness, for their identities rest entirely on the achievement of fame and honor. In it we see the primary problem with narcissism—its tendency to radically destabilize the social order as each hero becomes more concerned for his individual honor than the goals of the group. What Kohut adds to the above thinkers is an in-depth psychological understanding of why perfection and grandiosity are so essential to human beings, how they need to transform from infantile manifestations to mature ones, and how the self, which is the psychological vehicle that contains them, is extremely susceptible to traumatic disruptions.

If Kohut is right in saying that managing and transforming narcissistic pressures is crucial in order for persons to develop selves, mature, and become functioning members of a society, and it is also true that for most cultures during most of historical times, opportunities for self-actualization were minimal, then we ought to find all cultures offering their inhabitants general patterns for dealing with narcissistic stresses by telling them where to invest their idealizing needs and how to feel singularly great while still being part of a co-operative social order. I consider these cultural directives for how to organize and invest narcissistic energies to be so important that we find them in the highest values of any society. In order to understand the great shift in how narcissistic pressures were dealt with during the nineteenth century, we must first see how they were organized in the era that preceded this time, the religious era.

THE RELIGIOUS ERA

The thousand-year epoch which preceded the rise of modernity, the religious era, had an extraordinarily powerful and stable mechanism for dealing with the disturbing narcissistic pressures. It projected the perfection, grandiosity, and power that we associate with narcissism into a god-figure. This social projection was a cunning psychosocial move, for by connecting humans to a common ideal, it defused the dangerous tendencies for self-aggrandizement that makes community so difficult, gave life an authoritative meaning and purpose, and overcame the greatest narcissistic blow that humans must face, death.

Could it be that the universality of religion in human culture is an indication that it has been the most effective way for dealing with our basic narcissistic pressures? If we project our grandiosity and perfection into the fantasy of a god-figure who then cares for us, we re-enact at a more mature conceptual level what very young children do when they idealize their parents in order to rid themselves of the anxiety that arises when they are confronted with their helplessness. This self-psychological interpretation of religion seems far more likely than Freud's account of a father-murder and subsequent projection of the father into a godhead in *Totem and Taboo*.[1]

When modern states came into existence during the late Middle Ages, Renaissance, and early Modernity, the ideal of God ruling an organized universe became mirrored in the idea of a divinely sanctioned monarch ruling the state. As Ernst Kantorowitz shows, the monarch has two bodies—one that is mortal and subject to the law and the vicissitudes of the flesh and another which is immortal, contains the body politic, and has the capability of generating law that is, because of his position as the mirror of divinity on earth, immediately legitimate (1997). The king's mortal/immortal nature mirrors the Christian understanding of divinity in which God the father is immortal and the ground of law but becomes mortal and suffers in Christ.

In short, religious-era subjects found themselves in a profoundly coherent world in which God's rule over the universe is mirrored by the king's rule over the state. This kind of rule is supposed to be mirrored in each subject, whose fundamental task in life is to have the regal element in the soul overcome the fragmenting and rebellious urges that threaten to turn the soul away from the good. In this gloriously coherent worldview, the good soul mirrors the good state that in turn mirrors the good universe. This mirroring extended into the spaces of public life, for churches were located at the central foci of cities and towns, and their steeples rose higher than any other edifice, pointing toward the ultimate reality around which life must revolve. This mirroring of the metaphysical, political, physical, and psychological realms, combined with the understanding that the earth is at the center of the universe, humans are most important species on earth, and God's main concern is with the moral destiny of each human being, makes this worldview incredibly narcissistically gratifying. Each person had infinite individual worth in the eyes of God and each person desired to achieve moral perfection—a perfection that had mainly to do with the taming of the disruptive sexual drives and the narcissistic tendencies to pride and arrogance.

But when the absolute monarchs proved themselves too autocratic, irrational, and unfair to a rising middle class that was getting narcissistic gratification from successes in the socioeconomic realm, the organization of narcissistic energies around a divinely invested monarch was called into question. English and French kings were beheaded, the Napoleonic Wars spread democratic institutions throughout central Europe at the beginning of the nineteenth century, and the revolutions of 1848 turned the tide irrevocably away from monarchy to democracy. The dethroning of absolute monarchs completed itself at the end of WWI when the German Kaiser, Russian Czar, Ottoman Sultan, and Austro-Hungarian Emperor were all deposed.

At the same time that monarchs were being abolished, the belief in God and a trust in his divine representatives on earth was crumbling. The French Philosophes revealed the hypocrisies in Church doctrine and practice; Feuerbach convincingly showed that all concepts of God were psychological projections of what humans found to be most important in themselves; Hume and Kant proved that human knowledge has no access to a supernatural world hiding behind the world of sense; and Marx and Nietzsche exposed the oppressive and life-negating features of religious life. To these philosophic critiques must be added those of science: Copernicus disabused us of our narcissistic belief that our planet stands at the center of the universe and Darwin revealed that our origin is from nature, not divinity. On the basis of the rise of material concerns for the new middle class and these compelling critiques of the religious worldview, Nietzsche could announce the death of God, the death of a whole way of life organized around an authoritative set of values and beliefs that had been the great container for our narcissistic sense of perfection and sustained our narcissistic need for grandiosity and specialness for over a millennium. Freud was right in proclaiming that the killing of the king-father underlies society, but this event did not happen in prehistoric times but lies at the advent of late modernity. At the gateway to contemporary times lies both regicide and theodicide.

THE ASTONISHING NINETEENTH CENTURY

The nineteenth century is simply unparalleled in its artistic creativity, depth of philosophical thinking, life-transforming inventions, and breathtaking advances in political rights and freedoms. Even the Italian Renaissance and Athens' golden age have trouble rivaling what happened in Europe during this century. Here are a few lists, all drastically incomplete, all excluding geniuses in America. In music, think of Beethoven, Schubert, Schumann, Brahms, Mendelssohn, Gounod, Wagner, Verdi, Puccini, Tchaikovsky, Mahler, Grieg, Liszt, Chopin, and Schoenberg. In painting: Delacroix, Millet, Corot, Courbet, Turner, Constable, Monet, Manet, Cezanne, Van Gogh, Renoir, Gauguin, Pissarro, Matisse, and Toulouse-Lautrec. In literature: Dickens, Hardy, Wordsworth, Byron, Shelley, Flaubert, Balzac, Zola, Goethe, Rilke, Dostoevsky, Tolstoy, and Chekov. In philosophy there was Kant, Fichte, Feuerbach, Hegel, Kierkegaard, Nietzsche, Mill, Adam Smith, Marx, Schopenhauer, and Freud and in science we find such luminaries as Charles Darwin, Clerk Maxwell, Louis Pasteur, Helmholtz, and the young Einstein.

In the beginning of the century there was slavery and serfdom, and in many places women were virtual or actual property, but by its end slavery and serfdom had been abolished and women were poised to gain equal civil rights with men. At the beginning of the century, most Europeans were illiterate; by its end the great majority could read and write. When the century began, the fastest way to travel was the same as it had been since the beginning of history: by horse or sail; by the end of the long century people were taking trains and steamships, driving automobiles, and flying in airplanes. Communication at the beginning of the century was accomplished through hand-delivered mails; by its end there were telegraphs and telephones. Autocracies were the rule at the beginning of the century; democracies reigned at its end. Urban centers were dark, cold, and unsanitary at the beginning of the century; lit by electric lights, sanitized with plumbing, heated by great power plants, and sprouting skyscrapers at its end. There were bloodletting barbers and other medical incompetents providing health care at the beginning of the century and an organized medical profession working scientifically by its end.

The above are just the mere highlights of what happened during this incredible century of progress and creativity. However, the same Europeans who were being so creative and liberating also spent the century insensitively colonizing the rest of the world, destabilizing local populations and destroying ages-long traditions. They also become so aggressively nationalist, anti-Semitic, and grandiosely militaristic that the century culminates in the most devastating wars of all time and the horrific death camps of the twentieth century.

NARCISSISM AND THE NINETEENTH CENTURY

The narcissistic pressures of life that had been previously stored in the unlimited power of the monarch, directed toward satisfying the soul's ideals for salvation, and projected into a godhead—all that surplus of life that built great palaces for kings and cathedrals for God—now poured into the common life of the people and fueled the incredible creative burst in the arts, science, philosophy, inventions that transformed material life, medicine, architecture, commerce, and just about every other facet of modern life. The narcissistic idealization that had gone into esteeming the greatness of God and divinely sanctioned monarchs was re-invested in new democratic secular selves. These selves then poured their re-integrated narcissistic energies into their finite embodied lives, lives redefined away from a search for salvation toward an adventurous engagement in the socioeconomic world. God the creator was replaced by man the creator; the monarch's absolute authority was absorbed by each individual's proclamation that he was the absolute authority over his own life. This led to an outburst of creative energy in which originality in all forms of art shattered conventions, inventions in the realm of technology utterly transformed life, and the demand for the recognition of individual worth did away with slavery, gave women rights they had never had before, and opened up ever-expanding forms of political freedom.

To witness just one thread of what happened when this excess of life burst into Europe, let us take an overview of painting. In classical seventeenth- to eighteenth-century art, there is typically a spatial grid that is used to reveal the depth of space. This grid is a set of invisible lines that converge at a point of infinite distance, a metaphor that reveals an invisible infinite world lying behind and sustaining the visible world. The brushstrokes that brought the painting into being are hidden and the painting takes on the glow of a finished perfection. Geometry reigns, forms are stable, and movement—the imperfection of the world—is captured in an eternal moment in which the universal truth underlying the event is revealed. Think of the great paintings of Poussin, Claude de Lorrain, Jacques-Louis David, and Ingres.

And then the nineteenth century comes and everything changes. Brushstrokes erupt onto the canvas and the creative process of the painting becomes visible. The stable geometry collapses and space rushes to the surface of the canvas. Movement, flux, process, change, light, and the presencing of here/now particular places and people are portrayed as real, not an eternal perfection lying within or behind the world or expressed in mythological or religious depictions. Delacroix's ferocious tigers and dark sultans reveal to us a world in which force, emotion, the irrational, and turmoil replace geometry and order.

With the impressionists natural light rather than divine light makes every aspect of life—landscape, boating parties, maidens on terraces, railway stations, water lilies drifting on a pond, bowls of fruit—become so vivaciously present that we, too, commit to living in this world with all of its glorious sensuousness and aesthetic delight rather than preparing for a supposed afterlife. Unfinished or unpolished canvases reveal an openness to life, a nonclosure that reveals life as possibility rather than the completeness of a divinely ordered universe or a morally ordered soul. The purpose of life is not to perfect one's soul, come closer to the divine, or prepare for eternal life—it is simply to enjoy the sensuous beauties of this mortal life to its fullest. Manet's Olympia is not an example of eternal beauty like Titian's nudes, but a lady of the night unabashedly revealing earthly sexual desire. Cezanne's bathers reveal both our natural evolutionary past as slithery sea creatures and the openness of our future in unformed horizons.

But the unleashed excess of life would not stop with impressionism. It pushed against ordinary forms that sought to contain it and shattered them. Shapes and colors broke free from their usual boundaries and transformed into everything from Van Gogh's contorted portraits and geometrically skewed still-lives to Toulouse Lautrec's green faces revealing more life than we might want to admit. The cubists further deconstructed ordinary shapes to reveal the multiplicity underlying coherence, while Dali and Miro revealed the excesses of life flowing out of the unconscious container. Finally with abstract expressionism and Rothko's fields of color, art reveals its fundamental truth: that art is about art and only about art—it has no moral or metaphysical message to convey. Its purpose is not to express truth or even to be beautiful. It, like everything else, exists for its own narcissistic sake, and not in the service of any further kind of meaning. The artist is now god and his one aim is to exhibit originary brilliance.

However, while the gains in individual freedom, creativity, and productivity that arose from this shift in the organization of narcissistic energies were immense, so were the costs, for the loss of God and king constituted a trauma—perhaps the greatest non-war trauma that any civilization has experienced. When trauma occurs, we can expect to find not just creative readjustments to life, but also desperation about the ground of meaning, intense fragmentation, inner emptiness, narcissistic rage, and desperate attempts to restore an objective greatness and perfection in strange substitutions.

TRAUMA, SUBSTITUTIONS, AND NARCISSISTIC RAGE

If I am right that nineteenth-century Europe suffered a widespread narcissistic trauma with the deaths of God and king, then we can anticipate that we will find some strange substitutions for the connection to a godhead and a dark side—ways of expressing narcissistic rage. For instance, I think that the narcissistic gratification that came from being connected to God was to some extent displaced onto the startling new practice of vacationing at the beach, for the sea gives the feeling of an infinite expansive greatness. Brighton became the place to be in England, while the French not only flocked to the sea but were accompanied by their painters. Boudin, Manet, Monet, and others brilliantly captured the infinite expansiveness, grandeur, and lure of the beach with their sunny palettes and waves of brushstrokes.

I think that the nineteenth century's dramatic invention of new competitive sports or organization into leagues of old ones also is the result of this shift in narcissism. Tennis, soccer, cricket, rugby, football, baseball, basketball, and hockey are all invented in the century. The amount of public money that went (and still goes) into building stadiums rivals the resources once poured into churches, and sporting events have become almost as important part of national life as the church was previously. The intense interest with which sports are watched and followed reveals a significant amount of psychological over-determination. Sports are a place in which a number of people can win glory and an even greater number have the chance of identifying with a winning individual or team as a way of generating narcissistic grandiosity. If I can no longer be great because I matter to God, I can at least be great in my connection to the Yankees or Michael Jordan. Sports also present a medium by which anger and rage can be discharged by players and vicariously enjoyed by spectators without massive social mayhem.

However, narcissistic rage also took sinister forms of aggression in the nineteenth century. While the century saw the elimination of slavery and relaxation of anti-Semitic laws in the mid-century, by the end of the century anti-Semitism was present not just as a social fact but had become a powerful political platform. It was fueled by the rise of an insidious scientific racism—an attempt by narcissistically injured white Europeans to restore their sense of superiority by proving that they were the most advanced race and finding a scapegoat for problems in the supposedly "lower" races on which to focus their rage. This combination of rage and a restoration of grandiosity through racial superiority resulted, as we all know, in one of the most horrific events in human history, the Holocaust. I am not claiming that the narcissistic rage released from the trauma of the loss of king and God was the sole or most powerful cause of the Holocaust, for like all historical events, a dense multiplicity of factors are involved. However, I do want to say that narcissistic vulnerability, especially that surrounding grandiosity and self-esteem, seems to be an important psychological factor that needs to be taken into account.

Another way in which narcissistic rage expressed itself was in Europe's attempt to colonize the world, almost always with such insensitivity that local peoples were disrupted, killed, and/or had their ages-long traditions destroyed (Kiernan, 1969). While some of the motivation behind colonization was to acquire favored markets for goods and sources for raw materials, a great deal must be accounted for by the want to assert the "omnipotence" of

Europe over the rest of the world. It is as though Europeans were saying "We have lost our connection to a divine omnipotence, but we can still be connected to omnipotence by colonizing the world." Of course, Europe didn't colonize the world, individual states did, and did so out of a venomous nationalism in which each state sought to achieve superiority over the other states. "I am better than you because I have more colonies than you" was a common mantra. This narcissistic nationalism in which each nation sought to make itself superior to all other European nations also resulted in a tremendous arms race—especially a naval race between Germany and England—that was probably the most important factor for the outbreak of WWI. It is not hard to see that the rise of an insane nationalism and the attempts to dominate the rest of the world in colonialism as desperate measures to restore a connection to narcissistic grandiosity while at the same time releasing narcissistic rage.

World War I was, of course, Europe's great act of suicidal self-destruction. This extraordinary continent that invented modern science, produced the first modern forms of democracy, transformed the world with technology, and generated the most sustained century of artistic and philosophic creativity that the world has ever known ended its long century with an act of utter self-devastation. The insane rage with which WWI is conducted, its senseless destructiveness, its stalemated fronts of unresolved conflict, and its refusal to submit to any rational conclusion all point to this being the dénouement of the narcissistic wounding that occurred a century earlier. Unlike forms of ordinary aggression and anger which want to destroy obstacles that impede us and then are done, narcissistic rage is an unrelenting revengeful destructiveness that seeks total annihilation and won't stop until self structure is restored. The consequences of the rage of WWI were compounded in the sadistic, revengeful Treaty of Versailles, which in turn helped lead to the rise of Nazism and Fascism, enraged movements meant to restore grandiosity in the defeated countries. The country that, of course, suffered the most humiliation was Germany "whose thirst for revenge after the defeat of 1918 came close to destroying all of Western civilization" (Kohut, 1985b, p. 125). WWII and the unthinkably horrible death camps seemed to be the final expressions of the rage that has haunted modern European civilization since the twin deaths of God and king.

HAS THERE BEEN A SUCCESSFUL TRANSFORMATION OF NARCISSISM SINCE WWII?

It is now over half a century since WWII and we need to inquire as to whether Western society been able to find more stable ways to deal with narcissistic pressures than those which led to the disasters at the culmination of the nineteenth century. It would seem that the democratic practices of contemporary Western society in which individuals have authority over their lives, the freedom to choose their own ideals, and the opportunities to ambitiously achieve those ideals in a myriad of economic and recreational opportunities would be the ideal society for transforming narcissistic pressures into the most satisfying and secure structure—that of singular selves.

However, a number of disturbing symptoms tell us that Western society's (now represented as America) new way of dealing with narcissism has not been fully successful: the extraordinary amount of cheating that is happening at the individual, social, economic, and political sectors reveals that a significant portion of the populace feel that they are above the law and ethics (Callahan, 2004; Riker, 2010). The amount of drugging and overindulgence in alcohol and food reveal a huge portion the population desperate to soothe the inner emptiness of not having a self. It is difficult to go through a day without encountering someone expressing infantile entitlement—people demanding to go as fast as they want on the road, cutting into lines, demanding more recognition than they deserve, etc. Also the tremendous number of failed marriages (infantile narcissists have trouble living together), a strong regressive movement to re-instate the old religious way of being human, and our thinkers/poets proclaiming that life has no meaning all point toward the failure of the society to generate persons with mature selves who have integrated solid ideals and realistic ways to achieve recognition. So, we need to ask why the narcissistic wounding which occurred with the deaths of God and king hasn't been healed with a fresh set of cultural meanings that revolve around the values of becoming a democratic, autonomous human being competing in the marketplace for recognition and wondrous services and goods. I want to say that there are several crucial features of modern life that prevent the establishment of an adequate set of practices for dealing with narcissistic pressures.

First, values in the contemporary world seem incredibly fragile. When the king's law and God's will disappeared, questions of legitimacy arose and with them a malignant suspiciousness about any structure of meaning that claims to be authoritative, a suspiciousness that still haunts and undermines our contemporary life. Even values we create for ourselves fall under this suspiciousness and doubt—it is hard to find a person fully secure in whether what they have chosen for themselves is right.

Second, as we saw in the last chapter, the contemporary economic world is constructed in such a way as to undermine the very self structure individuals need to sustain themselves. The crucial condition for the formation of self structure out of infantile narcissistic energies is the presence of caring, empathic adults who allow themselves to be idealized, who empathically mirror children at every turn, and who gently and age-appropriately frustrate their children so that they can develop. As Kohut noted, the modern house is too empty, too void of meaningful interactions to affirm the nascent self and help it develop a realistic sense of self-esteem (1977). Why are the households empty? Because Mom and Dad are in the workplace desperately trying to establish their greatness in a brutally competitive economic world in which their self-esteem is in danger and challenged almost every day.

Not only have homes become increasingly devoid of the psychological nurturance so necessary for the development of selves, but the workplace, which has become the dominant site in which we live out our lives, has been ridding itself of all human connectivity, aside from that required to conduct professional activities. Empathy, care, and warmth are either optional or deeply discouraged so that justice, efficiency, and productivity can reign.

Lying behind both of these social deficits is a misguided concept of what it means to be a self—namely a rugged independent individual who seeks to maximize personal pleasures by competitively engaging in market activities. It is this notion of individuality that utterly dismisses the essential need for persons to be connected at the very core of their beings to others that lies behind the impoverished selfobject structures that haunt the home and workplace. Insofar as the usual instantiation of ideal individuality is equated with being a successful competitor in the capitalist market and reaping the pleasures which such success brings obscures the self's needs to have its singular nuclear program actualized, regardless of how it relates to market success and pleasure.

So, in late modernity everyone gets to be a little god and rule his own kingdom, but those kingdoms are increasingly lonely and riddled with anxiety. When we are not sure what life means beyond establishing our own narcissistic greatness, then we tend to get compulsively fixated on the markers of greatness—material wealth, sexual desirability, and socioeconomic status—a fixation that has driven us to a frenzy of competitiveness in which the few big winners get to horde most of the wealth, the world is ravaged for resources and polluted with garbage, and everyone seems to be taking some chemical fix to ameliorate the inner emptiness.

In sum, modernity has gotten rid of our relation to God and monarch as the primary way to organize our narcissistic needs to feel great and relate to perfection but it has also undermined the crucial conditions necessary for the transformation of infantile narcissism into coherent self structure. We are then left with too much untransformed narcissism. Given the vise-like grip the economic worldview has on contemporary society and the devastations to self development and seemingly unstoppable ravages of the environment brought about by this Weltanschauung, one would expect me to draw a conclusion of despair. But I remain in a state of hesitant hope, for I think that with self psychology's new understanding of the dynamics of narcissism, we have the ground for constructing social practices that will, in time, facilitate the general development and sustenance of persons with mature self structure, the one reality-based and fully satisfying organization of the narcissistic pressures that afflict human beings.

Although the transformation from economic to psychological society might seem improbable, I note that two of the most important social conditions for a psychologically robust society to come into existence are already in place. First, the larger world has exploded into countless small worlds in which fabulous numbers of persons have a chance to be local heroes and realize their idiosyncratic selves. These narcissistically satisfying worlds can be as small as a philosophy department at a small liberal arts college or the dancing crowd at Chicago's Willowbrook Ballroom. Second, the high value we place on romantic love is firmly established, if not often achieved. Romantic love and the nuclear family based upon it have had a great deal of difficulty replacing the clan, church, and state as the fundamental providers of selfobject needs, but it has within it the possibility of being the most adequate source of personal recognition, empathic mirroring, and a feeling of specialness ever invented. However, romantic love, while the most exhilarating form of human relationality, is also the most fragile and difficult to sustain over time. It typically takes two people with healthy, vital selves to foster it and such people are not easily come by in the contemporary world. In order for persons with robust selves to come into being, many of our social practices need to change, and these will change once we begin thinking with more adequate philosophical and psychological concepts about what it means to be human and live a worthy human life.

In sum, psychoanalysis has uncovered that we have primary narcissistic needs and pressures to orient our lives toward some forms of greatness and perfection. Our narcissism makes us the unique species that we are, striving for perfections and greatness beyond mere survival and reproduction. It has also made us the species that has been the most trouble to itself. Since we now understand much more profoundly what this narcissism is, we can, I hope, abandon our insidious and destructive ways of achieving superiority and generate social environments that truly foster the development and sustenance of persons with strong vital selves who care deeply about others and who do not have to fill up an insatiable inner emptiness with endless consumer goods, the production and disposal of which has had such devastating effects on the environment. Indeed, if we cannot move from the concept of the individual that undergirds economic society to the concept of self understood by self psychology, I fear for our planet and for the human community which dwells therein.

NOTES

1. I do not mean this analysis of how humans use religious concepts to organize narcissistic pressures to imply any metaphysical conclusions concerning the actual existence or non-exis-

tence of God. This is a book about the needs and dynamics of our psyches, not a careful metaphysical treatise about the nature of noumenal existence.

Conclusion

What I hope to have shown in this book is the importance and revolutionary significance of psychoanalytic self psychology. I believe that it constitutes an original human ontology—a new possibility for thinking about ourselves and what human life is all about. As such, it stands in strong opposition to the dominant, hegemonic ontology that proclaims the primacy of the rational ego and its ability to gain control over both the internal workings of the psyche and external circumstances. This regnant ontology, invented in ancient Greece and permutated through various forms including that of the scientist and economic subject, has transformed humanity and the earth, both for better and worse. We now have modern medicine and fabulous protection from the elements, a more moral world due to the presence of rational principles, more responsible and responsive forms of government, and delights of material life unimaginable to our forebears. However, with these great improvements have come extreme anxiety about attaining success in the socioeconomic world, overpopulation, ecological devastations, and a kind of nihilism in which we wonder whether we are just thrown up by chance events, doomed in the end to be nothing but food for worms.

Further, in its current instantiation in economic subjects, the old ontology unconsciously pushes us toward an unhealthy need for self-sufficiency and independence, causing dire trouble for the intimacies and friendships so crucial in sustaining the self. It also has us focus on pleasures, especially those that we can purchase in the market, and labor that is evaluated primarily on its ability to provide resources through which to purchase the pleasures. As such, it is easy for persons to fall into mechanical lifeless labor for an abstract end (money) and endless pleasure-filled diversions.

In addition, the rational soul tends to be arid, emotionally impoverished, and only thinly connected to others and environments. It attempts to solve ethical problems by reference to moral laws or general principles, rather than engaging face-to-face with persons, especially those who are other. Last, what psychoanalysis has discovered is how the rational ego might, itself, be repressive of the spontaneous, the erotic, and the irrational—that is, repressive of the particular, singular self. In short, this paradigm for how to be human is not the kind of soul capable of the fullest life, although it surely is the kind of soul capable of the most power and control. It is certainly the kind of soul that seems to be most prevalent in today's economic world.

To be fair, the development of the powers of the rational ego has been crucial, probably necessary, for the possibility of genuine selves to emerge. Without a highly developed ego for negotiating the precarious situations humans encounter in their natural and social environments, a form of life in which persons' selves could achieve a fullness of realization in work, recreation, and love could not have come into existence. Replacing the ego with the self as the core of psychological existence does not mean eliminating the ego, for this would be disastrous. It means de-centering the ego by placing it in a profound alliance with the self in which it attunes to the self's values.

The first great attempt to assert the primacy of the self was that of existentialism. These profound thinkers proclaimed the importance of the singular passionate individual, doubted the ability of reason to know truths or express the truth of the self, and negated the authority of religious institutions and generalized moral codes to direct human lives. They said that insofar as humans negate their particularity in order to become rational, moral, or religious beings, they lose the liveliness of life as they squeeze their robust, creative individualities into generalized templates. Although many have been greatly enlivened by this expansive philosophy, the individuality espoused in it demands loneliness and alienation from others, a retreat out of social life to live on the austere mountaintop of Zarathustra. Life is, in Kierkegaard's words, Either/Or. Either we can be rational or passionate, individual or social.

Self psychology, then, is an astonishingly new way of thinking about how to inhabit our humanity. It is an ontology in which the narcissistic self, if it matures, is the basis for living as both a passionate singularity and a caring ethical person. That is, self psychology offers a way to think about human life that offers genuine depth and meaning to human existence by profoundly validating the particularity of our selves, while at the same time revealing how selves can be fully developed only if one becomes an ethical human being living in a matrix of caring others. It not only re-invigorates our singular selves but also re-invigorates what has been dying since the mid-nineteenth century: ethical life.

With self psychology we can return to the ancient Greek theorem that the genuinely happy individual is also the virtuous person who cares for others. However, it is not a life based on the achievement of rationality, but on the vibrant presence of an internal, largely unconscious self, erotically choosing activities, friendships, and adventures that realize its deep values, while empathically attending to the self needs of others. It proclaims that humans have a core self on which to base agency and from which to resist the pressures of the massive socio-discursive contexts which dominate so much of modern life.

As such, psychoanalytic self psychology is a beacon of hope within contemporary ways of seeing the world, the most important of which cannot locate personal sources of creativity or uniqueness. The post-structuralists tend to find that we are mere pawns within the hegemonic power systems. They hold that the values of unique creativity and self-assertion are part of the old humanistic theory that cannot be sustained in the face of what we have learned about the invasive power of social discourse and disciplinary mechanisms in the production of persons. Likewise, scientific psychologists also cannot locate a source of spontaneous, free agency, as they find all psychological activity to be determined by chemico/electrical events in the brain or patterns of reinforcement.

While Freud thought his psychoanalysis was also locating new structures of psychological determinism, what his psychoanalytic work was meant to do was to free persons from unconscious constrictions so that they could more freely choose how to love and work. Working within the psychoanalytic tradition, Kohut discovered an unconscious self, the activation and expression of which gives us agency, freedom, and a deep source of meaningfulness. What is so different about this erotic self that can grant focus, coherence, and vitality to the whole of psychic life is that it is not a metaphysical entity that is granted at birth, but the precipitate of a tenuous developmental process that requires the nurturance, empathy, and robust presence of others. That is, the self is the most vulnerable of psychological structures and is constantly in need of empathic mirroring, shoring up, triumphs, affirmation, challenges, and opportunities for activation. It is this fusion of fragility with vitality, neediness with autonomy, and empathy with self-assertion that makes self psychology so philosophically and psychologically rich and compelling.

In the end, I hope I have shown how living erotically—full of passion for life and whatever moves one's core self—is the best way to live a human life, not only because it is the most individually fulfilling way to live but also because it leads to an empathic caring for others, a caring which to me is the essence of being an ethical person. It is that way of constructing the human psyche that allows the soul to fill with the most life.

It is now time for the life-transforming therapeutic concepts and empathic practices introduced by self psychology to enter the wider culture and give it their great gifts. If this book has taken a small step toward the transformation of an economic world into a self-psychological one, then it will have established its worth.

Is the self-centered soul then the final answer to the meaning of human life? Hardly. It is a psychology, not a metaphysics. As such, profound questions are left unexplored. Might there be something immortal about the soul, as so many great thinkers have held? Might there really be a divine force that resists conceptualization but which is a real presence in human existence? Might there be, as Jung held, a transpersonal realm of archetypes or, as Plato held, a world of forms that can fill the soul with a depth of meaningfulness? Might the mystics have experienced something extra-psychological, profoundly real and compelling? I address none of these questions and all of them are interesting. In the end human life and the universe remain wondrously mysterious. However, what I hope to have shown is that we do not need answers to these great questions to know how to live genuinely satisfying and ethically enriched human lives.

Bibliography

Arendt, H. (1968). *Eichmann in Jerusalem: A Report on the Banality of Evil:* New York: Viking Press.

_____. (2003). *Responsibility and Judgment.* New York: Schocken Books.

Aristotle. (1962). *Nicomachean Ethics.* Tr. M. Ostwald. New York: Bobbs-Merrill.

Beebe, B. & Lachmann, F. (2014). *The Origins of Attachment: Infant Research and Adult Treatment.* New York: Routledge.

Benjamin, J. (1988). *The Bonds of Love.* New York: Pantheon.

Bentham, J. (1789). *The Principles of Morals and Legislation.* New York: Haffner (1948).

Berman, M. (2006). *Dark Ages America.* New York: Norton.

Bernstein, H. E. (1990). *Being Human: The Art of Feeling Alive.* New York: Gardner Press.

Bollas, C. (2011). *The Christopher Bollas Reader.* New York: Routledge.

Brandchaft, B. (2007). "Systems of Pathological Accommodation and Change in Analysis." *Psychoanalytic Psychology,* 24, pp. 667-687.

Bromberg, P. (1998). *Standing in the Spaces.* Hinsdale, NJ: The Analytic Press.

Buber, M. (1923). *I and Thou.* New York: Charles Schribner's Sons (1970).

Callahan, D. (2004). *The Cheating Culture: Why More Americans Are Doing Wrong to Get Ahead.* New York: Harcourt, Inc.

Dewey, J. (1981). *The Philosophy of John Dewey.* Ed. J. McDermott. Chicago: University of Chicago Press.

Eigen, M. (1998). *The Psychoanalytic Mystic.* London: Free Association Books.

_____. (1999). *Toxic Nourishment.* London: Karnac Books.

Emerson, R. (1836). *Nature.* In *Nature, Addresses, and Lectures* (pp. 9-80). Cambridge, MA: The Riverside Press (1883).

_____. (1841). "Self-Reliance." In *Essays: First Series* (pp. 45-87). New York: Houghton, Mifflin, and Company (1883).

_____. (1841a). "Circles." In *Essays: First Series* (pp. 279-300). New York: Houghton, Mifflin, and Company (1883).

Erikson, E. (1980). *Identity and the Life Cycle.* New York: W. W. Norton.

Fenichel, O. (1951). "On the psychology of boredom." In D. Rapaport (Ed.), *Organization and Pathology of Thought,* 4th ed. (pp 349-372). New York: Columbia University Press.

Foucault, M. (1978). *Discipline and Punish: The Birth of the Prison.* Trs. A. Sheridan. New York: Vintage Books (1979).

Freud, S. (1953-1974). *Standard Edition of the Collected Works,* trs. & ed. James Strachey, et. al., 24 vols. London: Hogarth Press. Hereafter: SE.

_____. (1914). "On Narcissism: An Introduction." SE 14. pp. 73-102.

_____. (1915). "The Unconscious." SE 14: pp. 159-215.

_____. (1916-17). *Introductory Lectures on Psycho-analysis.* SE 15-16.

_____. (1919). *Beyond the Pleasure Principle.* SE 18: pp. 7-64.

_____. (1923). *The Ego and the Id.* SE 19: pp. 1-66.

_____. (1925). "The Resistances to Psychoanalysis." SE 19: pp. 213-222.

_____. (1930). *Civilization and Its Discontents.* SE 21: pp. 59-145.

Gass, M., Gillis, H. L., & Russell, K. (2012). *Adventure Therapy: Theory, Research, and Practice.* New York: Routledge.

Gewirth, A. (1978). *Reason and Morality.* Chicago: University of Chicago Press.

Goldberg, A. (1999). *Being of Two Minds.* Lanham, MD: The Analytic Press.

_____. (2007). *Moral Stealth.* Chicago: University of Chicago Press.

Grünbaum, A. (1984). *The Foundations of Psychoanalysis: A Philosophical Critique.* Berkeley, CA: University of California Press.

Hare, R. (1963). *Freedom and Reason.* Oxford: Oxford University Press.

Hegel, G. (1807). *Phenomenology of the Spirit.* Tr. A. Miller. Oxford: Oxford University Press (1977).

_____. (1821). *Elements in the Philosophy of Right.* Tr. H. Nisbet. Cambridge: Cambridge University Press (1991).

Heidegger, M. (1949). "The Question Concerning Technology" in D. Krell (Ed.), *Martin Heidegger: Basic Writings* (pp. 307-342). New York: Harper & Row (1993).

_____. (1927). *Being and Time.* Trs. J. Stambaugh. Albany, NY: SUNY Press (1996).

Hempel, C. (1965). "Problems and Changes in the Empiricist Criterion of Meaning." In Eds. E. Nagel & R. Brandt, *Meaning and Knowledge: Systematic Readings in Epistemology* (pp. 17-28). New York: Harcourt, Brace, and World.

Herodotus. (1972). *The Histories.* Tr. A. de Selincourt. New York: Penguin.

Hesiod. (1953). *Theogony.* Tr. N. Brown. Upper Saddle River, NJ: Prentice-Hall.

Hume, D. (1740). *A Treatise on Human Nature.* Oxford: Oxford University Press (1973).

James, W. (2000). "The One and the Many." In G. Gunn (Ed.), *Pragmatism and Other Writings* (pp. 58-73). New York: Penguin Books.

Johnson, A. (2002). "In the Gaze of the Other." *Free Association,* 9: 237-249.

Kant, I. (1787). *Critique of Pure Reason.* Tr. N. Smith. New York: St. Martin's Press (1965).

_____. (1797). *Foundations of the Metaphysics of Morals.* Tr. L. Beck. New York: Bobbs-Merrill (1959).

Kantorowicz, E. (1997). *The King's Two Bodies: A Study in Mediaeval Political Theology.* Princeton, NJ: Princeton University Press.

Kierkegaard, S. (1846). *Concluding Unscientific Postscript.* Trs. & eds. H. & E. Hong. Princeton, NJ: Princeton University Press (1992).

_____. (1849). *The Sickness Unto Death.* Trs. A. Hannay. New York: Penguin (1989).

Kiernan, V. (1969). *The Lords of Human Kind.* Chicago: University of Chicago Press.

Kohut, H. (1959). "Introspection, Empathy, and Psychoanalysis: An Examination of the Relationship between Mode of Observation and Theory." In P. Ornstein (Ed.), *The Search for the Self,* Vol. 1 (pp. 427-60). NY: International Universities Press (1978).

_____. (1966). "Forms and Transformations of Narcissism." In A. Morrison (Ed.), *Essential Papers on Narcissism* (pp. 61-87). New York: New York University Press (1986).

_____. (1977). *Restoration of the Self.* New York: International Universities Press.

_____. (1984). *How Does Analysis Cure?* Chicago: University of Chicago Press.

_____. (1985). *Self Psychology and the Humanities.* Ed. C. Strozier. New York: Norton.

_____. (1985a). "On Courage." In C. Strozier (Ed.), *Self Psychology and the Humanities* (pp. 5-50). New York: Norton.

_____. (1985b). "Thoughts on Narcissism and Narcissistic Rage." In C. Strozier (Ed.), *Self Psychology.and the Humanities* (pp.124-160). New York: Norton.

_____. (1985c). "Creativity, Charisma, and Group Psychology." In C. Strozier (Ed.), *Self Psychology and the Humanities* (pp. 171-223). New York: Norton.

Kohut, H. & Wolf, E. (1978). "The Disorders of the Self and Their Treatment: an Outline." In A Morrison (Ed.), *Essential Papers on Narcissism* (pp. 175-196). New York: New York University Press (1986).

Kulka, R. (2012). "Between Emergence and Dissolving: Contemporary Reflections on Greatness and Ideals in Kohut's Legacy." *International Journal of Psychoanalytic Self Psychology, 7* (2), pp. 264-283.

Lacan, J. (1966). *Ecrits.* Trs. B. Fink. New York: W. W. Norton & Co. (1996).

Layton, L. (2006). "Racial Identities, Racial Enactments, and Normative Unconscious Processes." *Psychoanalytic Quarterly,* 75: pp. 237- 269.

Lear, J. (1990). *Love and Its Place in Nature.* New York: Farrar, Straus, and Giroux.

_____. (2000). *Open-Minded: Working Out the Logic of the Soul.* Cambridge, MA: Harvard University Press.

_____. (2003). *Happiness, Death, and the Remainder of Life.* Cambridge, MA: Harvard University Press.

_____. (2004). *Therapeutic Action.* New York: The Other Press.

_____. (2005). "Give Dora a Break: A Tale of Eros and Emotional Disruption." In S. Bartsch & T. Bartscherer (Eds.), *Erotikon* (pp. 196-212). Chicago: University of Chicago Press.

Levinas, E. (1989). "Ethics as First Philosophy." Tr. S. Hand & M. Temple. In S. Hand (Ed.), *The Levinas Reader* (pp. 75-87). Oxford: Blackwell Publishers.

Levy, D. (1996). *Freud Among the Philosophers.* New Haven, CT: Yale University Press.

Lunbeck, E. (2014). *The Americanization of Narcissism.* Cambridge, MA: Harvard University Press.

Lyotard, J-F. (1979). *The Postmodern Condition.* Trs. G. Bennington & B. Massumi. Minneapolis: University of Minnesota Press (1984).

MacIntyre, A. (1958). *The Unconscious: A Conceptual Study.* London: Routledge.

Marcuse, H. (1955). *Eros and Civilization: A Philosophical Inquiry into Freud.* Boston: Beacon Press.

Margulies, A. (2012). Review of *The Christopher Bollas Reader. JAPA* 60:1071-1078.

Marion, J-L. (2003). *The Erotic Phenomenon.* Trs. S. Lewis. Chicago: University of Chicago Press (2007).

McCloskey, D. (2010). *Bourgeois Dignity.* Chicago: University of Chicago Press.

Mill, J. S. (1859). *On Liberty.* In *On Liberty and Utilitarianism* (pp. 3-133). New York: Bantam Press (1993).

_____. (1863). *Utilitarianism.* New York: Macmillan (1957).

Mills, C. (2007). "Intersecting Contracts." In C. Pateman & C. Mills (Eds.), *Contract and Domination* (pp. 169-186). Malden, MA: Polity Press.

Nagel, T. (1986). *The View from Nowhere.* Oxford: Oxford University Press.

Nietzsche, F. (1882). *The Gay Science.* Tr. W. Kaufmann. New York: Random House (1974).

_____. (1883). *Thus Spoke Zarathustra.* Tr. W. Kaufmann. New York: Viking Press (1978).

_____. (1887). *The Genealogy of Morals.* In F. Goffling (Trs.), *The Birth of Tragedy* and *The Genealogy of Morals* (pp.147-299). New York: Doubleday and Company (1956).

_____. (1968). *The Will to Power.* Tr. W. Kaufmann. New York: Random House.

Panksepp, J. (2012). *The Archeology of Mind: Neuroevolutionary Origins of Human Emotions.* New York: Norton.

Plato. (1961). *The Collected Dialogues of Plato.* Eds. E. Hamiliton & H. Cairns. New York: Pantheon Books.

Poole, R. (1991). *Morality and Modernity.* New York: Routledge.

Popper, K. (1963). *Conjectures and Refutations: the Growth of Scientific Knowledge.* New York: Harper & Row.

Putnam, R. (2000). *Bowling Alone.* New York: Simon & Schuster.

Oliver, K. (1998). "Identity, Difference, and Abjection." In C. Willett (Ed.), *Theorizing Multiculturalism* (pp. 169-186). Malden, MA & London: Blackwell Publishers.

Rawls, J. (1971). *A Theory of Justice.* Cambridge, MA: Harvard University Press.

Riker, J. (1991). *Human Excellence and an Ecological Conception of the Psyche.* Albany, NY: SUNY Press.

_____. (1997). *Ethics and the Discovery of the Unconscious.* Albany, NY: SUNY Press.

_____. (2010). *Why It Is Good to Be Good: Ethics, Kohut's Self Psychology, and Modern Society.* Lanham, MD: Jason Aronson.

Ruti, M. (2006). *Reinventing the Soul.* New York: The Other Press.

_____. (2014). *The Call of Character.* New York: Columbia University Press.

Santner, E. (2001). *The Psychotheology of Everyday Life.* Chicago: The University of Chicago Press.

Sartre, J-P. (1956). *Being and Nothingness.* Tr. H. Barnes. New York: Simon & Schuster.

Shaleen, J. (2015). "When the Wind Comes Sweeping Down the Plain: Embracing Atmospheric Interrelatedness." *International Journal of Psychoanaltyic Self Psychology,* 10 (1), pp. 14-32.

Shedler, J. (2010). "The Efficacy of Psychodynamic Psychotherapy." *American Psychologist,* 65 (2), pp. 98-109.

Sherburne, D. (1966). *A Key to Whitehead's Process and Reality.* New York: Macmillan.

Siegel, A. (1996). *Heinz Kohut and the Psychology of the Self.* New York: Routledge.

Stolorow, R. D. & Atwood, G. (2013). "The Tragic and the Metaphysical in Philosophy and Psychoanalysis." *Psychoanalytic Review,* 100 (3), pp. 405-419.

Strozier, C. (2001). *Heinz Kohut: The Making of a Psychoanalyst.* New York: Farrar, Straus, and Giroux.

Suchet, M. (2004). "A Relational Encounter with Race." *Psychoanalytic Dialogues,* 14: pp. 423-438.

Summers, F. (2005). *Self Creation.* Hillsdale, NJ: The Analytic Press.

_____. (2013). *The Psychoanalytic Vision: The Experiencing Subject, Transcendence, and the Therapeutic Process.* New York: Routledge.

Teicholz, J. (1999). *Kohut, Loewald, and the Postmoderns.* Hillsdale, NJ: The Analytic Press.

Thoreau, H. D. (1854). *Walden.* In *Walden and Other Writings* (pp. 1-312). Ed. B. Atkinson. New York: Modern Library (2000).

_____. (1861). *Walking.* In *Walden and Other Writings* (pp. 625-694). Ed. B. Atkinson. New York: Modern Library (2000).

Thucydides. (1996). *The Landmark Thucydides: A Comprehensive Guide to the Peloponnesian War.* Ed. R. Strassler. New York: The Free Press.

Tillich, P. (1952). *The Courage to Be.* New Haven, CT: Yale University Press.

Tolpin, M. (2002). "Doing Psychoanalysis of Normal Development: Forward Edge Transferences." In A. Goldberg (Ed.), *Progress in Self Psychology,* vol. 18 (pp. 167-190). New York: Guildford Press.

Wheelwright, P. (1966). *The Presocratics.* New York: The Odyssey Press.

Whitehead, A. (1925). *Science and the Modern World.* New York: Macmillan.

_____. (1929). *Process and Reality.* New York: Macmillan.

_____. (1933). *Adventures of Ideas.* New York: Macmillan.

Williams, B. (1982). *Ethics and the Limit of Philosophy.* Cambridge: Cambridge University Press.

Winnicott, D. (1960). "Ego Distortion in Terms of True and False Self." In *The Maturational Processes and Facilitating Environment* (pp. 140-152). New York: International Universities Press.

Wittgenstein, L. (1958). *Philosophical Investigations.* Tr. G. Anscombe. New York: Macmillan.

_____. (1958b). *The Blue and Brown Books.* Oxford: Blackwell.

Index

Made in the USA
Coppell, TX
01 December 2019